Plural Marriage for Our Times

Plural Marriage for Our Times

A Reinvented Option?

Second Edition

Philip L. Kilbride and Douglas R. Page

 PRAEGER

AN IMPRINT OF ABC-CLIO, LLC
Santa Barbara, California • Denver, Colorado • Oxford, England

Library of Congress Cataloging-in-Publication Data

Kilbride, Philip Leroy.
    Plural marriage for our times : a reinvented option? / Philip L. Kilbride and
Douglas R. Page. — 2nd ed.
        p. cm.
    Includes bibliographical references and index.
    ISBN 978-0-313-38478-3 (hardcopy : alk. paper) — ISBN 978-0-313-38479-0
(e-book) 1. Polygamy. 2. Marriage—United States. 3. Families—United
States. I. Page, Douglas R. II. Title.
    HQ988.K48 2012
    306.84'23—dc23   2012016711

ISBN: 978-0-313-38478-3
EISBN: 978-0-313-38479-0

16 15 14 13 12   1 2 3 4 5

This book is also available on the World Wide Web as an eBook.
Visit www.abc-clio.com for details.

Praeger
An Imprint of ABC-CLIO, LLC

ABC-CLIO, LLC
130 Cremona Drive, P.O. Box 1911
Santa Barbara, California 93116-1911

This book is printed on acid-free paper ∞

Manufactured in the United States of America

Contents

Preface

We, the authors of this book, although having pursued different careers, were brought together because of our mutual interests in family structures, marriages and finding some way, if possible, of alleviating the consequences of divorce, especially for children.

We met on the phone in the fall of 2010, when Page was assigned to write an article for a monthly parenting magazine in Massachusetts, *Bay State Parent*, about changing family structures. When Page conducted a Google search for experts on polygamy, also called plural marriage, Kilbride's name popped up. So he called his office and left a message.

Two days later, Page called back and interviewed Kilbride; many of his comments were included in the article, published in the February 2011 edition of the magazine. That led to a follow up conversation between Kilbride and Page about the former's publisher, Praeger, having an interest in updating the first edition of this book, which was released in 1994; hence, this book.

In the nearly 20 years since that first book a lot has changed. Some states recognize same-gender marriage. Gays and lesbians are adopting children or giving birth. And polygamists appear to be borrowing from the playbook of gays and lesbians, coming out of the closet with television shows and books, saying, basically, "We're here. Come and get us." Polygamy or plural marriage includes polygyny (one man married to more than one woman at the same time) and polyandry (one woman married to more than one man at the same time).

We attempt to show these many changes, explain the benefits and pitfalls of monogamous and plural marriage, and provide some insight into the legal and theological issues facing plural marriage today. We are cognizant that many readers will find this a highly controversial topic.

We have used a variety of sources, including ethnographic research conducted by Kilbride, interviews conducted by Page, the U.S. Census Bureau, and published sources from diverse perspectives. In addition, we have attempted to provide an "insider's" point of view. Many of the sources we cite and, when possible, interviewed provided us with their community's perspective on plural marriage. Our intent is to provide as comprehensive a picture as possible of plural marriage, at least in the United States, that many readers will find provocative and nuanced, one that we hope will prompt debate.

The people interviewed were told about the book's subject and why we wanted their insight on either plural marriage or, in some cases, plural relationships. Everyone was generous with their time but some of the people we spoke to wished to remain unnamed. We respected their wishes because, in some cases, they risked notoriety in their career or their families.

Let's make something clear: We do not support sexual or physical harassment; sexual or physical abuse; or any harm to anyone, regardless of their gender, their faith, their age, their ethnicity, or their sexual orientation. We're not selling any sort of sexual system. If there is one thing we seek, it is a world filled with more love and commitment that benefits not only adults but also their children. We are boosters of the family, seeing it as an institution, even in its many forms, that provides many benefits for all of its members. We are not advocating for a revolution. While we certainly think that plural marriage should be an option for all consenting adults, we also encourage our readers to follow the law and to seek change if they so desire it.

At its best, plural marriage can, potentially, allow aging widows and widowers to marry men or women already in a committed relationship who they also find attractive; provide an extended and caring family for single parents and their children; reduce the numbers of lonely adults; and provide, perhaps, a modern-day safety net that costs less than a government program.

But that doesn't mean it is perfect or any better than monogamous marriage. Like any relationship in a family setting, plural marriage has its own set of issues and possible drawbacks. Still, we think it should be an option for consenting adults.

The problem with plural marriage, for most Americans, is that they usually only see polygyny through the lens of a videotaped police raid on a polygynous compound, often located in the American West. Or, perhaps, they view the defendants in a court setting. These raids—the last biggest one conducted at the Yearning for Zion ranch near San Angelo, Texas, about four years ago—have led many Americans to understand polygyny as something that only sexually and physically abuses women and girls.

It is our opinion, however, that if most people only saw the downside to monogamous marriage—a divorce, a separation, a child yearning for the parent no longer at home, or physical or sexual abuse of one spouse by another—then they might have the same view of monogamy as they do of polygamy. They would consider it abusive.

What most Americans don't see is what one Canadian attorney told us: there are a number of underground Fundamentalist Latter Day Saint (FLDS) plural marriages in Salt Lake City, where men and women live together, hold down jobs, bring up children and carry on their family life as inconspicuously as possible. They live this way because they believe they're living within the boundaries of their religious faith.

In addition, unlike many Fundamentalist Latter-day Saint (FLDS, formerly Mormon) communities, the men in these more egalitarian marriages decide whom they marry and do so, often, with the consent of the other wives. They dress like anyone else, so, to look at them, you would never know they are polygynists.

Is there such a thing as a perfect relationship between people? Although there are numerous companionate marriages, can one person always be another person's everything—their spouse, their lover, their friend, and their compatriot? Do we want a society with more love or one with less? Perhaps, regrettably, monogamous marriages that remain filled with passion over their duration are unlikely.

These are some of the questions we'll explore in this book. We do not claim to have all the answers; but we might have a few. Future scholars and writers of this topic may ask different questions and arrive at alternative conclusions.

THE FIRST BOOK

There were many different reactions to the book's first edition. Some were positive; others were negative. It caused, when some readers were able to talk with Kilbride directly, a variety of emotional outbursts, too.

One of the reactions to the first book was when women considered the prospect of polyandry. About 1 percent of the world's cultures approve of this (notably Tibet, Nepal, India, parts of West Africa, and a few Native American). It's usually tied into a country's or culture's economics and provides for a low birthrate, necessary in some geographic areas because there's little fertile land available to grow the crops necessary to feed the population. Was this practice okay with Kilbride, asked feminists? His answer: Of course, depending on their circumstances. He provided the same answer for polygyny.

Some readers inquired if plural marriage is possible given that jealousy may be magnified when more than two people are involved in a marriage. Kilbride answered "yes," but asked the reader if monogamy is always free of jealousy. When Kilbride appeared on a radio talk show, one listener called in to say that she was leaving her cheating husband and bringing up their daughter alone. She asked, "Are men just plain selfish?"

Kilbride responded by asking, "Isn't it selfish also to deny your husband and daughter their relationship, especially for your child?" Her pain was clear but it also intruded on an important issue to be taken up in this book, child welfare in marriages of all types.

Religious objections to plural marriage were also common. On one talk show, a listener strongly objected to polygyny on biblical grounds. Did Kilbride not know that Jesus was against plural marriage, the listener asked? Kilbride answered the caller and similar ones, saying that African Christians differ strongly, often objecting to enforced monogamy. They hold that God, based on what's written in the Hebrew Bible, favored plural marriage.

Kilbride went on to say that St. Paul seemingly permitted polygynists to be Christians having said that Deacons could only have one wife, referring them to 1 Timothy 3:12, "Let the deacons be the husband of one wife ruling their children and their own houses as well." Even Martin Luther, the 16th-century priest who initiated the Reformation in Europe, appears to have supported plural marriage, albeit discreetly.

In Florida, the *Tallahassee News* reported that one minister's response was that "Kilbride has written a stupid book. Doesn't he know the word of God?" There were also favorable reactions to the first book. One college student, among others, thanked Kilbride for bringing some cultural perspective to her own family. She was Korean American and her grandmother had been a second wife. One student asked Kilbride, "Why bother to have any marriage in the first place?" Kilbride responded to the student, saying that that it has been the role of marriage, including plural ones, to do the work of child rearing for thousands of years across the globe. Besides, who among us have lost much sleep during our child's infancy and have been grateful to have helping hands?

After appearing on a television talk show in Philadelphia, Kilbride was approached by one of the panelists who thanked him for describing the situation of a mistress with children living in the shadows of respectability. She was in that very same place herself but kept silent about it so she wouldn't be stigmatized. She also observed that children, especially in America, are often absent from debates about marriage, urging Kilbride to keep promoting a child-focused dimension to this discussion.

Kilbride discussed plural marriage on some television shows outside of the United States and, in Kenya, advised the High Court about how to handle Muslim (thus plural) marriages in a predominantly Christian nation.

Since the first book, there's been a continuing decline of marriage and increased singleness and certainly single parenting. The latest divorce numbers are higher than previously calculated but also remain around the same percentage of the population: about 10 percent of U.S. adults tell the Census Bureau they are divorced.

We take no stand on lifestyles that are different from our own. We understand why some gays and lesbians object to the cry for marriage rights just as much as we understand why same-gender couples seek them. We think that plural marriage should be legally recognized. At the same time, we can appreciate the profound feelings the majority of Americans show for a preference for heterosexual, monogamous marriage. Such marriages are not threatened by allowing others a plural marriage option.

We wonder, given the numbers of broken families, at least in the United States, if the monogamous family today requires some sort of improvement and/or augmentation. Perhaps this can come about by the legal recognition of plural marriage. We should also say, at the outset, that the question of patriarchy remains crucial. Is widespread patriarchy in plural marriage an essential component of such marriages? Can the two be separated? Is monogamy somehow less patriarchal?

While monogamy is in all cultures the major marital form statistically, in practice the majority of the world's cultures value polygamy. Allowing some in the United States a plural marriage prerogative should not be feared as the start of a slippery slope away from monogamy. Readers will become familiar with the anthropological fact that plural marriage is a widely practiced form of the family around the world past and present and is not a sexual practice.

THE AUTHORS' BACKGROUNDS

As an anthropologist, Kilbride's primary technique in analyzing and studying how one society observes its rituals, customs, and traditions—and then compares it to another society—is through a technique called "participant observation." It involves living in a particular society or culture, learning its language and participating in many of its habits to gain an insider's perspective on the society's values.

He has spent many years conducting ethnographic research in Uganda and Kenya. It was during his years of studying those African countries that he became familiar with polygyny. By learning more about it, he came to understand what this marital institution means in Africa, a topic which will be discussed in this book.

When Kilbride isn't observing another culture, he's an anthropology professor at Bryn Mawr College in Pennsylvania, having taught there for 42 years. He holds a PhD in the subject from the University of Missouri and has written extensively about marriage, family, and childhood topics.

Page's background includes more than 20 years in the news industry. He's worked at United Press International, the *Chicago Sun-Times*, Tribune Media Services, and has recently been reporting for *Bay State Parent* and writing a column for a newspaper industry trade magazine, *News & Tech*. He holds a bachelor's degree from DePauw University in Greencastle, Indiana, and an MBA from Northwestern University in Evanston, Illinois.

Both authors are American, having experienced this national culture first-hand, and can, accordingly, speak as insiders on marriage and family issues presented in this book.

THE EVERLASTING EFFECTS OF DIVORCE

A parents' divorce can leave their children with chronic pain. Page has supposed—often—that he should just get over his parents' broken marriage and move on. But the pain of their divorce from nearly 30 years ago continues to return. Not every day. Not every week. But there are the odd days when it arrives, usually without warning.

The conventional wisdom, back in the late 1970s and early 1980s, when Page was growing up, was that it was best for parents to stick together until their children were out of the house so as to reduce a divorce's sting. As Page told his friends back then, that just means, after those many years of knowing his parents as a married couple, the heartache and sense of loss is greater than perhaps had they divorced in an earlier time.

Despite years of anger, finger pointing, and a few verbal fisticuffs with his parents over their split, today Page enjoys a healthy relationship with his father and his father's wife and oversees the care of his mother, now a dementia patient. He hopes his own marriage remains intact and that his sons will only know him as married to their mother.

Kilbride has also experienced divorce but in a much different fashion. His was a companionate divorce after many years of marriage and a teenage daughter. For him, it was painful to no longer live with his daughter, but after a subsequent marriage and a second daughter, with the cooperation of his wife and former wife, each committed to monogamy, they have allowed an open and free parental role for him with an ensuing friendship between his two daughters. Such wisdom is rare in his experience, but under a different cultural framework, it might have been permissible for him not to divorce, foregoing the economic penalties and, more importantly, the emotional turmoil of those who do.

Philip L. Kilbride, Bryn Mawr, Pennsylvania
Douglas R. Page, Boston, Massachusetts

Acknowledgments

No book is written alone, even if it has two authors. Many people play a vital and supporting role in making a book come to life. We are grateful to all who have helped us in our preparation, research and writing of this book.

Kilbride's former wife, Dr. Janet E. Kilbride, and he originally did field research in the 1980s on polygamy in Kenya. While she doesn't agree with his American applications of this work, she recognizes the ethnographic significance of its practice in Africa. The first edition of this book was dedicated to her.

They share a strong pronatal perspective (emphasized in this book) that's originally Roman Catholic. Working together enriched their lives. She provided careful editorial review of this edition of the book.

Kilbride also acknowledges the inspirational influence of the late Dr. Nancy (Penny) Schwartz, who shared his passion for African Studies in Kenya, and who did not oppose his views about polygamy in the United States. She regularly invited Kilbride to campuses, especially Western Michigan University and Washington College, to speak about polygamy.

Kilbride also acknowledges the small number of Fundamentalist Latter-day Saints specialists on marriage and family life who, after the book's first edition was published, invited him to lecture at their university, including William Jankowiak at the University of Nevada at Las Vegas, or to review their own books on polygamy, including Janet Bennion, Joseph Ginat, and Irwin Altman. He has learned much from them, although he alone is responsible for the policy direction of this book.

The late Ralph Vigoda did a superb piece of reporting on the 1994 edition of this book for the *Philadelphia Inquirer* in 1995. His story was reproduced in numerous newspapers and led to many radio and television invitations, all good learning opportunities to discover American national cultural values about plural marriage. Professors Aaron Podolefsky and Roger Brown published an article by Kilbride, based on the original book, in their coedited volume, *Applying Cultural Anthropology*. This article was widely read by college and university students. These three individuals are especially noteworthy for promoting a modest public response to the first book and another opportunity to discover from readers' responses younger American and international views about plural marriage today.

This public exposure became a good source of data for the present book. Only a few mentioned here fully support the advocacy position taken by Kilbride, although as fair-minded colleagues, they provided a public audience for his book that they considered scholarly and worthwhile. He is grateful for their collegiality.

Kilbride also acknowledges the fine editorial assistance by Valentina Tursini of Praeger Publishers, especially her suggestion that he should pay more attention to tax issues in the revised edition. Both Kilbride and Page thank Karen Sulpizio for her professional typing and editorial work, crucial in working through materials for this book. Kilbride also thanks Sara O'Connor, a talented undergraduate at Bryn Mawr College, for her helpful editorial comment. Neither, of course, is responsible in any way for the views presented in this book. To all of the many colleagues, friends, informants, and others who have shared with Kilbride his life in anthropology in Africa and the United States, he extends a special hand of gratitude for the gift of their learning and support; Kilbride also thanks Professor Collette Suda of the University of Nairobi, Kenya for her work on polygamy in Africa. It was inspirational.

Page comes to this topic as the outsider. Prior to writing an article about the evolution (or disintegration, depending on your perspective) of U.S. family life for a monthly parenting magazine in Massachusetts, *Bay State Parent,* he didn't know much about plural marriage, other than what he had read in newspapers and magazines and watched on television news networks. It has been a fascinating and intriguing intellectual and journalistic exercise to coauthor this book and for that Page thanks Kilbride, who he interviewed for the article, for the opportunity.

Being a coauthor of anything can be treacherous. There's often a conflict between the first author's ideas and the second author's ability to express them so they're understood by the general reader. Page feels very fortunate to have worked with Kilbride; both Kilbride and Page recognized each other's strengths and skill set and, as a result, they were able to form a fun, happy and close working relationship with one another. In fact, Kilbride emphasizes to readers that this book is equally coauthored.

Page also offers a special thanks to Carrie Wattu, the editor of *Bay State Parent.* If it hadn't been for Carrie, this project would never have come about for Page. When he pitched her on the idea of writing about the changing nature of families in October 2010, Carrie was very enthusiastic and supportive.

Stories about plural marriage, the polyamorous, divorce, and changing family structures can be risky for a magazine that stakes its claim as a must-read for parents, especially mothers, as well as being a must-buy for businesses targeting the magazine's audience. Page is grateful for Carrie's willingness and fortitude to run a story about a controversial topic.

Page also wants to acknowledge everyone who generously gave their time to be interviewed by him for this book, including Robyn Trask; Adrien Wing; Dr. Patricia Dixon-Spear; Dr. Jankowiak; a Boston suburban couple involved in the polyamorous community whose names have been changed; two Salt Lake City attorneys, including Rod Parker; Paul Murphy, a spokesman for Utah's attorney general; the attorney working on behalf of the Fundamentalist Latter-day Saints in Canada's British Columbia, Robert Wickett. He also wants to extend a special thanks to two Boston University professors, Linda McClain and Bruce Schulman; Dr. Bennion; and University of Virginia sociologist Andrea Press for answering his many questions when writing the original article for *Bay State Parent.*

Page also wants to offer up a special thanks to Tia Costello and Arthur Bakis, two employees at the United States Census Bureau in Boston, who provided invaluable information and interpretation of the data the Bureau collects. Both are high-performing, dedicated professionals.

Page also wants to acknowledge Mary Van Meter and Chuck Moozakis, the publisher and editor-in-chief, respectively, of *News & Tech,* a newspaper trade magazine. They encouraged Page to write a column for their magazine about four years ago. Chuck knocked out all the cobwebs in Page's writing ability, which had lain dormant for many years.

No writer or reporter comes to the profession without some excellent teachers. Page's writing and journalism "professors" included a number of editors at United Press International, where he first worked, among them Lou Carr, Jerry Berger, Dave Haskell, Dick Taffe, Ken Cafarell, and Ed Lyon. There are many others. Each was relentless editing Page during his career's early years; each time they ripped him apart, Page knew what he had to improve.

Page extends his hand in gratitude to Craig Klugman, editor of the *Journal-Gazette* in Fort Wayne, Indiana, for his constant, moral support—although he may not agree with this book's conclusion—as well as to his many friends and colleagues he's met during his career.

Page also wishes to thank his dad, Robert E. Page, a former newspaper publisher and UPI executive. He was Page's first writing "professor" and was as tough on his son's first forays into writing and journalism as were the editors at UPI. No son could ask for a better teacher.

Page acknowledges his love for his mother, Barbara Page. He wishes she could read the book. He also wishes to acknowledge his love for Rebeca Page, his dad's wife, who's also a terrific grandmother to his two sons.

Last but not least, there are never enough words to effectively articulate the gratitude one man can to express to his wife. Thank you just doesn't do it. That said, Page is very, very grateful for all of Liz's love and support on this project. Page also wants to thank their sons, Jeff and Chris, for their understanding the many times he couldn't play because he was working on the book. Daddy loves you.

1

Slow-Motion Polygamy in America: Why a Second Edition

By all appearances, Dr. Norman J. Lewiston led a normal life. In fact, it was likely one that most would envy.

He was a leading and respected figure at Stanford University's Medical School, faithful to his patients, raised money for cystic fibrosis research, a devoted father to his three children, and he always kept his Friday lunch date with Diana, his wife of more than 20 years. There was only one minor glitch.

He had two other wives.

Not legally of course. In the eyes of the law, Dr. Lewiston was only married to Diana. But behind Diana's back, he married Katy and behind Katy's back, he married Robyn.

Robyn, a nurse who continued to live in San Diego after they were married, became suspicious of how her new husband, who remained near the Stanford University campus, conducted his personal life in the Bay Area and instructed her attorney, Gregory Alford, to investigate. He uncovered that Norman was not the divorced man he claimed.

Meanwhile, Diana, as the *Los Angeles Times* reported, was more than willing to put up with Norman's infidelity as long as he slept at the house he shared with her.[1]

While Robyn knew Norman wasn't divorced, neither Diana nor Katy knew about his other marriages until one day the good doctor did something completely unexpected—he died.

"Typically, [bigamy] occurs by virtue of oversight. What seems to be emerging is that he was truly a man who was capable of having an intimate relationship and a legitimate one with more than one woman. He had a concern and care for each one of them and just kind of overlooked the obvious—which is, we have rules in this society and he chose to ignore them," Alford told the *San Jose Mercury News* in October 1991, shortly after Norman's death, when the details of his private life became public.[2]

Robyn, who had also worked with him, was far more sympathetic. "Once you had a relationship with Norm, you had a relationship for the rest of your life," she told the *Los Angeles Times*.[3]

To others, Dr. Lewiston, a bearded and overweight man, wasn't so much a villain but, perhaps, a man who loved too much. The *Times* reported that "to many who knew him, he was a caring person who couldn't say no; a doctor who often witnessed the deaths of patients but had difficulty parting with people; a man whose life went quietly out of control and who did not have the inner strength to be honest."[4]

In the process of executing his estate, Diana found out about Katy and Robyn and, at last report, was attempting to secure any property that was hers since she was his first—and only legal—wife.

To be sure, Lewiston's actions caused a lot of pain. Katy, his second wife, purchased a house with the doctor. He made the mortgage payments but she made the down payment. Upon learning she was the victim of bigamy, she worried about losing the house, telling the *San Jose Mercury News* that the doctor had taken out an equity loan on the house to finance his children's college education.[5]

While this may be one of the more interesting bigamy and/or plural marriage cases in U.S. legal history, it's far from the last. Bigamy, or being married to more than one person at the same time, is against the law. Warren Jeffs, a polygynist, was convicted for sexually molesting children, and reality television star Kody Brown, of *Sister Wives*, along with his four wives and their children, recently moved to Nevada because, unlike Utah, where they'd lived previously, cohabitating with more than one woman in the Silver State isn't against state law.

There are numerous cases of bigamy, and they're not all in Utah, the spiritual home of Mormonism, the faith that introduced polygamy, or plural marriage, to the United States in the 19th century. Bigamy charges have also been investigated in North Carolina, Maryland, Ohio, Tennessee, Georgia, Washington, Florida, Virginia, Vermont, and Wisconsin, to name a few states, in the last 12 years.[6]

Add to these cases some of the recent stories of public men misbehaving: former President Bill Clinton nearly thrown out of office because he had an affair with a White House intern; former Speaker of the House Newt Gingrich's numerous marriages and affairs; and former New York Governor Eliot Spitzer's dalliance with a prostitute.

Such affairs sometimes approach marriage-like status. Former California governor Arnold Schwarzenegger fathered a son with the housekeeper who cared for the home he shared with his wife, Maria Shriver; we've also learned that former U.S. Senator John Edwards fathered a daughter with a film producer while married to his wife, Elizabeth, who is now deceased.

Given the political affiliations of all the men involved—both Republicans and Democrats—we might conclude that fathering children outside of wedlock and sexual affairs outside of marriage are bipartisan afflictions.

Coincidentally, with regard to Schwarzenegger and Edwards, their stories contain the same characters: there's a bad husband; an embarrassed wife; and a mother. The men are condemned; the wives placed on a pedestal; the mothers are in some sort of moral nebulousness.

But for all the Sturm und Drang, there's little concern, made public at least, for the stories' most innocent and vulnerable players—the stigmatized children from these hidden unions who, just like children from traditional marriages, had no say in choosing their parents. If we believe that a parent's love for their child is paramount and that every kid deserves at least two parents or surrogates, then these progeny are also victims, perhaps even more so than their mothers and the spurned wives, because they aren't receiving loving, nurturing attention from both parents. Much of society, including the media, appears to treat these children as nonpersons.

How should they be treated and viewed by society? Like bastards? Or like a "Love Child, Never Meant to be," as the singer Diana Ross once crooned. This is one of the issues we take up in this book concerning children living in informal plural circumstances who often suffer discrimination and stigma.

PLURAL MARRIAGE STATISTICS

According to the best statistics anyone can find—reported by the *New York Times* and National Public Radio—there are between 50,000 and 100,000 people living in polygamous families in the United States.[7] Certainly bringing up plural marriage as a possible option to either augment monogamous, heterosexual marriage, because the number of those who are married has fallen sizably, or even same-gender marriage, or to improve the living conditions of children, is highly controversial, especially in a culture that values monogamous marriage and often misconstrues plural marriage as being barbarian and a sexual system that's only for the benefit of men.

But if we can support, after considering all the facts, same-gender marriage, which is gaining legal acceptance in the United States, what's the problem considering the facts for allowing one more marriage option for those who find themselves attracted to someone who is already married, especially when there are children involved? Shouldn't our society allow many options that anyone may choose so long as no one is coerced into some sort of living arrangement they may not want? People who previously didn't accept same-gender marriage are accepting it today because they've looked at all the facts and realize gays and lesbians are just as entitled to marriage and family life as heterosexuals are.

The criticism that's been published, so far, against plural marriage is that it abuses women and, indeed, some of that is very true. This viewpoint also prohibits people from considering that polygamy, if it became legal, would not remain as it has traditionally been practiced, an institution, because of its long history, that's only for one husband with multiple wives. We also explore the opportunity for women to have more than one husband at the same time.

Indeed, this is where University of Chicago Law School Professor Martha Nussbaum sees an opening, when she asks, "What about . . . a practice of plural contractual marriage, by mutual consent, among adult, informed parties, all of whom have equal legal rights to contract such plural marriages? What interest might the state (the government) have that would justify refusing recognition of such marriages?"[8] She goes on to write:

> Well, children would have to be protected, so the law would have to make sure that issues such as maternity/paternity and child support were well articulated . . . a regime of polygamous unions would, no doubt, be difficult to administer—but not impossible. . . . It is already difficult to deal with sequential marriages and the responsibilities they entail.[9]

If plural marriages were contracted or somehow legally recognized, as Nussbaum suggests, a husband or wife, knowing their spouses would retain legal rights, might reconsider their enthusiasm for adding additional spouses because legally recognized spouses would no longer be easily discarded. In this book, we will consider plural marriage as an option or alternative to divorce in some cases.

In the United States, we live in the culture of the divorced and the never married. The heterosexual, monogamous family is under duress. It seemingly cannot do all of the work expected of it as America's only marital option. In 1960, the Pew Research Center reported, 72 percent of all American adults were married. Today, however, the number of married adults has fallen, to just over 51 percent, with a 5 percent decline between 2009 and 2010, the Pew Research Center reported.[10]

But upon further examination of the Census Bureau data, less than 50 percent of all adults in the United States are living with their spouse. The Bureau reports there about 243,858,000 adults with 120,309,000 living with their spouse. Another 3.5 million adults are separated, perhaps making one wonder how committed these adults are to their marriages.[11] To be sure, the Census Bureau doesn't measure attitudes about separated adults or, for that matter, anyone's emotions and feelings. The separated spouses they've counted could be fully committed to their marriages, hoping to resume living with their wives or husbands.

Why is one marriage successful and another one a failure? We develop the concept of "it depends," in this book. It means that some people are better at collaboration than others; it means that some people are fortunate enough to have a personality that melds well with their spouse; it means that some people are lucky enough to find the right person to marry. And, then, let's face it, some don't. They marry the wrong person, eventually undergoing a divorce which is painful, not only for them and their partner but, perhaps, even more so, for their children. We expand the concept of "it depends" to the situation of children in plural marriages.

To say that all plural marriages are inherently filled with abuse is to say that all monogamous marriages are completely healthy. In the United States, there are statistics that show about 25,000 women are abused each week by their intimate partner.[12] Some of them are suffering abuse at the hands of their monogamous husbands. We don't have any reliable statistics about the harm that polygyny causes because it's so far underground. If it was legal or at least decriminalized, we would be better able to track how one system of marriage compares to another.

There's also an issue, which we'll go through in a later chapter, about African American living arrangements, dating and marriage. Given some of these issues African America faces—which are, overall, far different than their white counterparts—there are today African American scholars calling for plural marriage as an option and, for that matter, some who aren't.

THE DIFFICULTY OF DISCUSSING MARRIAGE

Marriage is not a simple topic. It's impossible to discuss marriage—in whatever form, monogamous, plural, or same-gender—without looking into history, political ideas, government actions and religious thought. Marriage can be just as much about romance and love as it can be about a number of day-to-day issues and obligations, like careers and employment, child rearing, health insurance, education, taxes, faith, home ownership and inheritance rights, to name a few issues. The reason marriage isn't simple—and becomes so controversial when it delves into the topics of same-gender or plural unions—is because, in whatever form it takes, marriage touches nearly every area of peoples' lives.

No less important is the fact that marriage is also about the shape and culture of society. As one legal scholar, Gregory C. Pingree, wrote, debates about marriage are about "the relative virtues of autonomy and community (and) are . . . variations on the fundamental question that motivated Socrates, Plato and Aristotle: what makes a good society? In every epoch this core social question has particular context and character; in the last two centuries, issues that have shaped this question include the nature of human subjectivity, the politics of state and social power."[13]

In fact, a Cato Institute writer, David Boaz, in an article for Slate magazine in 1997, asked, "Why should the government be in the business of decreeing who can and cannot be married?" He goes on to say, "the history of marriage and the state is more complicated than modern debaters imagine, as one of its scholars, Lawrence Stone, writes, 'In the early Middle Ages all that marriage implied in the eyes of the laity seems to have been a private contract between two individuals, enforced by the community.'"[14]

Boaz also says that in colonial New England, "marriages were performed by justices of the peace or other magistrates . . . even then common-law unions were valid."[15]

Boaz recommended making marriage a private agreement between two people. While he was specifically addressing the issue of same-gender marriage, it's not difficult to imagine how his prescription could also work for a variety of unions, including plural ones. Marriages, whatever their form, would be drawn up in mutually, binding legal agreements, which could then be subjected to review by the judiciary, meaning, just like today, they would still be subjected to some government regulation. Religious institutions, suggests Boaz in his scenario, would retain the right to determine which marriages they would bless.

In the Western world, marriage became part of civil society with the ancient Greeks and was very much part of ancient Rome. Christians, like the Jews, took an interest in marriage, eventually making it, in some parts of the faith, a sacrament. We're not here to determine whether marriage is sacred, but religious involvement with marriage provides much of the foundation over the debate being held about it today. We consider religion and plural marriage in a later chapter.

Given the declining rates of marriage in the United States and the country's steady rate of divorce, is it time to consider ways to augment this institution so it continues well into the future? Or should we do nothing—which is tantamount to casually accepting divorce as part of today's U.S. culture—which will only hurt more people by either condemning them to a future divorce or keeping them single and, potentially, lonely?

THE MEDIA

What is the effect of television shows like *Big Love* and *Sister Wives* on the American public's attitude toward polygamy? Do they begin to change the minds of those who might have been adverse to plural marriage? Some experts think so. "These shows help people imagine the alternative and start normalizing our own experience against them," said University of Virginia sociologist Andrea Press.[16] "*Sister Wives* and *Big Love* show that polygamy can work," said Janet Bennion, an anthropologist at Lyndon State College in Vermont. "They show that polygamists are just regular people trying their best. They're trying to live the American Dream."[17]

Congress rolled back the policy against openly gay people serving in the U.S. military, referred to as "Don't Ask, Don't Tell," with President Obama's approval. What consequences will this new policy have for same-gender marriage? Will the federal government recognize same-gender marriage but not some state governments? Will this prompt a legal battle? In the United States, nearly a dozen states allow civil unions between two adults who may or may not share the same gender. Civil unions allow couples the same legal rights and responsibilities—specifically the ability to transfer property and money to one another—as married couples without saying "I do." Will there be a fight to expand civil unions so that more than two people can enter into one simultaneously? Could this become the forerunner for plural marriage just the way it was, in some instances, the forerunner to same-gender marriage?

EVERYONE'S MARRIAGE CRISIS, OR, WHO WILL RAISE THE CHILDREN?

As one person told Page, and we're paraphrasing, why will our kids get married if they see their own parents remaining single or divorcing? Unless there's something that comes along to alter this trend, fewer and fewer people will marry, at least in the United States. The issue that seems to go undiscussed and unexamined—because we appear to be on this brink of seeing families disappear—is who will make sure the children are nurtured, loved and brought up from infancy to adulthood?

For centuries, marriage and child rearing have gone hand in hand. Sure, there are different attitudes today about marriage than in previous times. But if one generation is built on another generation's experience, what happens to child rearing 20 or 30 years from now? Who will bring up tomorrow's children if today's children are seeing their parents and other adults as only single and divorced? Will today's kids, when they're adults, want to have and to raise children, especially if they've only seen their mothers living alone while suffering in emotional and economic turmoil, partly because they remained single and had kids. Fathers missing from active child-rearing and other familial responsibilities are not good role models.

Another trend to consider, as reported by the Pew Foundation, is about religion, which shows there are fewer Protestants than there were 40 years ago.

Catholics still hold about 30 percent of all adults but that percentage hasn't changed. The biggest increase faith is seeing is—if you can call it a faith—the number of people who are unaffiliated with any religion.[18] That doesn't mean they're atheists; it just means they're not going to church or professing any one faith.

It also likely means they're not learning the values and benefits of marriage, which becomes a powerful basis for being attentive to one's spouse and the children they conceive.

But if the trends continue—a continuing fall off in marriage and a continuing decline in the numbers who are faithful to one religion or another—there are some possible outcomes, including the following:

1. The ranks of the married decline so much so they become a minority of the adult population because those who have either never married or divorced outnumber them.
2. Faith and church attendance continues to slide so anyone who professes any kind of faith will also be a minority. A current institution and resource for, hopefully, expanded family values faces the possibility of being diminished, perhaps extinct, with no alternative in place. We return to this subject later in the book.
3. It's possible married couples and their families could be perceived as awkward by the majority of the population.

How do we turn this around?

Unless there's some radical thinking about marriage across ideological spectrums, including those believing in established religions, we're very likely to see a further deterioration of the numbers of married adults in the United States. What are the consequences for the babies and children a generation from now? Given what we know about what's in the best interests for children, is this the outcome we want?

Let's make something clear—we're making a new argument on behalf of families, and especially children. Plural marriage should not be thought of as a sexual system. It isn't. It's about marriage and responsibility and, hopefully, bringing up children in such a manner that they go on to become self-sufficient, well-educated, well-adjusted adults.

We should also make something else clear—we think and know that single parenting just might be the hardest job there is. Kilbride, between his two marriages, gained some insight into the demands of single parenting when living apart from his wife while sharing in caring for his eldest daughter. Page gained a similar insight into the issue when his wife was working in one city while he remained at home with their children in a distant one.

American family life is changing. The landscape is no longer *Ozzie and Harriett, Father Knows Best,* or *Leave It to Beaver,* popular television shows from an earlier era that reflected happy, monogamous marriages with children.

It's more like a version of *The Brady Bunch,* a television show from 1969–1974, that demonstrated that blended families—in this case, two widowers with children from their first marriages—can provide a caring, nurturing and loving environment as those where both parents, married to one another, have a biological connection to their kids.

In fact, according to the latest data from the United States Census Bureau, just above 20 percent of all households, about 23.5 million, are married and bringing up children they conceived together, which is down by more than 1 million households from the previous Census in 2000.[19]

In the wake of this decline, there's been a significant increase in both single parent households and unmarried partner households. The only thing that seems to have remained steady is divorce. It's about 10 percent of the adult population in both the 2000 and 2010 Census.

As Dr. Press, a sociologist at the University of Virginia, told the coauthor of this book, in an article he wrote for *Bay State Parent* magazine, "The family structure has been changing rapidly. There are so many unorthodox looking families compared to 10, 20 or even 30 years ago. The blended family is common. The single parent family is common because of divorce. Unmarried people are having children or adopting children. More and more parents are gay (or lesbian) so you have an increasing proportion of parents and children that look nothing like the traditional nuclear family," she said.[20]

There are many issues that presently complicate any debate about the acceptance of plural marriage in the United States. Here are some of them:

- Same-gender marriage, which remains severely contested, is allowed in six states—Connecticut, Iowa, Massachusetts, New Hampshire, New York, and Vermont—but other states, as well as Congress, have passed laws defining marriage as an institution that's the exclusive province of one man to one woman. But given the U.S. Constitution's Full Faith and Credit Clause—meaning that one state's laws are recognized by all other states—will one state's recognition or nonrecognition of same-gender marriage face a Supreme Court challenge?
- Presently, U.S. Attorney General Eric Holder says the Obama administration will not defend exclusive heterosexual monogamy in the Defense of Marriage Act, which was signed into law by former President Bill Clinton in 1996.
- If the United States legalizes same-gender marriage, will other alternative marital arrangements, which might challenge preconceived

notions of what constitutes normal family life and normal sexual relationships between adults, be accepted? This is the "slippery slope into polygamy" argument, which we will consider later.

- In the last 10 years, some Muslim immigrants to the United States and Canada entered into polygamous marriages in their native countries. Should these marriages be recognized by their adopted homelands? Canada will be considered later for its cultural and political similarity to the United States.

- In the United States, individual states are billions of dollars in debt, and the federal government is about $14 trillion in debt and growing, meaning there's a chance this will force funding cuts in social safety-net programs. In fact, the National Association of State Budget Officers announced last year that states will cut spending on public assistance programs.[21] With the unemployment rate at a high for the foreseeable future and some companies transferring jobs from one state to another or even out of the country, the U.S. economy is very unstable. Can more plural relations, which can bring about increased extended family, become a new family-based social safety net for those unemployed or who require financial assistance? This is one advantage argued in defense of Fundamentalist Latter-day Saints (FLDS) polygamy by advocates for its decriminalization. We consider plural marriage in several American communities, including the FLDS and some African American communities.

- Kay S. Hymowitz, in her 2012 book *Manning Up: How the Rise of Women Has Turned Men into Boys,* says that the numbers of marriageable men for highly educated and professional women is declining because fewer men are attending college.[22] If these women want to marry their cultural, economic, and intellectual equal, will they become the one thing that their feminist sisters in the 1960s never expected—advocates for plural marriage as an option? They may need too, especially if they hope to marry someone whose values they share and if they want to share parenting responsibilities with a like-minded man.

- Marital change over the lifecycle is another situation where plural relations in marriage may be helpful. One might think, based on the statistics, that Americans are bipolar about marriage. One the one hand, reports the U.S. Census Bureau, more than 70 percent of all American adults—more than 167 million—describe themselves as "ever married," meaning that at one point in their life, or when the Census Bureau was surveying the population, they'd been married, at least once.[23] On the other hand, the Census Bureau also reports they're seeing more long-term couples divorce. Marriage for these long-term couples, one possible conclusion says, worked while they were bringing up children but failed when they became empty nesters or were facing the end of their professional careers. Maybe that's one way to explain the divorce of former vice president Al Gore and his wife, Tipper, who had been married for 40 years by time they brought their marriage to an end. Finally, the Census Bureau also reports they're seeing more second and third marriages among older people.

People seek out companionship and love and parenting possibilities, whether or not it's with someone with whom they share the same gender; these unions can provide children and, therefore, families and obligations. Some people, as the late Dr. Lewiston showed, who was anything but a Fundamentalist member of the Latter Day Saints, have the capacity to love more than one woman. Should that be a crime?

It's our feeling that the next social frontier for Americans to cross—which could be quite revolutionary—will be plural marriage and other partnership options. Plural family relations will likely be met with fierce resistance, a subject we will consider later, that has been put up against same-gender marriage. Given the debate on same-gender marriage and some of the issues it has spawned, including the rights of the transgendered, it appears the argument isn't so much about marriage rights but the right of individuals to decide how they want to constitute their family, even if it is far from traditional looking. This debate, it appears, will continue, perhaps become more complicated, as different lifestyles, including plural marriage, gain acceptance by the American public.

We should also make another point clear. Our support for plural marriage isn't limited to just polygyny, one husband with more than one wife. We're equally in favor of polyandry, one wife with many husbands. Indeed, we can support many combinations of marriage, both plural and monogamous, so long as they consist of consenting adults committed to loving one another as well as the children who may become part of any marital union.

The traditional American family is moving closer to a blended family reality even though the monogamous, nuclear version remains the ideal. In the blended family, as we shall see, the "wife-in-law" trap (ongoing relations among women with a common past or current husband) is all too common in our family life. Africans (in conversations with Kilbride) refer to this as "non-simultaneous polygamy" or "slow-motion polygamy" with frequent divorce and remarriage as a source of conflict in an exclusive nuclear family model ideal.

With the United States, like other countries, facing an unstable economy, single parent households, unmarried households, questions about health insurance, same-gender marriage, divorce and remarriage, questions about the best way to bring up children, and the culture as defined and discussed in popular television shows and the potential decline of marriageable men for highly educated and professional women, the time is right to engage in a thoughtful conversation about the merits and pitfalls of plural marriage. That's what we intend to do with this book.

Let's also make something clear: we don't advocate plural marriage the way it's commonly seen in the United States—with the police arresting an adult man because he's "married" to an underage girl, not a frequent but usually sensationalized abuse by some polygamists. Only consenting adults should be allowed to enter into any type marriage, whether it's monogamous, plural, gay, lesbian, or straight.

As Dr. Bennion has suggested, FLDS plural marriage should be decriminalized in the United States so it can be examined, out in the open, by the country's citizens.[24] In fact, she suggests, there's a feminist argument on its behalf: because it involves more than one wife, polygyny allows the possibility of one or more of the wives to pursue a professional career outside the home or advance their education while taking comfort and reassurance in knowing other family members—the other wives in this case—will provide the same love and care for her children that they would.[25]

For those who view plural marriage as only an abuse of women, it sometimes is. There is, however, no singular argument to be made here. We develop a theme of "it depends" to better understand examples of well-adjusted polygamy in the FLDS situation and in other communities, both in the United States and abroad. Moreover, it's important to keep in mind that there are lots of shelters throughout the United States for women from monogamous marriages. If plural marriage were decriminalized, it would make it far easier for a battered wife in a plural setting to run to the authorities—without risking the breakup of a family she may cherish.

WHY A SECOND BOOK

This book, which first appeared in 1994, was partially a response to the high number of divorces in the United States, which often resulted in negative consequences for the couple's children. More so than the first edition, this book is a child-centered approach to marriage and the family. We will consider, again, the idea that some divorces may be avoided by adding a spouse to what is to be a blended family, a potential solution to avoid the hostile separation and remarriage that often produce conflicts and dilemma for women and children and even men. In fact, our pattern of serial monogamy is often called "slow-motion polygamy," so why not make it legal?

Plural marriage, which is widely recognized around the world, isn't about to bring monogamous marriage to an end. Even in those societies where polygamy is the ideal, the majority of marriages are always monogamous. We intend to show the reasons for this and the social circumstances where polygamy has been successfully practiced. And plural marriage should not be seen as plural sexuality. It isn't. It's about marriage and family, with its many obligations and restrictions.

This book is not a retreat into moral relativism, a primer on sexuality, or a call for undisciplined family life only in pursuit of multiple sexual partners. It is one where concern for the children must be the highest priority. As Dr. Kilbride tells his introductory anthropology students, it is insightful to note that there is a reason why polygamy is described in their textbook in the chapter on marriage and the family, not one on sexuality. Many Americans see polygamy as only a sexual practice and this common cultural construction needs to be undone.

Much has changed since 1994, including fewer people marrying, a sharp increase in single parent households and, now, a rising number of divorces among people who are 50 and older. In addition, television shows, like *Big Love* and *Sister Wives*, have provided a glimpse of how polygyny is practiced in the United States.

More so than in the first edition of this book, in this one we've quoted and attempted to interview many American experts in their field of expertise. No one has told us plural marriage is perfect. If anything, they've said it's a very difficult lifestyle to maintain. They have also said it should be a legal option because, for some people, it's the only way they'll experience the benefits of marriage and their children will be ensured of knowing both of their parents.

Since the first edition, the issue of same-gender marriage is more so at the forefront, with more and more states giving it legal approval. One of the advantages that same-gender marriage has, one legal writer says, is that "Gays have many straight friends and family members who are part of the American mainstream."[26] Polygamists, in comparison, are isolated and in a minority—similar to what heterosexual married couples may become in the future—and suffer in their attempts to bring their marriages into the open legally because plural marriages are "chiefly practiced by separatist Mormon communities, whose political connections are limited by their living apart."[27]

Can a society that claims to be progressive reject a lifestyle simply because it's a minority, isolated and not understood by the majority?

This book is not the final word on plural marriage. We have looked at a variety of sources, including Kilbride's expertise on the topic, as we updated and prepared this book. We are sure others will also examine this issue and may very likely come up with different conclusions.

We look at how plural marriage—both polygyny (one man married to more than one women at the same time) and polyandry (one woman married to more than one man at the same time)—are practiced outside the United

States; the history of monogamous marriage; and the economics of marriage, both plural and monogamous.

In addition, we also review some recent Supreme Court rulings about relationships. Some of them may very well provide a legal opening for either legalizing or decriminalizing plural marriages. We have also looked at a variety of legal opinions that have studied plural marriages and offer a means by which these unions could be legally managed. Much of it is based on how some monogamous marriages are reviewed in some states.

We also examine religion's influence on marriage and show why plural marriage should not be feared, which is now the dominant American viewpoint.

While the authors of this book certainly think plural marriage should be an option for consenting adults, we understand that many people have a very different point of view on this issue. We especially invite them to read this book. In many ways it's for them that we write. We also know that plural marriage is not likely to be legally accepted anytime soon. But one thing is for sure—before people react viscerally against plural marriage, they would be better served reading and learning more about it. There are many demographic groups in the United States, we believe, whose lives would improve if they had a plural marriage option.

A FURTHER NOTE ABOUT THE AUTHORS

The authors have very different professional backgrounds. Kilbride has been an anthropology professor for more than 40 years, evaluating various cultural practices, and Page has worked in and around the newspaper industry for more than 20. They teamed up to write and update this book because the topic is still so compelling. It is our hope that many people, of all backgrounds, will read this book. Everyone, even if they remain single throughout their lives, is likely touched by marriage. We have all experienced childhood, and we all have a stake in the quality of life of our children.

In spite of their different professions, Kilbride's and Page's jobs have something in common: they both study the human condition and human behavior. Anthropology is the study of cultural influences as they are applied to human behavior. Journalism, usually less intellectual because it's written and produced on short, tight deadlines, tells the story, any given day, about how people live in their communities.

We suggest, too, that there be more professional pairings of journalists and academics. It is one more way to facilitate a much broader understanding of some very difficult topics as they are applied to public audiences.

While it's likely no surprise that Kilbride, an anthropologist with many years of study in Africa, where polygamy is a cultural norm, supports plural marriage as an option, some in the journalistic community might wonder why a reporter would do the same. There's an answer for that: his love of the Bill of Rights provides him with an appreciation for human freedom so long as those rights and freedoms do not impinge on anyone else.

NOTES

1. Richard C. Paddock, "Doctor Led Three Lives with Three Wives: Polygamy: Stanford University Professor never Divorced and Kept Households with each Woman. Truth Emerged after his Death in August," *Los Angeles Times*, October 14, 1991, http://articles.latimes.com/1991-10-14/news/mn-436_1_stanford-professor.

2. S. L. Wykes, "Bigamist's Family Stunned, Anger Outweighs Grief after Physicians Death," *San Jose Mercury News*, October 11, 1991.

3. Paddock, "Doctor Led Three Lives."

4. Ibid.

5. S. L. Wykes, "Respected Doctor had Multiple Wives, Secret Bank Account," *San Jose Mercury News*, October 8, 1991. Also see S. L. Wykes, "Stanford Doctor Had Secret Life—Three Wives," *San Jose Mercury News*, October 8, 1991. All *San Jose Mercury News* articles were accessed via the newspaper's archives, hosted at http://nl.newsbank.com.

6. From http://www.fightbigamy.typepad.com, a blog that keeps tabs on bigamy cases in the United States.

7. Felicia R. Lee, "*Big Love*: Real Polygamists Look at HBO Polygamists and Find Sex," *The New York Times*, March 28, 2006, http://www.nytimes.com/2006/03/28/arts/television/28poly.html?_r=1&pagewanted=all; and "Philly's Black Muslims Increasingly Turn to Polygamy," National Public Radio, May 28, 2008, http://www.npr.org/templates/story/story.php?storyId=90857818.

8. Martha Nussbaum, "Debating Polygamy," the University of Chicago Law School Blog, May 19, 2008, http://uchicagolaw.typepad.com/faculty/2008/05/debating-polyga.html.

9. Nussbaum, "Debating Polygamy."

10. "Barely Half of U.S. Adults are Married—A Record Low," Pew Research Center, December 14, 2011, http://www.pewsocialtrends.org/2011/12/14/barely-half-of-u-s-adults-are-married-a-record-low/.

11. "Table A1. Marital Status of People 15 Years and Over, By Age, Sex, Personal Earnings, Race and Hispanic Origin," United States Census Bureau, November 2011, http://www.census.gov/population/www/socdemo/hh-fam/cps2011.html.

12. "Domestic Violence Facts," National Coalition Against Domestic Violence, July 2007, http://www.ncadv.org.

13. Gregory C. Pingree, "Rhetorical Holy War: Polygamy, Homosexuality, and the Paradox of Community and Autonomy," *Journal of Gender, Social Policy and The Law* 14:2 (2006): pp. 314–383.

14. David Boaz, "Privatize Marriage: A Simple Solution to the Gay Marriage Debate," Slate.com, April 25, 1997, http://www.slate.com/articles/briefing/articles/1997/04/privatize_marriage.html.

15. Ibid.

16. Dr. Andrea Press, interview by Doug Page.

17. Dr. Janet Bennion, interview by Doug Page.

18. "The Religious Composition of the United States," Pew Forum on Religion & Public Life, 2007, http://religions.pewforum.org/pdf/report-religious-landscape-study-chapter-1.pdf.

19. U.S. Census Bureau data from http://www.census.gov. The 2010 data from the Census Bureau is available at http://factfinder2.census.gov/faces/tableservices/jsf/pages/productview.xhtml?pid=DEC_10_DP_DPDP1. The 2000 data from the Census Bureau is available at http://censtats.census.gov/data/US/01000.pdf.

20. Doug Page, "Changing Families: From Traditional to Whatever Works?" *Bay State Parent*, February 2011, pp. 10 and 11.

21. Michael Cooper, "Improved Tax Collections Can't Keep Pace with States' Fiscal Needs, Survey Finds," *The New York Times*, June 2, 2011, http://www.nytimes.com/2011/06/02/us/02states.html?_r=1.

22. Kay S. Hymowitz, "Where Have The Good Men Gone," *The Wall Street Journal*, February 19, 2011, http://online.wsj.com/article/SB10001424052748704409004576146321725889448.html?KEYWORDS=where+have+the+good+men+gone.

23. "Number of Times Married by Sex by Marital Status for the Population 15 years and Over," 2009 American Community Survey, http://www.census.gov/prod/2011pubs/p70-125.pdf.

24. Page, "Changing Families," pp. 10 and 11.

25. Ibid.

26. Eugene Volokh, "Same Sex Marriage and Slippery Slopes," *Hofstra Law Review*, May 22, 2008, p. 122.

27. Ibid.

2

The Monogamous Ideal in Western Tradition and America: Variations

Any book about plural marriage in America must provide an overview into the origin and history of monogamous marriage in Western civilization.

Our intent is not to provide a complete history of monogamous marriage but to show that marriage has undergone a transformation from being something that was strictly a civil institution (as was the case in Roman and Athenian days) to a religious one (as was the case when the Catholic Church dominated Europe) and continuing into the Protestant Reformation.

Monogamous marriage, like plural marriage, is powerful, both as an idea and in practice. It ties people together through a ritual ceremony and, if children are born, can extend and transfer a family's name, property, and wealth into perpetuity. While plural marriage is illegal in some countries, including the United States, monogamous marriage is found in virtually all cultures and is legally recognized throughout the world.

Monogamous marriage in America is about social control. As E. J. Graff discusses in her book *What's Marriage For?*, marriage was about controlling women because they had little or no legal standing.[1] Men, depending on their social standing, have always had political rights. But women, whether they lived during antiquity, the Middle Ages or even, as some might argue, as late as the middle of the 20th century, were with few political and economic rights and, in some cases, could be treated as being just above chattel.

Today's monogamous marriage in America is rooted in antiquity. As for its particular values, including social control, well, much of that depends on where the marriage takes place and the cultural, social, and legal norms in that particular country.

TRADITION IN THE WESTERN WORLD

In the Western world, marriage customs date back to ancient Greece as a societal practice. Men and women weren't marrying for the same reasons they do today—because, ideally, they're romantically in love with one another. They were creating a domestic life in which to bring up their children, and, for the men at least, show that they were mature and responsible, even if they weren't sexually faithful to their wives.

As stated in the Magnus Hirschfeld Archive for Sexology website, marriage was considered so important to the Greeks that, in some cases, bachelors were prevented from holding government jobs. Marriage was seen as "a practical matter without much romantic significance." As one Greek statesman, Demosthenes, said, "We have prostitutes for our pleasure, concubines for our health and wives to bear us lawful offspring."[2]

The Roman Empire created much of the foundation for marriage as it is understood and practiced today. Marriage was a civil institution, not a religious one, with contracts and, like the Greeks, allowed for divorce.

There were two kinds of marriage in Rome, "dignitas" and "concubinatus." The former, as detailed by the late sociologist Carle C. Zimmerman (1949), was a binding contract while the latter was a version of marriage that would likely find opposition today among people who might be considered cultural conservatives.

Dignitas marriage, as the Romans created it, involved a husband-wife relationship with children. The wife lived with her husband, tended to the house, and even brought a dowry to the marriage. Her family retained an interest in the dowry and, as Zimmerman wrote in his book, *Family and Civilization,* the couple continued to have a relationship with both his family as well as hers. Any offspring the couple produced took the father's name and became his legitimate heirs. It was at this time that social control of women, mentioned earlier, was most evident.

A concubinatus marriage was entirely different. As Zimmerman details, it was a much looser relationship but still "subject to legal regulation and social consequences." If this union produced children, they remained with their mother and were her legal heirs; they could be adopted by the father and, thus, have the same kind of legal standing as a child born into a dignitas marriage.[3]

In both versions of marriage, as well as the one that happened in Greece, the man was completely in charge of the relationship. Wives had limited rights, including the ability to ask for a divorce.

Unlike the Germanic and Irish cultures on their borders, polygamy was not practiced in Rome. But Roman monogamy, instead, was marked with married men carrying on affairs and sexual dalliances with concubines who had no legal family rights.

JEWISH INFLUENCE

Discussing sex and morality in the Western tradition, the authors Herant Katchadourian and Donald Lunde (1975) note a positive attitude, starting with the Jewish tradition, to marriage and the family in the Hebrew Bible or the Old Testament, as Christians refer to the book. The Jews saw procreation as the primary obligation of sexual activity between a husband and his wife. The Talmud stresses a religious obligation to marry and raise a family. Men, in particular, had an obligation to carry on the family name.

Because Jewish tradition holds marriage in high regard, Katchadourian and Lunde write, "There seemed to be a very positive feeling among Jews about sexual intercourse, within the confines of marriage at least, which contrasts rather sharply with the attitude prevalent in the early Christian Church, an attitude that has persisted to some extent until very recent times: that sex is intrinsically evil."[4]

In its earliest form, Jewish law even allowed polygamy. The book of Deuteronomy 25: 5–6, describes the custom whereby a deceased brother's widow goes to his brother (levirate) to "take her as his wife and perform the duty of a husband's brother to her."[5] The surviving brother was frequently already married. In fact, examples of polygamy are so common in the Hebrew Bible, such as Abraham and David, that non-European Christians are mystified as to why polygamy is so much opposed by Christian missionaries.

Hebrew religious laws permitted concubines and polygamy, with some patriarchs having numerous wives. Adultery was not permitted; however, it appears that adultery only means having sex with a married woman, thus, leaving all men, married and single, free to have sexual relations with all nonmarried women because they could, in theory, become wives.

CHRISTIAN INFLUENCE

As Christianity gained influence across the Roman Empire, it flexed its muscles. The Church of Rome, which would become the Catholic Church, had assistance from Roman emperors who became Christian. The church said it would only recognize dignitas marriages, insisting they be made sacred and lasting unions and, in time, the concubinatus marriages went away, at least as an approved relationship.

Between the end of the Roman Empire and the Council of Trent in the 16th century, the church set down rules and regulations of married life. As the church saw European family life, it was very much in need of reform by regulation and law.

The Roman Church, at this time, defined marriage with 10 points, saying, among other things, that Christians could only marry other Christians; that marriage was a sacrament not just a ceremony, and, thus, a way of receiving God's grace; incest was prohibited (there was to be no marriage between first cousins); placed limits on divorce; made marriage independent of both the husband's and wife's family; abortion was not allowed; quarrels between families were not to be settled by fighting one another; last wills and testaments were introduced; and, finally, people were married to one another until one of them died. At this time, celibacy was elevated over marriage as the highest virtue in sexual conduct.

The Roman Church, earlier, was also fighting two major influences— Roman culture and the barbarian, nomadic, Germanic tribes of northern Europe, both of which were considered morally derelict, at least in the eyes of the church; the Germanic tribes, which also practiced plural marriage, as we have noted, were also considered a threat to civilization. As the Roman Church saw their role, it was up to them to define morality and, thus, what constituted a marriage and family that would be pleasing to God.

Writing in the fifth century, St. Augustine, one of the church's most influential theologians, said there were three fundamental tenets of marriage, including fides (loyalty), proles (children), and sacramentum (indissoluble unity of husbands and wives).

St. Augustine was not opposed to polygamy in principle, but he didn't think it would work in the West. His position was similar to the one taken much later by Martin Luther, the Catholic priest who instigated the Protestant Reformation in the 16th century.

One of the biggest differences between Luther and the church was how marriage would be controlled—by civil or religious authorities—the availability of divorce, and whether marriage led to eternal salvation.

As Luther saw it, marriage was very important—a way to make a sacrifice on God's behalf—Zimmerman wrote, but it was not a sacrament. He also felt that marriage laws should only be made by civil authorities—not one, single, worldwide religious body—because each country "has its own marriage customs" and thus, only the local governing authorities should regulate it. In a time when the Catholic Church was an example of a transnational, regulating body, Luther was, as Zimmerman sees him, a nationalist.[6]

While Luther didn't personally approve of divorce, he said it was permissible for adultery, refusal of conjugal duty, and if the couple wasn't in agreement on their religious faith. Luther, as E. J. Graff writes, also saw sexual desire as very powerful, maybe even, at times, all-consuming. Marriage, as Luther saw it, was a way to release pent-up sexual desire.

John Cairncross writes in his book *After Polygamy Was Made a Sin*, that, "If Luther rejected pleas for the re-introduction of polygamy, this is not because he thought such a move would be morally wrong but because he was convinced that it was not all expedient, since it would be bound to discourage potential converts to the new faith."[7]

In fact, Luther was so opposed to divorce that he wrote, "Indeed, I detest divorce so much, that I prefer bigamy rather than divorce, but whether it may be permitted, I do not dare to determine by myself."[8]

Soon after the Reformation began, Philip of Hess ruled over one of the first states in Germany to become Lutheran. His marriage to Christiana of Saxony produced seven children in 16 years, but Philip was not satisfied with the marriage. He requested Luther's advice on whether he might follow the example of the Hebrew Bible and marry another wife.

Luther replied, "Therefore I am not able to advise this, rather must advise against, especially for Christians, unless there be the highest need, as for example, if the wife has leprosy or is taken away from the husband in some other way."[9]

In another correspondence, Luther wrote in regard to the idea of polygamy being entertained by other reformers, "I confess, indeed, I cannot forbid anyone who wishes to marry several wives, nor is that against Holy Scripture; however, I do not want that custom introduced among Christians among whom it is proper to pass up even things which are permissible, to avoid scandal and to live respectably, which Paul everywhere enjoins."[10]

In 1539, Philip of Hess, with the written consent of Martin Luther and other Lutheran theologians and priests, approved a bigamist marriage that was consecrated by a wedding ceremony performed on March 4, 1540 by Philip's court preacher. His first wife had given her written permission for the ceremony.

We see that Martin Luther tolerated polygamy at least for special circumstances, and personally approved it over divorce, although he did not wish it to be extended to the masses.

Interestingly, in the privacy of their own home, Frau Luther reportedly sometimes debated her husband on polygamy, generally taking a negative stance. On one occasion, she was reported to have responded in reference to polygamy, "Before I put up with that, I would rather go back into the convent and leave you and all your children."[11]

ENGLAND'S KING HENRY VIII

The Church of England arose as a result of the marriage controversy centering on King Henry VIII's first marriage to Catherine of Aragon and his subsequent desire to marry Anne Boleyn, as described by Miller (1974, see also Alison Weir 1991).[12] In the 1520s, Henry met and courted Anne and was captivated by her French education and charm. Henry then approached Rome about an annulment from his first marriage. But Pope Clement VII refused, owing to theological objections and to political alliances in Europe. Catherine was an aunt of the French Emperor Charles V, a potentially powerful enemy of the Pope.

In the meantime, Anne had become pregnant with what Henry hoped would not be an illegitimate child. At this point, the Archbishop of Canterbury declared King Henry's marriage to Catherine annulled, resulting in Henry's excommunication from Rome.

But within the advisory group of cardinals with whom Pope Clement consulted, there was one prominent cardinal, Cardinal Cajetan, who many believe is the unnamed eminent divine the Pope cited who favored a bigamous resolution to their differences. Cajetan referred to some of St. Augustine's writings; Augustine said that polygamy was neither a sin nor a custom in Europe.

Even John Milton, one of England's great 17th-century poets, advocated for plural marriage. Leon Miller (1974) explored Milton's thoughts on divorce and polygamy. Soon after marrying, Milton was deserted by his wife. Because England's laws at the time didn't allow divorce, he couldn't end his marriage to the wife who had left him.

Spurred on by an attraction to another woman, Milton wrote in favor of reversing the divorce laws. Although he never published anything directly in favor of legalizing polygamy, it is known from his private testimony that Milton favored bigamy over divorce, particularly in situations such as his own where there was difficulty obtaining divorce.

Milton's published writings defend polygamy, primarily by referencing the patriarchs of the Hebrew Bible and to the theological rationales for their marriages. For example, Milton maintained theologians who attempted to deny the appropriateness of polygamy had to compose their opinions by interpretation or by basically quoting biblical verses out of context, a method he believed permitted virtually anything to be proven.

Miller (1974) also describes how Milton treated the subject of King David who was "no mortal more dear to God" and who was polygamous at a time when he was "entirely occupied in the study of the law and of God and in the right regulation of his life" (11). Miller concludes, "David perceived that Jehovah had established him King over Israel . . . and David took himself more concubines and wives" (11).

In 1536, in response to the Protestant Reformation, the Catholic Church held the Council of Trent. It released its conclusions about marriage nearly 30 years later, in 1563. To summarize, the church's leaders declared that only monogamy was permissible; celibacy is a higher state of life than marriage (something Luther had said was the exact opposite); marriage was to be regulated by the church; and there was no allowance for divorce.

MARRIAGE COMES TO AMERICA

If the Puritans were anything, they were all about that old-time religion. They weren't Puritan because they saw sex as sinful. They were Puritan because they rejected the role of bishops.

As they read the Bible, Jesus and his disciples didn't mention bishops and, thus, the Puritans struggled to reconcile why there should be any. In addition, the bishops of the Church of England did the monarch's bidding, working to keep their country free from any religious movement that might be suspected of upsetting or overthrowing governing institutions, including the church. This is why so many Puritans were forced to go into hiding, eventually taking refuge in Holland before embarking on their trans-Atlantic voyage to Massachusetts.

Puritans viewed sex as holy when it was confined to marriage. They were open about sex and thought it was a natural and joyous part of marriage. In fact, James Mattock was expelled from the First Church of Boston for refusing to sleep with his wife.

But keep something in mind—in 17th century America, marriage wasn't about love. It was more like a job two people shared to provide for one another. The husbands worked in the fields while the "wives tended to animals and a vegetable garden, sewed clothes, cooked, canned and did the washing" (Cherlin 2009, 43, 44).

The house any family lived in during those days didn't allow for privacy, especially if they were anything like what's on display at the Pilgrims' Plimoth Plantation in Massachusetts today. There was one main room, which was for cooking, sleeping, and any other activity. As for privacy, forget it. Everyone knew everyone else's business.

By 1700, 80 years after the Pilgrims arrived, church membership was lower than it had been in the early 1600s. Marriage unions, especially in some of the frontier areas, were also marked by what became called "informal marriage." Because the Anglican Church didn't have enough ministers for the colonies, a number of people, especially in the frontier areas, proclaimed their love and loyalty to one another and lived as a married couple.[13]

As the decades passed, and the colonies became the United States, and the new country went from the 18th to the 19th century, marriage didn't look all that different than it did with the Puritans, until just prior to the Civil War.

This is when the issue of divorce and, to some degree the rights of women (as well as men), within marriage, started coming up for debate.

Divorce had always been available but it was limited, usually, to adultery and abandonment. Another issue was how marriage was controlled and regulated.

In 1860, with North and South headed toward a fight, and with the availability of cross-country train travel, something happened that likely few had thought about: It was possible to seek and obtain a divorce in one state, sometimes with little difficulty, and have it recognized as legitimate and legal by another.

The 19th century's great, crusading, New York City newspaper editor, Horace Greely wrote that Indiana, a "paradise of free-lovers," was where a "prominent citizen of an Eastern manufacturing city, came to Indiana . . . obtained his divorce about dinner-time, and in the course of the evening was married to his new inamorata. . . . They soon started home . . . he introduced his new wife to her astonished predecessor, whom he notified that she must pack up and go."[14]

Robert Dale Owen, a former member of Indiana's House of Representatives, and someone who, by the standards of the 19th century, was a leading feminist, responded to Greeley's criticism about the ease of this divorce, saying, "The question remains, whether it be more pleasing in the sight of God and more conducive to virtue in man, to part decently in peace, or to live in shameful discord."[15]

After the Civil War, with the 19th century heading toward conclusion, the issues discussed about marriage included birth control, sexual intercourse for anything but procreation, the marriages of former slaves, the rising divorce rate, informal marriages, and the decline of traditional ones.

Cherlin describes this as a time of transformational change in the United States, as it went from an agrarian to manufacturing economy, with people flocking to cities for jobs and a husband and wife often not as close to one another as before, when they were living and working on a farm, because he was now at a factory. "Urbanization put people closer together in settings where their behavior was often unsupervised by family and neighbors."[16]

In the 19th century United States, there was also a debate about plural marriage. The territory of Utah was attempting to become a state but the Mormons, members of the Church of Jesus Christ of Latter-day Saints (LDS), practiced polygamy, saying that it was very religious because it dated back to Abraham. They also maintained that the Constitution's First Amendment, which allows the free expression of religion, provided the right to practice polygamy. But the federal government refused to allow polygamous marriage—there was even Supreme Court ruling on the issue—and, eventually, in 1890, the Mormon Church stopped allowing plural marriage, too. We will later consider the LDS historical polygamy and its current practice among Fundamentalist Latter Day Saints (FLDS).

20TH-CENTURY MARRIAGE: ROMANTIC LOVE

The single biggest difference between marriage in the 20th century in the United States and the ones in prior centuries was the idea of romantic love. Perhaps because more and more people were living in cities, working in factories or offices, the notion that couples share a pragmatic, rather than romantic, relationship dimmed. Nevertheless, there were many examples of marital love prior to this time. One notable example is that of the second president of the United States, John Adams, and his wife, Abigail. Adams held great passion and love for his wife and became nearly inconsolable after she died:

> It all came to a sudden end in October 1818. Abigail collapsed with typhoid and probably suffered an accompanying stroke that made it difficult for her to speak . . . John first reached out to Jefferson, who had lost his own wife many years earlier: "The dear partner of my life for fifty-four years and for many years more as a lover, now lies in extremis, forbidden to speak or be spoken to." Abigail was in great pain and at one point murmured to John that she knew she was dying. . . . After leaving her bedside in tears, John was inconsolable: "I wish I could lie down beside her and die too . . . I cannot bear to see her in this state." Despite Abigail's chronic ailments, as almost ten years her senior, John had always expected to go first. With John at her bedside, Abigail died on October 28. She was seventy-four. The music they had made together for so long finally stopped.
>   . . . John remained adrift and in mourning for nearly a year: "My House is a Region of Sorrow," he explained to one friend. "Inhabited by a sorrowful Widower . . . burdened with Multitudes of Letters from total strangers, teasing me with impertinent inquiries." He felt strangely alone.[17]

As with any idea, it didn't just start in the 20th century. The idea of an emotional bond between men and women, as the foundation of marriage, started in the late 19th century.

After World War I, the idea came into its own with books, like Theodor van de Velde's *Ideal of Marriage: Its Physiology and Technique*, which, as Cherlin describes, told readers that for marriages to succeed, the couple needed a robust, mutually satisfying sex life. Lovemaking was so important to the marriage, according to van de Velde, that if it didn't include variety and satisfaction, especially for the wife, the couple would drift apart and likely divorce.[18]

Family life during this time, post-World War I and pre-World War II, according to convention, was about a man married to a woman and together they would have children. He would work outside of the home while she tended to the house and child rearing.

The 1950s was a time of great conformity and much of how society looked—a man and woman married to one another with children—was seen on some of the more popular television shows, like *Leave It to Beaver*. The husband worked outside of the home while his wife tended to the domestic duties, including managing and bringing up the children on a daily basis.

An earlier generation of observers on the American family scene in the 1950s included anthropologist Margaret Mead who, among other writings, published *Male and Female* (1949) soon after World War II. In this classic work Mead stated that the American family life of her generation often fell short of satisfying human need.

She observed, for example, that the American family, which was predicated on the assumption that each family would have a home of its own, represented a narrowing of family life. That is, it excluded from the home the grandmother, the unmarried sister, the unmarried daughter, and even the domestic servant who in earlier generations sometimes took on a family role. "We have multiplied the number of homes in which the whole life of the family has to be integrated each day, meals cooked, lunches packed, children bathed, doors locked, dogs walked, cats put out, food ordered, washing-machines set in motion, flowers sent to the sick, birthday cakes baked, pocket-money sorted, mechanical refrigerators defrosted."[19]

She also noted that the fragmentation of household units had resulted in more work for women. Now, she said, there was only one pair of woman's hands to feed the baby, answer the telephone, turn off the gas under the pot boiling over, soothe the child who has broken a toy, and open both doors at once. Women had become nutritionists, child psychologists, engineers, production managers, and expert buyers, all in one.

Mead, an outspoken person on many public issues, believed that marriage customs in the United States were quite restrictive, based on the assumption that marriage must be for life. Remarkably, she wrote about divorce at a time when considerable stigma was attached to the divorced person and the rate was less than 10 percent.

The American marriage ideal, she observed, "is one of the most difficult marriage forms that the human race has ever attempted, and the casualties are surprisingly few, considering the complexities of the task. But the ideal is so high, and the difficulties so many, that it is definitely an area of American life in which a very rigorous reexamination of the relationship between idea and practices is called for."[20] As to divorce, "this hope for a complete commitment fits *very* well with our traditional marriage form, in which Church and State combine to insist that all marriages are for life, and that no marriage can be broken without branding the one who breaks it as a failure, if not a criminal and an enemy of society."[21]

Barbara Dafoe Whitehead has documented a pattern of stressful outcomes for family members in what she calls our "divorce culture" in a widely read article in *The Atlantic Monthly* (1993) and subsequent book called *The Divorce Culture* (1997).[22]

Mead disapproved of condemnation of divorce while favoring it when the rate was very low. In opposition to this thought, as represented by Barbara Whitehead, which came from both pulpit and bench, a criticism that assumes "that all those who get divorces are selfish, self-indulgent creatures."[23] She was committed instead to a "cultural constructionist" or "cultural reinvention" framework; specifically, she pointed out that "there is no reason why we cannot develop manners and customs appropriate to the greater fragility of marriage in the United States."[24]

Mead had particularly keen insights into the importance of family life for children and into the potential threat of un-reinvented marriage and divorce with children's welfare in mind: "In a pattern for marriage which accepts the fact that marriage *may* be for life, *can* be for life, but also may not be, it is possible to set to work to find ways of establishing that permanence which is most congruent with bringing up children, who are defined as immature until the early twenties."[25]

How would Mead have reacted to Whitehead's conservative view on divorce? Certainly, Mead's fundamental message today, regardless of any specific domain of cultural life involved, is that we should always be ready to change. Generally as an anthropologist and specifically in her book, *Male and Female*, Mead set out a strategy for change guided by knowledge of our own culture and its history and that of cultures elsewhere. In her view we, as humans, are primarily cultural, and it is within our grasp to address problems from a cultural constructionist perspective.

Insightful observers of American marriage and family life in the pre-1960s, post-World War II era were in fact observing and critiquing what in our culture continues to be considered the "traditional" form of the family. Hernandez writes concerning this ideal that, "in the 1950s the U.S. television program called *Ozzie and Harriet* idealized the . . . family in which the father was a full time, year around worker, the mother was a full time homemaker . . . and all the children were born after the parents' only marriage" (1998, 208). This ideal also included a small, nuclear unit consisting of a man and a woman and their children, each unit residing in a separate domicile and constituting a kind of isolated social unit, with marriage and betrothal activities occurring in the school years or soon thereafter, resulting in a relatively early entrance into marriage by current standards. Divorce was stigmatized, as was birth out of wedlock, and they occurred less frequently than they do today.

The nuclear family pattern could itself be contrasted with an earlier generation of traditional family life when the family farm was the ideal. The modern nuclear family, which we now take to be traditional, evolved, as Mead observed, from earlier traditional experiences in American life in which the extended family of two or more generations often lived in the same house. Those who cling to the idea of the "traditional" as the absolute baseline against which all other change must be measured need only reflect on our own marital and family patterns over the last century or so to see that the idea of the traditional is itself always subject to changing circumstances.

In the 1960s, the next idea in marriage was that of individual space and self-development. The notion here, as Cherlin writes, is that husbands and wives were expected to develop themselves—or take up their own interests— so as to maintain their own identity rather than simply be a spouse sacrificing oneself to their spouse. This idea also included that gender roles were "flexible and negotiable," and that "communication and openness in confronting problems are essential."[26]

The '60s—marked as it was by the Vietnam War, great political and social upheaval, which included the pill, allowing women to determine when they would procreate—saw self-development within marriage as something that perhaps encouraged "people to find personal satisfaction outside of their marriage."[27]

As for the pill, while there were those who thought it would strengthen marriage—because it allowed a couple to have sex without worrying about pregnancy—it also allowed "people to lead active sex lives outside of marriage"—without fear of pregnancy![28]

Over the last 40 years, marriage has experienced considerable disruption, including no-fault divorce laws, which, in some states, Cherlin notes, doesn't allow courts any reason to reject the divorce sought by the couple; the legal recognition, in some states, of same gender marriage; civil unions, which provide many of the same legal benefits of marriage without the marriage; the reduced legal standing of a husband to his wife; and the rise of cohabitating couples.[29]

In the United States, there's an argument that the easing of divorce laws has contributed to the emancipation of women. They're no longer stuck in a bad marriage for social, economic, or even legal reasons. They retain the legal ability to free themselves from a man (and, in some cases, a woman) who doesn't love them in the manner they prefer.

For that matter, the same is true for men. Today's culture—and certainly the law—no longer forces a man to feel obligated to stay in a marriage he neither likes nor wants.

Boston University Law School professor Linda McClain, in an interview with the coauthor for an article in *Bay State Parent* magazine, wondered if today's legal interpretation of marriage law, at least in Massachusetts, one of the first states to recognize same-gender marriage, still means that the law's original intent—to channel adults into being responsible parents— holds up.[30]

Perhaps now, more so than in previous decades and centuries, when both genders needed one another to survive, the people who are marrying and staying married today are, to borrow a phrase, a group of the truly willing. And while we celebrate the freedom women enjoy, we wonder, at the same time, if there's any price, potentially negative, as a result of the many changes that occurred to marriage and divorce. It appears the institution has returned, in some ways, to its Greco-Roman roots, becoming more of a civil institution because it's easier to divorce.

The changes to marriage have resulted in adults living in a variety of types of households. According to the latest census (in 2010), about 50 percent of all adults, around 120 million, are married. But more than 30 percent of all adults, around 74 million, have never been married. And just so we're clear, at this point, the Census Bureau hasn't tracked the numbers of same-gender married couples.

All of these changes bring up many questions about U.S. society. Are we lonelier nation than previously? Are today's married couples happier than previous generations of married couples? Are single people, because they're seeing married couples experience difficulties, averse to marrying?

As for child rearing, the census shows that of the country's 74 million children, 23 million live in single parent (both men and women) households while about 50 million are living in married-couple households. Will the living arrangement of today's child—especially if they're in a single-parent household—affect their take on marriage?

Can a single parent teach a child the value of the gender that's not living with them? In other words, can a single father teach his son why he should appreciate the talents and perspectives a woman brings to life, love, or any situation? And vice-versa? Can gay parents teach their sons the value of women? Can lesbian parents teach their daughters the value of men? These and similar questions have been answered in the affirmative, as we shall see.

Hansen and Garey (1998) write about recent household types including single-parent households, singles, and continuing multigenerational households. To these we would add even more recently the "boomerang" household in response to a downturn in the United States economy in which adult children increasingly return to live with their parents, demonstrating the close connection between family structure and economy.

Don Edgar writes about contemporary, blended family forms, "There is growing evidence that divorced and reconstituted families are emerging as a new form (the Lattice family) as couples ensure ongoing contacts with children" (2004, 14). He believes the Lattice family often pools resources, a fact which we will relate to plural marriage later.

The intersection between ethnicity and class in family life is well documented in Japanese anthropologist Yasushi Watanabe's book (2004) comparing the "Yankee" family with that of the South Boston Irish. The former are historically wealthy families who still overall value individualism and economic achievement to a greater extent than the more communitarian-oriented Irish American families of South Boston. The latter are overall loyal to the Catholic Church, neighborhood and their ethnic roots.

Watanabe writes that in the Yankee family culture the principle of "serial monogamy" is alive and well. He reports, "The timing of divorce differs significantly . . . informants testify that the 1960s was a 'confused and confusing' era . . . and the conventional notion of marriage . . . began to be openly contested" (2004, 86). The less wealthy Irish are also experiencing change, for example, with more husbands staying at home while their wives work on the weekends. Concerning divorce, Watanabe states that in South Boston, divorce appears to be about 25–35 percent below the national average and that such impersonal devices as prenuptial agreements are unheard of, or, as one informant said, "We ain't so rich" (170).

In this regard, the *Philadelphia Inquirer* ran a story by Sandy Bauers on December 9, 1992, called "Seasonal Adjustments," which described the stresses associated with holiday routines and blended families. She states, "for children of divorced parents, the holiday routine may include two batches of presents. It also may include a tug of war between their mother and father."

The parents involved reported a great deal of anxiety over the intrusion of stepchildren into their new marriage; the husband's decision not to have a second family, complaints over the other's parenting skills, visitation rights, and the emotional price imposed on their children.

Jan Pryor and Liz Trinder have summarized studies of children's views of family transitions after divorce. These are diverse; nevertheless, there are themes. They report that, "children are usually sad and bewildered . . . long for reconciliation" (2004, 334). Adults too often report high levels of unhappiness. Similarly, Crytser concludes, "children from former marriages often walk a difficult road. They not only have to deal with their mother's bitterness toward the new step family; they must also relate to a stepmother and stepsiblings who may not be ready or willing to accept them" (1990, 76). Some research shows that a significant minority of children have neutral or mildly positive reactions to their parents' marital break up. This is not unexpected. Divorce can be positive for children; the argument here, once again, is not essentialist.

MONOGAMY AND ADULTERY

Marital infidelity in recent decades is the gift that never stops giving in our national political culture and media. Infidelity involving presidents, governors, senators and other elected officials appears to be almost commonplace.

Add to that the well-worn image of the loyal wife standing by her man, which is now offset by that of wifely hostility and opposition. This was seen with Hillary Clinton as details of her husband's dalliance with a White House intern went public; with Elin Nordegren, the ex-wife of golf star Tiger Woods; and with Elizabeth Edwards, the late and former wife of John Edwards, a former U.S. senator from North Carolina.

One of the most recent cases bears directly on the theme of this book, the affair of Senator Edwards, nearly elected vice president in 2004. While previous senators have covered up out-of-wedlock children (Senator Strom Thurmond is a famous example), the Edwards affair provides a good perspective on how husband, wife, and mistress evaluate their situation from a child-centered perspective. After a lengthy delay, Edwards eventually recognized his daughter, a move that should be applauded. A child-centered perspective, even if it violates the nuclear family ideal, is difficult and sometimes requires courage in the absence of cultural support.

The public posture in this affair illustrates a cultural script of moral panic about adultery, especially with children involved. Within a framework of romantic love about which marriage is "supposed" to be all about, consequences for children are absent, as in the Edward's affair. In a March 15, 2009, story, we learned that Ms. Hunter loves "Johnny," as she referred to the former senator, and that he is very supportive. She believed, at least then, that they would be forever together, but they have not discussed any plans to marry.

Assuming Elizabeth Edwards had not been stricken with cancer, could this story and many like it have had a different outcome for all concerned, especially the child, if plural marriage were a culturally sanctioned option?

One of the reasons the divorce rate is so high, of course, is that many marriages break up over adultery, which also holds consequences for the children who are also invested in the husband-wife relationship. Media queries are so culturally specific that rarely does anyone questioning an affair or looking into a similar event ever challenge the Edwards-Hunter trilogy to think about ways a child, and perhaps a new spouse, can be incorporated into a new family life. Instead, in multiple television shows, for example, Mrs. Edwards was asked repeatedly about such things, for example, as her bedtime conversations with her husband and other intimate details of their private life.

Kilbride's African and European colleagues expressed shock over the extent to which private sexual topics are public in American political discourse compared to the privacy still enjoyed elsewhere in the world. Kilbride reminded them that such privacy was once very American, certainly so during the Kennedy presidency in the 1960s. Things had changed by the 1990s when former President Clinton's sexuality preoccupied the United States much to the dismay of the world at large.

By all public accounts, Clinton and Kennedy were superb fathers, but this perspective on them was seemingly lost by the 1990s. It seems fatherhood is overridden by sexuality as a master cultural symbol. A child-centered perspective, on the other hand, includes considering fatherhood both within marriage and even on those occasions when it involves "outside" or "illegitimate" children, terms in need of reinvention and separation from social stigma.

In a landmark study, Annette Lawson (1988) reports that, according to surveys, even in the liberal San Francisco area, about 80 percent believe extramarital sex to be wrong. She concludes that most people still consider adultery to be deviant sexual behavior. Her investigation does, however, show some loosening in attitudes among married people: 60 percent of married men and nearly as many married women, for example, disagreed to some extent with the statement, "Adultery is always wrong under all circumstances."

Interestingly, those who are remarried tended to take a stronger view against adultery than those who had stayed married to one spouse. The latter's attitudes apparently become comparatively more liberal over time. Overall, however, and significantly, based on her review of the literature and her own research findings, Lawson came to the striking conclusion that women have fewer lovers than men. Nevertheless, she reports, as female lifestyles become more similar to male lifestyles, the pattern of their adulterous relations tend to look similar. For example, she indicates that if a wife is better educated than her husband, she tends to have a greater number of liaisons than he does.

One factor contributing to adultery in U.S. culture is the seemingly strong attraction between older men (frequently already married) and younger women. In other cultures, this attraction seems to find expression in polygamous marriage and concubinage. For instance, in many societies, the youngest wife is often particularly favored and the one the husband loves the most whereas, he has a more respectful and less amorous relationship with the eldest wife. In our own culture, the age attraction has been described in terms of the so-called Jennifer principle. In her book, *Jennifer Fever*, Barbara Gordon (1988) links the Jennifer principle to the pattern of divorce in the United States. She writes,

> But statistics from the U.S. census reveal that there are millions of American men who choose to add a younger woman to their lives, and they "do" marry them. The first time around, American men marry women close to their own age, but in second marriages they marry women five or more years younger If a man is in his forties when he decides to take the plunge again, it is likely he will marry a woman ten or more years younger. (1988, 9)

Gordon accepts the Darwinian principle of evolutionary significance in seeking to account for the "Jennifer fever" pattern of behavior. For example, men who opt for younger women are choosing women who are in their reproductive years; at the same time, Gordon points out that younger women are selecting men who are older and more powerful and who may be better suited for mates. Some studies she reviewed show that only in humans can this pattern of older male-younger female interaction be observed.

Among nonhuman primates, there is no such pattern; females primates do not experience menopause and they can reproduce even when old, and, in some cases, males even prefer them as mates. Whatever its cause, the Jennifer principle is widespread, but once again we need not opt solely for a biological explanation here. One of the most recent changes in sexual mating patterns in our own society, for instance, is that of, so called cougars, older women choosing younger men. Once again the more similar man and woman's social role becomes, the closer their actual behavior is, not only in sexuality but in many other areas of life as well.

On January 15, 1992, in an hour-long radio talk show originating in Los Angeles, the *Tom Likus Show*, sought responses from listeners regarding their opinions on dating married men. "Why would one want to date a married man?" was the question posed to listeners who either dated married men exclusively, or dated both single and married men. All of the callers to the show were women. The range of variation that surfaced in terms of background and responses was considerable, and it emphasized the importance of social convention and particular circumstance in both adultery and its various patternings in our society.

One caller, for example, enjoyed the total control she felt in her adulterous relationships: at any time, she said, she could call his wife and report him. When she wished to end the relationship, it would be because she felt the man had little recourse but to let her end it lest she tell his wife about the two of them. Thus, this feeling of power was what attracted her most to married men.

Another woman said that she thought the majority of single women spoil single men so much that the men cheat on them, whereas a married man treats a woman like a queen. She herself was now involved with a married man she had known for four years. They had only recently started having sex, because she showed some anxiety about AIDS and was taking precautions. She believed that the problems of marriage had nothing to do with an affair; in fact, she thought that having an affair would keep a married man from running around even more and keep him married.

One other woman admitted that she had dated a married man for nine years, from the age of 21 to 30. He was wealthy and saw her in Europe every month. She said that she was divorced at the time after having been married earlier at the age of 19. She had no interest in wanting to break up the man's marriage, in part because her father had left her mother and she had no interest in breaking up any marriage. The man still called her on a regular basis. Interestingly, the callers did not feel that the consequences of these adulterous relationships for children were central, although one caller did insist that adultery should be illegal because it leads to divorce, breaks up families, and damages the children involved. Children grow up in single-parent families as a result of adultery, she said, and, as a result don't do as well as those children in nuclear families.

The final caller stated she had an affair with a married man and that it was no one's business. She loved the man and his wife, and she thought his wife was grateful under the circumstances. She explained, "I nurtured him through a crisis; I never would steal him from his wife, and she knew it. At the time they were sweating out the birth of a potentially defective child. His wife was pregnant, and my friendship and counsel was very important at that time."

In linking sexuality to marriage, we generally view having multiple marital partners in our own or other cultures as resulting predominantly from the sex drive. As we will see in the next chapter, however, of the various reasons polygamy occurs, the idea of a sexual outlet is minimized within a wider, more general body of needs and functions considered important for both individuals and the wider society. Disentangling issues of marriage, family, and sex life is an important task that remains to be done by those of us critiquing the modern American family system, but it is just as important for those defending the status quo?

MARRIAGE IN THE UNITED STATES TODAY

The most significant change in marriage today is that people are older when they marry for the first time—from 23 for men in 1950 to 28 in 2009 and from 20 for women in 1950 to 26 in 2009. In addition, people marrying today tend to be better educated than previous generations and "better off socioeconomically," the Census Bureau reports.[31]

There's another noticeable change compared to prior years and generations, there's a different attitude about marriage, especially among young people. "Today's 18- to 29-year-olds value parenthood far more than marriage," the Pew Research Center reports.

The Pew Research Center discovered that just over 52 percent of adults between the ages of 18 and 29 "say being a good parent is 'one of the most important things' in life. Just 30 percent say the same thing about having a successful marriage."[32] Could this attitude spell a further decrease in marriage in the future?

Statistics about monogamous marriage in the United States still show that Americans are very prone to marry. According to the Centers for Disease Control, about two million weddings are performed annually in the United States.[33]

Nearly 70 percent of all adults—more than 167 million—described themselves, according to a 2009 U.S. Census Bureau study, as "ever married," meaning that at some point in their life they either had been married or were married during the time of the survey. That's more than twice as many adults who described themselves as "never married," just over 78 million, in the same survey.[34] The Census Bureau goes on to say that more than 126 million American adults have married once; more than 32 million have married twice; and nearly nine million have married "three or more times."[35]

As one social commentator writes, this is what sets Americans apart from their counterparts in the Western world. Being married is a sign that things are going well. It is a status symbol, says Andrew Cherlin. "There are more partners in the personal lives of Americans than in the lives of people of any other Western country," writes Cherlin in his book *The Marriage-Go-Round*. "The most distinctive characteristics of American family life, then, the trait that most clearly differentiates it from family life in other Western countries, are sheer movement: frequent transitions, shorter relationships. . . . Americans step on and off the carousel of intimate partnerships (by which I mean marriages and cohabitating relationships) more often."[36] In fact, perhaps no Western nation is better equipped to make plural marital relations legal for some, if there are advantages, than the United States!

The data from the Census Bureau—which shows that as men and women age, there's an increasing likelihood they'll experience a second marriage, a divorce or that their spouse will die—seems to prove Cherlin's point.

In the picture of the country presented for 2009, the Census Bureau reported that about 1.5 percent of all men, between the ages of 25 and 29, who had married once, were likely to be on their second marriage; that percentage increases to 22.1 percent for men between the ages of 60 and 69. In the same survey, the Census Bureau reported, about 2.3 percent of all women, between the ages of 25 and 29, who had married once, were likely to be on their second marriage; that percentage increases to more than 20 percent for women between 60 and 69.[37]

There's also an increasing prevalence of divorce for both genders as they age. In 2009, 5 percent of men, between the ages 25 and 29 were "ever divorced," meaning they'd experienced at least one divorce; that percentage peaks, at 36.5 percent, for men between the ages of 60 and 69. Meantime, just 7 percent of women between the ages of 25 and 29 said they were "ever divorced" in 2009; that percentage tops out, at just over 37 percent, for women between the ages of 50 and 59.[38]

Do these divorce statistics spell the death knell for marriage in the United States?

Hardly. Because, as the data from 2009 shows, there's an increase in second and third marriages by both men and women, especially as they age.

Why do people, who had a failed first or second marriage, remarry? It's hard to say. But, as Andrew Cherlin suggests, being married is a sign of successful personal life and, thus, its "ultimate merit badge."[39] Or maybe American idealism is even extended to marriage. Even if their first marriage failed, divorced Americans are convinced the next partner will be the right one.

DIVORCE

Divorce statistics are less conclusive than those on marriage. But there are some things we do know about divorce: According to the Centers for Disease Control, there are about one million divorces granted each year.[40]

According to the latest U.S. census, in 2010, about 10 percent of the adult population—just over 27 million people—was divorced. Coincidentally, this percentage is the same as the Census Bureau's previous survey of the population, in 2000, when 21 million adults, just under 10 percent of the adult population, reported it was divorced.

Based on what the surface numbers say in the United States—two million weddings and about one million divorces annually—it is easy to see how the adage "half of all marriages fail" is formulated. The problem with this mantra is that it's not clear how long each couple is married before becoming part of the one million divorces granted each year.

The closest approximation we have to the length of U.S. marriages is an estimate from a 2001 survey by the Centers for Disease Control. That survey, which only looked at women between the ages of 15–44, said that 20 percent of all first marriages fail within five years and that another third of marriages among this age group fail within 10 years.[41]

If it could be proven that half of all couples marrying one year divorce the following year, then, yes, the adage "half of all marriages fail" holds up. While we're not attempting to prove or disprove this adage, it appears to be very questionable.

Part of the explanation for divorce, at least for people who are in their 60s and 70s today, is that breaking up became easier when they were younger, in their 30s, back in the 1970s, when no-fault divorce laws started being approved. This allowed people to divorce on the basis of "irreconcilable differences," whatever they may be.

The data from the Census Bureau also shows that divorce is decreasing. For example, fewer than 2 percent of the men and women, born between 1940 and 1944, by the time they reached their 20th birthday, had experienced a divorce. For both men and women born between 1980 and 1984, no more than 1 percent of each gender was divorced by the time they turned 20.[42]

Of course, there's something else that might also be considered about the reduced divorce rate among younger adults: Simply because someone is married and in their early 30s today—as they are if they were born in 1980—doesn't mean there's a guaranteed outcome they will remain married until they are parted by death from their (original) spouse.

The most recent estimates show that about 1 million children are affected by their parents divorce any given year; what's more surprising about the most recent information available about divorce is that the petitioner—that is, the person who files for the legal break up of the marriage—is more likely to be the wife than the husband.[43]

In 2010, the Census Bureau reports, there were just over 4.1 million births. Of those, about 1.5 million were estimated to be to single women. Add in the number of kids likely to be affected by divorce any given year—just over 1 million—and that means that a sizeable number of children, at least for the foreseeable future, will be affected by family break up or a family that was never constructed—because their parents divorced or their parents never married.

If we believe that children, overall, when all factors are considered, are better off growing up in two-parent households, is there something else the government can offer as a marital option, especially so the living conditions—and futures—of children improve? Not every single parent is gay or lesbian, so the option of same-gender marriage, which is gaining legal acceptance in the United States, works for some but not for all.

The biggest risk any single mother is likely to face, especially if she only has a high school diploma, is poverty. In fact, one research study says, "7 in 10 children living with a single mother are poor or low income, compared to less than a third of children living in other types of families."[44] Should kids, living in numerous, single mother households, be condemned to poverty simply because their mothers didn't marry their fathers or they have no legal or financial means of gaining the support, financial or otherwise, that they—and most certainly their children—deserve?

There's an argument to be made that single men who are also fathers who aren't contributing to their child's or children's welfare are being let off the hook, especially when it comes to being a responsible parent. Is this what we want, a further erosion in responsibility?

THE EFFECTS OF DIVORCE

The authors of this book both experienced divorce—Dr. Kilbride as an adult, when his first marriage came to an end, and Page when he witnessed his parents' marital breakup as he was completing his bachelor's degree. If there's any one thing that's true of divorce, it's this: It frequently causes a considerable amount of emotional upheaval, especially for a couple's children. They see the only life they've ever known come to a crashing end and watch their parents go from partners to enemies and, in some cases, hold a visceral hatred for one another.

More commonly, unfortunately, divorce can completely alter a child's relationship with their parents, making them wonder which one they're supposed to love, trust, believe and support, maybe even live with, because the family unit, which they held so dear, and by which they defined life, and which offered security, disintegrates. The harshest lesson children of divorced parents learn is that love doesn't last. How, then, when they reach adulthood, are they supposed to view any potential marital commitment?

Divorce is expensive. In Kilbride's case of a companionate divorce, although there are no interactions between his current and previous wife (no "wife-in-law" trap), their good will has enabled him to be a good father for his daughters who enjoy a strong and enduring sibling relationship in spite of the fact that they're more than a decade apart in age. We think that one of the advantages of promoting community in plural relations, however achieved, is to enhance sibling solidarity.

If the most precarious thing any adult does is marry, then the next most precarious thing any adult does is undergo a divorce, and for this the children are usually implicated, too. It can be emotionally and financially ruinous for one or both partners and their children. We need to consider alternative remedies to reduce divorce, even slightly, so a couple's children will be spared this turmoil. Some of those proposals will be presented in this book.

SAME-GENDER PARTNERSHIPS AND CHILDREN

In our current customs, sexuality is linked strongly to heterosexuality. Marriage is generally thought of in terms of heterosexual couples. In May 1993, however, a controversy arose over a domestic partner bill in Philadelphia. The place of homosexuals in our legal life has been made even more visible by the continuing debate about gays and lesbians in the military, precipitated by the Clinton administration's "Don't Ask, Don't Tell" policy in 1993 and recently taken up again by the Obama administration.

It is informative that the assumption that sexuality should be confined to marriage is even more singularly defined to the exclusion of homosexuality from marital recognition. Sometimes those who favor a domestic partner-only solution to gays and lesbians—so they don't face a lack of access to health-care benefits—are sometimes not among those advocating for legalizing same-gender marriage.

Also, support for domestic partner benefits is sometimes withheld for fear that it might lead to same-gender marriage rights. The real or hidden issue in the discourse of domestic partner benefits—a.k.a. same-gender benefits to health insurance—is that some people see this issue as a challenge to heterosexual marriage.

Opponents feel that the only issue that should be debated is that of legalizing same-gender marriage. Much of the current opposition comes from churches, so we will consider the religious context for plural marriage later. Whatever one's personal views on marriage and sexuality, undeniably millions of Americans presently feel that it is time to reconsider the place of same-gender relationships in married life in light of better information that's now available.

There are now studies showing that one's sexual orientation has no bearing on their ability bring up kids. Kilbride, in fact, when appearing on a radio program, was asked about gay and lesbian family issues by a woman who wanted to know why lesbians were only given children "no one else wanted."

Kilbride felt this woman's pain and, since that appearance on that radio show, nearly 20 years ago, there's research on how children from lesbian and gay parents turn out. It shows children are no better and no worse than those brought up by heterosexual parents.

The American Psychological Association (APA) reports, "Results of social science research have failed to confirm any . . . concerns about children of gay and lesbian parents . . . sexual identities . . . develop in much the same way . . . as among children of heterosexual parents."[45]

The APA, two years earlier, in 2002, resolved that psychologists "eliminate all discrimination based on sexual orientation in matters of adoption, child custody, visitation, foster care, and reproductive health services."[46]

The APA's position was later backed up another study of lesbian parents in the United States, in 2010, that found "17-year-old daughters and sons of lesbian mothers were rated significantly higher in social, school/academic and total competence and significantly lower in social problems . . . than . . . their age match counterparts."[47]

Based on their extensive review of the research the APA wrote an ethical resolution, stating, "Therefore, be if further resolved that APA encourages psychologists to act to eliminate all discrimination based on sexual orientation in matters of adoption, child custody, visitation, foster care, and reproductive health services" (APA 2004). One of the shocking features of marriage and family life today is the disconnect between same-gender parental practices and scholarly evidence on the one hand and widespread ignorance and often public stigma on the other. Children are among those who suffer the most by this state of affairs.

IMMIGRANT FAMILIES

Compared to previous centuries, when the United States and Canada were destinations almost solely for Europeans, the two countries, recently, have become places for immigrants from countries that practice polygamy. Both countries have seen an increase of immigrants from the Middle East and Africa, parts of the world where polygamy is often part of the culture.

Part of this pattern is due to a shift if immigration policy in the 1960s, from a "favored nation" status (such as Ireland) to one of a family-based policy, where relatives, instead of favored nations, determine immigration practices.

Immigration patterns have changed so much, in the United States lately, that immigrants from Europe are now the minority. One recent book says that, today, 36 percent of the people living in New York City were born outside of the United States, in Latin America, the Caribbean, Asian, and African countries.[48]

For some foreign-born U.S. residents, polygamy is a cultural value, religious belief or even a family practice (back in the "old country"). Unlike other cultural or religious beliefs, polygamy is one that candidates must renounce to become U.S. citizens.

In spite of the government efforts, polygamy is practiced by some immigrants, as the *New York Times* reported. As the reporter wrote, some African men have one wife in New York, and another back home, in their former country.

U.S. ALLIES AND POLYGAMY

The Hmong from Laos immigrated to the United States shortly after South Vietnam fell to North Vietnam in the mid-1970s. Allied with the United States during the Vietnam War, the Hmong engaged in combat against the North Vietnamese army. Just like recent immigrants from Africa and the Middle East, the Hmong practice polygamy, and it is now estimated several thousand Hmong are living in polygamous marriages in the United States, especially in Minnesota.[49]

THE TRANSNATIONAL FAMILY

In another child-related pattern, Arlie Hochschild (2010) identifies "global care chains" where female domestics, often from Mexico or the Philippines, are in the United States raising the child of their employer while the mother works outside the home. While in the service of "imported maternal love," some of these women struggle to financially help their families back in their native countries. Filipina women, especially, work around the world in such care situations, including in Israel with elderly and medically challenged individuals.

Plural marriages and "global care chains," for example, cry out for a policy of legalized public recognition. The transnational family, which doesn't always adhere to nice, neat borders, consists of people from different countries, should be legalized.

In Australia, there are examples of transnational families, involving Australian women and men from countries where polygamy is accepted. Annie Stopford notes that, in Australia, sometimes women will marry or have children with men from Africa, some of whom are already married and have families in their native homelands. She concludes that the Western assumption that the monogamous nuclear family is superior to others doesn't hold up in these cases.[50]

Transnational families in the West might well turn to Africa for guidance. As Stopford writes, "My ongoing responsibilities toward my Ghanian husband and my active support of his bringing a second wife from Ghana are part of a system of reciprocity in which he continues to provide an African paternal function and a positive African male role model for my son."[51]

The disparity between the "ideal" of the monogamous, nuclear, heterosexual family and the "real" family on the ground, which can vary by ethnicity, sexual orientation, country of origin reveals a widening gap. One solution to close this gap is to see to the return of the idealized past whereas another, as Margaret Mead did, is to examine our own situation, our own history and that of other cultures, keeping in mind that change is possible and need not be feared.

SOME THOUGHTS AND QUESTIONS

Because of all the changes that have been made to marriage, what's next? Monogamous marriage isn't about to end and, in fact, should be encouraged and supported, but now other kinds of familial relationships—whether its two people sharing the same gender, two people signing a legal agreement, as is the case with civil unions, or even plural marriages among immigrants—are gaining ground.

The next civil rights battle, which has yet to completely unfold, may very well be the right to self-determination of a family. In other words, people may soon demand that they retain the legal right to bring anyone they want into their family to create a family. This idea may be very challenging to those who retain a very conservative view of what families are suppose to be—only a man and a woman together, as husband and wife, perhaps with children.

Are there overriding economic and legal reasons that the civil society should or should not allow plural marriage? We'll explore these thoughts in the coming chapters.

NOTES

1. E. J. Graff, *What's Marriage For? The Strange Social History of our Most Intimate Institution* (Boston: Beacon Press, 2004), p. 53.

2. Magnus Hirschfeld Archive for Sexology, 1981, http://www2.huberlin.de/sexology/ATLAS_EN/html/history_of_marriage_in_western.html.

3. Carle C. Zimmerman, *Family and Civilization*, ed. James Kurth (Wilmington, DE: ISI Books, 2008), p. 3.

4. Herant Katchadourian and Donald Lunde, *Fundamentals of Human Sexuality*, 3rd ed. (New York: Holt, Rinehart & Winston, 1975), p. 475.

5. Book of Deuteronomy, chapter 25, verses 5–6, Holy Bible (with the Apocryphal/Deuterocanonical Books), the New Revised Standard Version (New York: American Bible Society, 1989).

6. Zimmerman, *Family and Civilization*, p. 82.

7. John Cairncross, *After Polygamy Was Made a Sin: The Social History of Christian Polygamy* (London: Routledge and Kegan Paul, 1974), p. 2.

8. Leon Miller, *John Milton among the Polygamophiles* (New York: Loewenthal Press, 1974), p. 17.

9. Ibid., p. 15.

10. Ibid.

11. Ibid., p. 23.

12. Ibid.; and Alison Weir, *The Six Wives of Henry VIII* (New York: Grove Press, 1991).

13. Andrew J. Cherlin, *The Marriage-Go-Round: The State of Marriage and the Family in America Today* (New York: Alfred K. Knopf, 2009), pp. 43 and 44.

14. Zimmerman, *Family and Civilization*, p. 168.

15. Ibid., p. 169.

16. Cherlin, *The Marriage-Go-Round*, p. 55.

17. Joseph Ellis, *First Family: Abigail and John Adams* (New York: Vintage Books, 2010), pp. 244 and 245.

18. Cherlin, *The Marriage-Go-Round*, p. 68.

19. Margaret Mead, *Male and Female* (New York: HarperCollins Publishers, 1949), p. 334.

20. Ibid., p. 342.

21. Ibid., p. 354.

22. Whitehead wrote a lengthy article about divorce in the *Atlantic Monthly* in April 1993 titled "Dan Quayle Was Right." The article's title came from the former vice president's reaction to the popular television show *Murphy Brown*, in which the lead character gave birth outside of marriage. Many of Whitehead's observations on divorce's consequences for children and single mothers were correct. She followed up this article with a 1997 book titled *The Divorce Culture*.

23. Mead, *Male and Female*, p. 355.

24. Ibid., p. 358.

25. Ibid.

26. Cherlin, *The Marriage-Go-Round*, p. 88.

27. Ibid., p. 88.

28. Ibid., p. 90.

29. Ibid., p. 97.

30. Doug Page, "Changing Families: From Traditional to Whatever Works," *Bay State Parent*, February 2011, pp. 10 and 11.

31. "Number, Timing, and Duration of Marriages and Divorces: 2009," U.S. Census Bureau, May 2011, http://www.census.gov/prod/2011pubs/p70-125.pdf.

32. "For Millennials, Parenthood Trumps Marriage," Pew Research Center, March 9, 2011, http://www.pewsocialtrends.org/2011/03/09/for-millennials-parenthood-trumps-marriage/.

33. "First Marriage Dissolution, Divorce and Remarriage: United States," Advance Data, Centers for Disease Control and Prevention, May 31, 2001. http://www.cdc.gov/nchs/pressroom/01news/firstmarr.htm. The Centers for Disease Control tabulates the number of marriages and divorces from the country's 50 states. Also see "People who got Married, and Divorced in the Past 12 Months by State: 2009," from the U.S. Census Bureau, American Community Survey in 2009, which shows that 4.496 million people were married and another 2.319 million were divorced between January 2008 and January 2009. http://www.census.gov/compendia/statab/2012/tables/12s0132.pdf.

34. "Number of Times Married by Sex by Marital Status for the Population 15 years and Over," 2009 American Community Survey, U.S. Census Bureau.

35. Ibid.

36. Cherlin, *The Marriage-Go-Round*, p. 5.

37. "Number of Times Married by Sex."

38. Ibid.

39. Quoted in Belinda Luscombe, "Who Needs Marriage? A Changing Institution," *Time*, November 18, 2010, http://www.time.com.

40. "Births, Marriages, Divorces, and Deaths: Provisional Data for 2009," National Vital Statistics Reports, U.S. Department of Health and Human Services, Centers for Disease Control and Prevention, August 27, 2010.

41. "First Marriage Dissolution, Divorce, and Remarriage."

42. "Number of Times Married by Sex."

43. "Monthly Vital Statistics Report," National Center for Disease Statistics, U.S. Department of Health and Human Services, May 21, 1991, "'These Boots are Made for Walking': Why Most Divorce Filers are Women," American Law and Economics Association, 2000, pp. 126–169.

44. "U.S. Children in Single-Mother Families," the Population Reference Bureau, May 2010, http://www.prb.org/Publications/PolicyBriefs/singlemotherfamilies.aspx.

45. American Psychological Association (APA), *Sexual Orientation, Parents & Children*, American Psychological Association, July 18, 2004.

46. Quoted in Ann Wrixon, "Children Raised by Lesbian Parents Have Excellent Outcomes," *IAC* June 10, 2010.

47. Nanette Gartrell and Henry Bos, "U.S. National Longitudinal Lesbian Family Study: Psychological Adjustment of 17-year-old Adolescents," *Pediatrics* June 7, 2010.

48. Ayumi Takenaka and Mary Osirim, *Global Philadelphia: Immigrant Communities Old and New* (Philadelphia: Temple University Press, 2010), pp. 1–22.

49. Miriam Zeitzen, *Polygamy: A Cross-Cultural Analysis* (Oxford: Berg, 2008), p. 166.

50. Annie Stopford, "Trans Global Families: The Application of African Ethical and Conceptual Systems to African-Western Relationships and Families," *A Journal of Culture and African Women Studies (JENDA)* no. 8 (2006): pp. 62–74.

51. Ibid.

3

Critical Influences on Plural Marriage

Nearly every form of marriage—polygyny, monogamy, and polyandry—and, for that matter, any kind of adult relationship, whether in a Western country or anywhere in the world, between people of the same age or differing ages, holds something in common: economics.

Of equal importance, in many family settings, especially marriage, is religion as well as the community's culture and parental influences received by a marrying partner. Some social scientists also think marriage and other intimate, adult relationships are influenced by each partner's attempt at ensuring the propagation and survival of their DNA.[1]

Since this book is focused on plural marriage, we'll go through how religion, culture, parental influences, biological and economics push plural marriages, reserving for the next chapter a more comprehensive American discussion of economics, the most significant factor in all types of marriage.

ECONOMICS

In the book *Families in Global and Multicultural Perspective*, Bron B. Ingoldsby that the "explanation that has shown the most promise (explaining polygyny) . . . has been the link between marital type and economic subsistence patterns." Thus, he writes, "in polygynous societies, the wealthiest families are most likely to be polygynous. . . . The implication is that the more women and their children can contribute to the production of wealth, the more likely polygyny is to be practiced. We find this in light agriculture and animal husbandry economies, where the more wives a man has, the more fields can be tended and the more animals cared for."[2]

Ingoldsby also discusses other reasons for polygyny that might receive a better reception in parts of the world where plural marriage isn't accepted—sex. But he mentions that the only reason men take extra wives is because it improves his chances of having more sons "who will be workers in a male-oriented economy."[3]

Lawyer and journalist Elizabeth Joseph, while married to her polygamist husband, Alex, in Big Water, Utah, in the mid-1990s, was an outspoken advocate on the economic and social benefits of polygyny, saying her sister-wives cared for her son while she worked, preventing her from spending money on daycare. In addition, she said, her sister-wives' talents and interests were different from hers, allowing her to pursue her career full time, thus making polygyny beneficial for career-oriented mothers.

One of cries of America's feminists, starting in the 1960s, was about economics and labor—that women could do practically any job that was assigned to men. What they hadn't taken into consideration, perhaps, was childcare.

Polygyny, as experienced by Joseph, and as detailed by anthropologist Janet Bennion, is about women forming female-to-female networks, as sister-wives, to share the family's work. Thus, some sister-wives pursue careers outside the home while others supervise the family's children and tend to other domestic jobs.

In Saudi Arabia, Maha Yamani (2008) investigated how educated men and women created a new, polygamous culture. Both traditional and emergent types of Saudi polygamy reflect two preconditions seen elsewhere. She notes that polygyny is part and parcel of Islam, expected as a duty for women and men as a sign of their religious devotion. There's also a second pillar, one that might not have been expected. "Following an increase in oil wealth . . . in the 1970s providing for two (or more) homes . . . bringing polygamy within the reach of many."[4]

Oil wealth, then, created an incentive for some women to accept a polygamous relationship with a wealthy husband. Yamani also notes a rise in the divorce, which prompted previously married women to marry a man who's already married.

Yamani was told by one woman, "I am divorced with several children, although I have a fulfilling job . . . I needed a man in my life . . . I specifically wanted a married man with a family as I did not want to have more children . . . and needed time to pursue my responsibilities."[5]

Another example of plural marriage in the Arab world concerns "travel marriages." Investors, Yamani notes, from Persian Gulf countries sometimes start new families during their travels throughout the Arab world. Such travel marriages, while having precedence in Islamic history, may not always work out for the children of such unions. "Difficulties naturally arise when the husband returns to his country of origin, leaving a pregnant wife behind. Since these marriages are registered, the children will carry the nationality of their father and may, therefore, be ineligible for domestic social service such as free education."[6]

Kilbride, while visiting Kenya, introduced his college students to a married man whose mother was pressuring him to take another wife for one simple reason—she needed help running the farm.

There's a widespread practice in Africa of the "sugar daddy." He's typically older, married, and takes up with a younger, unmarried woman; in exchange for sex and romance, he pays her bills and then some.

Suda notes that while poverty in Africa drives many young women into these relationships for economic gain, some of these mistresses are only out for fun; others just want a baby "with a man" so they can move on—to the next relationship and, hopefully, with money from their first sugar daddy.[7]

The idea of the "sugar parent" isn't limited to just men in Africa. Suda notes that there is a growing tendency for rich "sugar mummies"— divorced, married, or single women—to date younger men who need money.[8] The sugar parent relationship is no stranger in the United States. Much of the typical sugar daddy relationship was detailed in a *New York Times Magazine* article titled, "Keeping Up with Being Kept" (Padawer 2009).

Another *New York Times Magazine* article, titled "Rethinking the Older Woman-Younger Man Relationship" (Kershaw 2009), said that there are more women dating and marrying younger men. The reporter wrote that while the numbers of older women-younger man couples remain small, about 6 percent of all married couples in the United States, the number of older woman-younger man couples doubled between 1960 and 2007.

Both sex and economics play a role in attracting older women and younger men to one another. As Kershaw's *New York Times* story pointed out, some older women are looking for a "boy toy," while younger men are searching for a woman who's sexually knowledgeable. Men are also comfortable with their female partners earning more money than they do. The article also noted that in older women-younger men relationships, from her standpoint, "she's less likely to be focused on the [economic] status of her partner than women of previous generations" because her income is likely bigger than her spouse's.

In cultures practicing polyandry—a woman with more than one husband—economics also plays a role. In South Asia, whether it's Tibet, Nepal, or Sri Lanka, where fertile land is in short supply, fraternal polyandry (brothers married to the same woman) serves to prevent the dispersal of property and fragmentation of the family's landholdings.[9] Polyandry's other advantage is that it lowers the birthrate in a part of the world where the land isn't conducive to feeding many people.

RELIGION

We consider the Fundamentalist Latter-day Saints' (FLDS) plural marriage in detail later, but one of the best known cases of polygyny is also found in Islam. A book by al-Ghazali is an excellent source on the classic rationale for polygynous and other marital and sexual patterns and customs in Islam. This book notes that marriage is not merely a secular contract in Islam but, instead, has religious overtones because it is defined in the Koran, which was received, as Islam says, by the Prophet Mohammed, through an angel, who was in direct communication with God.

Polygyny is also limited in Islam, with Mohammed saying men could only take four wives. "And if you fear that you cannot act equitably toward orphans, then marry such women as seem good to you, two, three, or four, or if you fear you will not do justice (between them) then marry only one," Mohammed wrote. Just like in American polygamy, as we shall see—where a husband is expected to visit each wife—Islam makes the same requirement. And should a husband miss his turn in visiting a particular wife, he must make up for it.

Al-Ghazali writes that, "The message of God said, 'Whoever has two wives and favors one over the other—that is to say—does not deal equitably between them, he comes to the day of judgment bent to one side.'" As set forth in the religious thinking of the Koran, polygyny is understood best in a humanitarian, communitarian, and religious context. Polygyny is legal in some Islamic countries, such as Saudi Arabia, but it's illegal in others, like Turkey.

In the United States, the only people practicing polygyny, besides recent African immigrants hiding multiple wives, are FLDS believers. They practice this form of marriage because, as they see it, they're keeping with their faith. In addition, some African American Muslims and other communities in the African cultural tradition also practice polygyny, we will see later in this book.

CULTURE AND PARENTAL INFLUENCES

There are also other reasons for accepting a polygamous husband. Among Saudi women, Yamani (2008, 231) found, those reasons included a fear of spinsterhood and an urge for motherhood; family pressure to marry a cousin; falling in love and then marrying to avoid breaking Islam's rules about engaging in sexual relations outside of marriage; and a socially imposed need for marriage.[10]

As Kilbride's college students learned, a Kenyan husband—using a philosophy that's similar to justify polygyny in the United States—said that while his mother was pressuring him to marry again because she needed help on her farm, she also said there were many single women in the village who needed husbands. And there was a slightly selfish motive from his mother: She wanted grandchildren who lived near her.[11]

The man's wife was opposed to adding a second wife because she was afraid there wouldn't be enough money to pay for her own children's school. Besides, his wife added, a second wife living in a rural area might want to live in the same city she resided. He reassured his wife that he'd make sure she remained on the farm.

Whatever the value orientation is toward polygyny, the reality is that most African men are monogamous. A study among the Zulu of southern Africa by Moller and Welch (1990) helps explain this male viewpoint toward polygyny, which is only about 10 percent of rural married men in the tribe.[12]

There's a shift from overt polygyny to covert polygyny or monogamy owing to several factors. They include a shortage of agriculturally productive land; social pressures to accept the values of the politically and socially dominant whites; the teachings of Christian mission churches.

From their research, Moller and Welch found that a majority of monogamist and polygynist men reported both advantages and disadvantages with polygyny. Among those men who favored monogamy, the largest disadvantage of polygyny was its economics. They found, for example, that the notion of the large polygynous family as a social security investment is being replaced by the challenge of educating children—because they have so many—for a long time in their own lives.[13]

Those Zulu men favoring polygyny reported higher job satisfaction, feeling far less lonely, more voluntary retirement, better health, higher degrees of social adjustment, including a better adjustment to aging and retirement, than their monogamist brethren, Moller and Welch reported.[14] Of course, more research needs to be completed in this area before we can conclude that polygyny has a positive health effect on these men.

As for growing up in a polygynous household, in interviews conducted by Kilbride, East Africans report both negative and positive experiences in this family setting. Marjorie, who is now 40 years old, whose father is a wealthy agriculture officer, recalls, positively, living with her father's second wife and her children so she could attend school near their residence. On school holidays, she returned to her mother.

Marjorie says the children treated each other well. "Myself and the stepsisters, we don't say, 'Who is your mother?'" Marjorie reported. "We are all like brothers and sisters."[15]

But for Robert, a man in his 20s, the exact opposite is true. His father also has four wives. But his economic situation, unlike Marjorie's dad, is much less favorable. Plus he has 31 children, so far, with the youngest being less than a year old. Robert's mother is not in as favorable a position economically or in terms of respect. She's his dad's second wife. In Robert's early childhood, his father had only two wives, both of whom Robert called "mother."

When he was seven years old, Robert began to question his status. When he was eight, he recollects going to school with the sons of the first wife. It was not a pleasant memory. His step-brothers beat him, made him carry their books, and forced him to get money from his own mother so he could buy their lunches. He eventually refused to go to that school and transferred to another one near his home, which he wound up leaving before finally settling on a school near the home where his father's fourth wife lived. Life still didn't get any better. Robert says he was forced to perform many household chores, including cooking, cleaning, and tending to livestock.

As an adult, Robert understands the advantages of polygyny, such as sharing the workload, protection from outsiders, caring for other family members when they're sick or their children and preventing childlessness. Still, the disadvantages he experienced, which he sees as being the result of his father's insufficient economic resources, makes him unfavorable to polygyny. In addition, he says, the other problems with polygyny include jealousy plus a conflict over the lack of money for food, clothing, and education. Robert reports that during times of food shortages, each mother looked after only her own children while his father tended to "disappear" until the worst was over.

Polyandry, found in less than 1 percent of the world's cultures, always exists in combination with polygyny. Among the Irigwe of Nigeria, there are two basic types of marriage. The first type, the primary marriage, is arranged by both sets of parents, prior to the couple's adolescence; the second type or marriage, called the secondary marriage, is arranged by the couple.[16] When a woman leaves her primary husband and goes to a secondary one or, later, to a third husband, she leaves behind everything except the clothes and jewelry she's wearing. The traditional Irigwe marriage system didn't allow divorce until the late 1960s. A woman's marriages are not terminated simply because she switches her living arrangements from one husband to another. If she bears children, she remains with the husband who's deemed the father.

Sangree (1969) reported that the older Irigwe women he interviewed had a plurality of husbands. He also discovered that about half of the middle-aged women had borne children for two or more husbands.[17] "It is usual for a woman to settle down for a relatively protracted period with a husband for whom she has borne a child or two. Sooner or later, however, she almost inevitably moves either back to an old or on to a new husband."[18]

Sangree wrote that polyandry provides a source of excitement and pleasure for women and is a source of pride for fathers who value daughters with plural marriages. The practice also results in uniting various tribal subgroups, enhancing tribal cohesion and creating ever-widening social networks. While polyandry increases competition between men, Ingoldsby writes, it also reduces it. "Once a man's wife has cohabitated with another man, that man must be treated with caution and respect because of the Irigwe belief that a co-husband can cause the first husband's death."[19] This results in men with the same wife being polite to one another.

Leanna Wolfe, a U.S. anthropologist, also observed African polygyny, writing that, more often than not, "a woman wants her co-wife to help with domestic chores and be a loving mother to her children." She also says that co-wives can provide "mothering insurance," meaning that if one dies, the others would take responsibility for the children of the deceased mother. Finally, she says, there are cases of African, polygynous woman living apart from their husbands in distant cities. Wolfe says "they may find value in the status of being a married woman, in terms of being a recipient of their husband's wealth . . . they may also enjoy the freedom of having a social life apart from his."[20]

Being an American, Wolfe found it strange that two people, married to one another, would want to live far apart. But, as her African friends told her, they could not "understand our American need for such constant reassurance of love, commitment and intimacy" by living in the same house.[21]

IN IT FOR LOVE

There is a gathering and hunting society in southern Africa known as !Kung San. In a widely read book about a !Kung woman named *Nisa* by Marjorie Shostak (1981), we learn that love exists in !Kung marriages and is expressed in many ways.

For example, married couples travel alone together to engage in hunting and gathering activities; they make presents for one another; and women will acknowledge their intense emotional involvements with their husbands. Sometimes, however, early in their marriage, women in this society enjoy having lovers, Shostak writes:

> To succeed at and to benefit from extramarital affairs, one must accept that one's feelings for one's husband—"the important one," "the one from inside the hut" and for one's lover—"the little one," "the one from the bush"—are necessarily different. One is rich, warm and secure. The other is passionate and exciting, although often fleeting and undependable. . . . The appeal of affairs, they say, is not merely sexual; secret glances, stolen kisses, and brief encounters, make for a more complex enticement. Often described as thrilling adventures, these relationships are one of the subjects women spend much time discussing among themselves.[22]

Among the Turu of Tanzania, the word *mbuyu* means "friend" and can be used among ordinary friends or lovers (Schneider 1972). But when someone calls a person of the opposite gender by this term, this is an indication that they are lovers.

Schneider reports that Turu women must be very mannerly in public but, on the sly, they can be aggressive in propositioning potential lovers. Although a man usually initiates an extramarital relationship, his wife often assists him.

"The quality of the *mbuyu* relationship is best indicated by comparing it to romantic love as it is understood in the West; mbuyu partners tend to engage in the same mooning, jealous and possessive behavior Westerners associate with this term," Schneider writes. Other similarities are whispering "sweet nothings" in each other's ears and "consummating their love" with kisses and sexual intercourse.[23]

JEALOUSY WITHIN POLYGYNY

Romantic love and its relationship to sex and marriage is an endless topic in the Western world because, more often than not, it's very much a priority for men and women.

One of the objections monogamists in the United States hold against polygyny is that romantic love is considered to be at odds with plural marriage. Polygyny is also often seen as injurious to women, at least in the United States, because the only time most Americans see plural marriage is when someone, like Warren Jeffs, is put on trial or his home is raided by police.

Still, there's also the issue of jealousy. Many monogamist women in the West cannot reconcile how the wives of a polygamist husband cannot be jealous of one another. As reported in *National Geographic* magazine, in a 2010 article about polygyny, there's very little jealousy, in the United States, among the FLDS wives. In this article, by Scott Anderson, the division of labor among the wives and the responsibility for their own children lessens or eliminates jealousy.

Gregory White and Paul Mullen (1989) report that in those societies where polygynous relationships are significant, "Most available ethnographic evidence suggests that multiple wives in polygynous societies do not become jealous unless the husband shows favoritism to one wife or her children that is not in accordance with cultural prescriptions about how attention and reward should be distributed among wives. . . . similarly in most societies in which polyandry is acceptable or the norm, the multiple 'husbands' . . . tend to show little jealousy as long as status differences are observed."[24]

In an extended discussion of jealousy as it pertains to polyandry, Zeitzen observes that there's been a lack of male sexual jealousy for his co-husband, perhaps in favor of making things work out in an inhospitable environment. Zeitzen concludes that "the inability or unwillingness to control feelings of sexual jealousy is nonetheless a challenge all polygamous spouses, regardless of their gender, face."[25]

BIOLOGICAL TENDENCIES AND POLYGYNY

Socio-biologists, biological anthropologists, natural historians, and many others have adopted a Darwinian perspective on polygamy. This group believes that family life, as expressed through marriage and other sexual practices, reveals a process of reproductive success. Through marriage, males and females, unconsciously, seek strategies to ensure the successful propagation of their own and their families' genes (c.f. Fisher 1992; Barash and Lipton 2001).

Helen Fisher, for example, writes that during courtship, mating, marriage, and divorce, that men and women are involved in "mating games," or what biologists call "reproductive strategies." Men and women, Fisher states, have two choices in mating games, mating with a single mate at a time or with numerous mates at a time (1992, 69). She believes that polyandry and polygyny are strategies that arise in particular social and economic circumstances and enhance the inclusive fitness of all those involved through a differential reproduction process.

The most fundamentally adaptive form, she says, is monogamy because pair bonding is a trademark of the human animal. She believes monogamy is the most widespread adaptation since in most societies that permit polygyny, it's only practiced by 5 to 10 percent of men. This is similar to women, "Because women in 99.5 percent of cultures around the world marry only one man at once, it is fair to conclude that monandry, one spouse, is the overwhelmingly predominant marriage pattern for the human female."[26]

Fisher says polygyny has genetic payoffs for men. It is a secondary opportunistic reproductive strategy. Polygyny is much less practiced than monogamy, but for powerful men who can enhance their number of progeny, there is a clear benefit. She writes that "the most successful harem builder on record was . . . an emperor of Morocco . . . that Ismail sired 888 children with his many wives."[27]

Given that there are reproductive limits for females in polygyny, Fisher concludes, "women in most societies try to prevent their husbands from taking a junior wife, although they are less reluctant to accept a younger sister as a co-wife."[28] We note here that such a sororal arrangement actually serves to assist sisters in passing on their genes with a powerful, advantageous male too.

Fisher summarizes her overall position in her writings by pointing out that men seek polygyny to spread their genes whereas women, through either monogamy or polygamy, seek personal resources and assets for their children.

Laura Betzig (1986) points to considerable evidence that a major function of marriage has, in fact, been reproduction. Out of 104 sample societies she investigated, sterility was considered grounds for conjugal dissolution in 37 of them. This figure rises to 53 if other factors related to infertility are taken into account, including impotence, the death of children, or the wife producing too few children. Fisher, while noting a worldwide divorce peak around the fourth year, writes this represents, "the remains of specific ancestral hominid reproductive strategy to remain together at least to raise a single child through infancy."[29]

Monogamy, though the predominant marital practice, should not be confused with sexual monogamy which is not natural as a biological, sexual practice. Barash and Lipton point out that sexual monogamy, polyandry, and adultery taken together, for example, implicate women though less than men in a nonmonogamous sexual pattern of behavior.

Their view is "for any of several reasons, females can find themselves paired with males who are not genetically the best . . . if the species is socially monogamous only one female gets the best male. Everyone else is 'settling.'"[30]

Although data is hard to come by, a significant number of children are conceived in extra marital sexual encounters either as sanctioned by a given culture or by secretive encounters. Estimates are that about 30 percent of married U.S. men and about 20 percent of married U.S. women have committed adultery and frequent extra pair copulations occur cross culturally. Fear of adultery is a central tenant in most cultures, including the Abrahamic faiths.

There are considerable exceptions to the views argued by biologically oriented social scientists. Celibacy, for example, a widespread, acceptable practice, is also a preferred custom in some cultural traditions. Similarly, same-gender relationships do not assume reproductive outcomes, and there is a growing tendency for individuals to live solitary lifestyles.

Other families consciously decide to remain childless. In sum, many sexual and family orientations offer no genetic advantages such that biological needs are often overridden by culturally constituted choices and options. Perhaps the best lessons from biologically based theories are those that point out the tremendous behavioral adaptability inherent in our cultural institutions.

Mating flexibility is part of the human primate heritage. Our closest relatives, the great apes, for example, show considerable variation in mating tendencies. Gibbons emphasize long-term monogamous-like bonds in exclusive territories; gorillas live in polygamous-like groups with a male and females; and bonobo chimps prefer strong bonds among females and a comparatively promiscuous mating pattern.[31]

Barash and Lipton conclude that monogamy has been described for 10 or 15 percent of all primate species so that, "there is no reason to think that human beings represent a mammal group that is predisposed to monogamy."[32]

Lila Leibowitz (1978) observes that human beings have as our most significant biological heritage the capacity to be socially flexible, thus human family arrangements must be understood in terms of flexibility and great variability. In short, there may be some natural tendencies, but they are based on the culture.

Walter Goldschmidt (2006) reminds us concerning genetic causes for human behaviors that what he calls "affect hunger" throughout his book trumps what is widely understood to be the "selfish gene." Goldschmidt argues that a need for positive affect among humans results in an almost unlimited capacity to learn from others beginning in the cradle and extending throughout life through social interaction. People hold a mental capacity for cultural, symbolic learning and are not slaves of their biological heritage. People need not be governed by practices of patriarchy, monogamy, polygamy, or other cultural institutions, defined as essential to their human nature by determinant biological arguments alone.

POLYGAMY AND GENDER

There is data showing traditional African women valuing polygyny, at least under certain circumstances. In an extensive survey by Ware that was undertaken in Nigeria in 1979, she learned that there were many wives who viewed polygyny as a means of companionship and also as providing them with a partner with whom they could share a variety of responsibilities, including housework, caring for their mutual husband and the family's children.

Ware surveyed more than 6,000 Yoruba females, ranging in age from 15 to 59, from the city of Ibadan, Nigeria's second largest city. Ware states that in Ibadan about one wife in two lives in a polygamous marriage; about 60 percent of the women in the survey reported that they would be "pleased" when asked how they would react if their husbands took another wife, explaining that this additional wife could help them with the many tasks she faces any given day. Only 23 percent expressed any anger at the idea of having another wife. The more traditionally oriented women without an education (about 67%) were more favorable toward polygamy than were those with some formal education (about 54%).

Ware proposes that sharing economic and domestic responsibilities among women might well appeal to modern feminists. The sharing of a husband might be viewed as a detriment or an advantage, depending on the extent to which husbands are considered assets or liabilities. Some Ibadan wives see little value in having a husband except as a "recognized progenitor for their children" (p. 190).

When these women, who live in a society where 99 percent of women marry by the age of 40, were asked whether they was a need for a husband apart from his role in begetting children, about 47 percent answered that women do not need husbands. They felt that there were many disadvantages in marriage, and since women were equal to men they often did better on their own. Other women who considered other roles that a husband could play—as in someone who provides companionship—tended to have a more favorable view of marriage.

Suda (2007) shows us that formal monogamy and informal polygyny as parallel marital institutions is the prevailing model for Africans. The older, more traditional polygyny model remains more acceptable and functional in rural areas compared to urban locations where its stigma often illegal status has been replaced by informal de facto practices in response to European cultural influences. While sub-Saharan Africa still widely practices polygamy despite restrictive legal and religious codes, Bledsoe and Pison (1994) note that, "Many of the new marriage forms that outwardly resemble monogamy actually follow patterns of de facto polygyny: serial marriage, 'outside mar-riage, and . . . sugar daddy relationships" (7).

Suda's (2007) overview of marriage on Africa also shows a number of rea-sons for polygyny's decline, especially in urban areas: Expense, the high cost of a bride price; scarcity of land; Christianity; Western values through educa-tion; the Internet; media, and HIV/AIDS (25). Zeitzen (2008) while noting that women who bear the heavier burden of HIV/AIDS in Africa, are even at a greater risk for being infected with the disease due to polygyny. A new wife, especially if she's a widow, could infect her new husband, who was previously her brother-in-law, and he might then pass on the disease to his other wife and/or wives.

Another example that Zeitzen mentions is that older men frequently mo-nopolize younger women as wives and these women may have contracted the virus before marriage from young boyfriends who often visit prostitutes (Zeitzen 2008, 176). Many women's groups, local politicians and church leaders oppose polygyny for its association with "wife inheritance" (which is also described in the Hebrew Bible), and HIV/AIDS. But in so doing, "local women's rights groups campaign not against traditional, rural polygyny, which often serves important purposes, but against the urban forms of plural unions involving multiple mistresses rather than wives" (Zeitzen 2008, 177). While this is true, international groups and western-oriented African women often oppose any form of polygyny in favor of monogamy for cultural, politi-cal or religious reasons. In a telling case, Uganda developed an indigenous policy of "zero grazing," an African solution to combat HIV/AIDS, one that would promote "ABC" (abstinence, faithfulness, and condom use). Being faithful would include fidelity to one spouse or multiple spouses but, wrote one observer, "Western conservatives couldn't stomach a program that coun-tenanced polygamy" (Rice 2007, 31).

The present state of marital flux in Africa is especially harmful for chil-dren. There is often little distinction between more traditional, surviving patterns of polygyny, legal in some countries, and a plethora of de facto prac-

tices under the cloud of illegitimacy. Imagine when a head of state, who has 3 wives and 20 children, is denounced in South Africa by the Roman Catholic and Anglican Churches as well as the psychological impact on the polygamist's children and countless others in the same situation in that country (Solomon 2010).

Suda points out that, overall, the current monogamous system, including de facto polygyny, primarily affects the poorest women who must often support their children alone, outside of any formal marriage obligations.

In her Nairobi, Kenya, research, Suda found that men prefer cohabitation over formal marriage because they are not obliged to assume responsibilities required in formal marriage. Discussing cohabitation, one man said, "the man is free as a bird since there is no marriage bond, there is no obligation to provide for his partner's needs, including his children's" (Suda 2007, 54). There is a strong correlation between the rise of street children in Nairobi and the breakdown of family structure and parental obligations (cf. Kilbride, Suda, and Njeru 2001). While it follows that many children are better off in the formal, now unregulated sector of urban family life, we agree with Bledsoe and Pison (1994) that, "the fact that new forms of polygyny are emerging throws into share relief the legitimacy status of different kinds of partners and children. . . . They also can comprise idioms for marginalizing some women and giving them and their children less recognition and support" (19).

MONOGAMY RECONSIDERED AND POLYGYNY REINVENTED

A persistence of both de facto and de jure polygyny across Africa suggests that both monogamy and polygyny as an essentialized singular practice must be, considering the conditions, rethought and reinvented. Widow inheritance, female circumcision, parent-arranged marriage, extended family ideology over individual rights have been modified or eliminated in various nations. Nevertheless, concerning sub-Saharan Africa, "other practices have been retained such as extended family loyalty and, to a smaller extent, the practice of polygyny . . . the Western bias toward . . . nuclear families seem unlikely to simply replace the traditional beliefs" (Wilson and Ngige 2006, 271).

What must be resolved in the short term is the question of HIV/AIDS, an issue that Kilbride frequently is asked about in response to the first edition of this book, especially as it pertains to plural marriage in both the United States and Africa. The Ugandan situation seems instructive. By moving de facto forms of sexuality into the daylight of public acceptance and recognition (as in foreign aid programs to Uganda mentioned previously), one makes men more responsible and, at the same time, one increases the power

of women in all marriages and, thus, in control of their own sexuality and provides them with the right to refuse their spouses on other matters, too.

The most vulnerable victims of HIV/AIDS today in Africa are poor women, especially those who are not married, either polygamously or monogamously (cf. Bledsoe and Pison 1994), who must often accept sexual opportunities for profit by going along with male refusals to use condoms (see also Washington and Nangendo 1997).

The extended family, so strong in Africa, is returning to the West for economic reasons as we have seen earlier in this book (e.g., boomerang children) or as a transnational ideology in Australia for better economic and social outcomes. The power of the economy is an important factor in any discussion about marriage, whether it's plural or monogamous. It is important to remind ourselves that Africa is appropriate to consider not only for its richness in family culture (distorted so much by colonialism, poverty and HIV/AIDS), but also because we are all struggling with the same issues found on that continent, including child-bearing, family life, and sexuality—at work in all marriages—regardless of the type of marriage, monogamous or polygamous. Critical influences, like religion, culture and family pressure, can influence marriage patterns anywhere in the world, whether it's a first-world country like the United States or a third-world country, like some of those found in Africa. Everywhere, however, the role of economics is crucial.

NOTES

1. Helen Fisher, *Anatomy of Love: The National History of Monogamy, Adultery and Divorce* (New York: W. W. Norton & Co., 1992), p. 69.

2. Bron B. Ingoldsby, *Families in Global and Multicultural Perspective* (Thousand Oaks, CA: Sage Publications, 2006), pp. 101 and 102.

3. Ibid., p. 102.

4. Maha A. Z. Yamani, *Polygamy and Law in Contemporary Saudi Arabia* (Berkshire, UK: Ithaca Press, 2008), p. 215.

5. Ibid., p. 231.

6. Ibid., p. 105.

7. Collette Suda, "Formal Monogamy and Informal Polygyny in Parallel: African Family Traditions in Transition," Inaugural Lecture, University of Nairobi, October 4, 2007.

8. Ibid.

9. Nancy Levine and Walter Sangree, "Women with Many Husbands: Polyandrous Alliance and Marital Flexibility in Africa and Asia," special issue of *Journal of Comparative Family Studies* vol. 11, no. 3 (1980): i–14.

10. Yamani, *Polygamy and Law in Contemporary Saudi Arabia*, p. 231.

11. Philip L. Kilbride, "African Polygamy: Family Values and Contemporary Changes," in *Applied Cultural Anthropology: An Introductory Reader*, 6th ed., ed. Aaron

Podolefsky and Peter Brown, pp. 201–209 (Mountain View, CA: Mayfield Publishing Company, 2003).

12. Valerie Moller and Gary John Welch, "Polygamy, Economic Security and Well-Being of Retired Zulu Migrant Workers," *Journal of Cross-Cultural Gerontology* 5 (1990): pp. 205–216.

13. Ibid.

14. Ibid.

15. Kilbride, "African Polygamy."

16. Walter Sangree, "Going Home to Mother: Traditional Marriage among the Irigwe of Benue-Plateau State, Nigeria," *Journal of the American Anthropological Association*, vol. 71, no. 6 (1969): 1046–1056.

17. Ibid., p. 1053.

18. Ibid.

19. Ingoldsby, *Families in Global and Multicultural Perspective*, p. 108.

20. Leanna Wolfe, "Adding a Co-Wife," *Loving More Magazine* 15 (1998): pp. 22–25.

21. Ibid.

22. Marjorie Shostak, *Nisa: The Life and Words of a !Kung Woman* (New York: Random House, 1981), pp. 267–268.

23. Harold Schneider, "Human Sexuality from an Intercultural Perspective," in *Human Sexual Behavior: Variations in the Ethnographic Spectrum*, ed. Donald Marshall and Robert Suggs (Englewood Cliffs, NJ: Prentice-Hall, 1972), p. 62.

24. Gregory White and Paul Mullen, *Jealousy: Theory, Research and Clinical Strategies* (New York: Guilford Press, 1989), p. 146.

25. Miriam Zeitzen, *Polygamy: A Cross-Cultural Analysis* (Oxford: Berg, 2008), p. 112.

26. Fisher, *Anatomy of Love*, p. 69.

27. Ibid., p. 66.

28. Ibid., p. 67.

29. Helen Fisher, "The Drive to Love: The Neural Mechanism for Mate Selection in the New Psychology of Love," in *The New Psychology of Love*, ed. Robert J. Sternberg and Karin Weis (New Haven, CT: Yale University Press, 2006), pp. 87–115.

30. David Barash and Judith E. Lipton, *The Myth of Monogamy: Fidelity and Infidelity in Animals and People* (New York: Henry Holt and Company, 2001), p. 68.

31. Frans de Waal, "Bonobo Sex and Society," *Scientific American*, March 1995, pp. 82–88.

32. Barash and Lipton, *The Myth of Monogamy*, p. 146.

4

Economics and Decline of Monogamous Marriage in the United States

If marriage were simply an issue about love—and all we had to do in this book is write an analysis about how emotions make one person marry and another person not marry—the topic would be so much easier. But marriage is complicated and also fundamentally involves economics. Money and wealth can be a reason why people marry—because, for example, they think they'll improve their living conditions by marrying someone who's rich—or a reason why people don't marry—because they're doing a fine job of earning all the money they need by themselves.

Less than 100 years ago, women often married so their economic future would be secure. Today, Western countries, and even some Asian ones, are seeing a decline in marriage because women are educated, in the workforce, with high paying jobs. They don't require marriage for their economic well being the way they once did. In fact, some men are saying women in their country are on "marriage strike."[1]

Still, as this chapter will show, married couples in the United States have an advantage that their never married and divorced counterparts don't have—they often accumulate more wealth together than single people do.

History Professor Stephanie Coontz, who's written extensively about marriage, reminds us that the "dismal science," as economics is sometimes called, has long been a reason that people have married over the centuries. She also shows that marrying for money—or to maintain one's economic status—is hardly new. The institution of marriage, she writes, "was more about getting the right in-laws than picking the right partner to love. . . . People maneuvered to orchestrate advantageous marriage connections with some families and avoid incurring obligations to others. Marriage became the main way that the upper classes consolidated wealth, forged military coalitions, finalized peace treaties, and bolstered claims to social status or political authority."[2]

Coontz also writes that making sure the economic part of any marital relationship wasn't the exclusive domain of just those who are well healed. It also involved the middle class. "Getting 'well-connected' in-laws was a preoccupation of the middle classes as well, while the dowry a man received at marriage was often the biggest economic stake he would acquire before his parents died. Peasants, farmers, and craftsmen acquired new workers for the family enterprise and forged cooperative bonds with neighbors through their marriages."[3]

Even hundreds of years ago, wives knew their husband's wealth would determine their living conditions. And, occasionally, they fought for it. As we show here, there's a long Western history of marriage and economics, and even religion, being intertwined with one another.

EARLY ECONOMICS AND THE EUROPEAN CHURCH

It was in the context of religious values, still significant in the United States, that opposed pleasure, including sexual pleasure, that the present marital form with its preference for monogamy and the nuclear family came to be institutionalized. Toward the middle of the first millennium, the conversion of the Roman Empire to Christianity set in motion a series of changes in social organization and kinship that were consistent with the sexual ideology that developed alongside these changes.

Marriages between first cousins were prohibited; in addition, around AD 393, the Roman Church also forbade unions with the wife of a dead brother (the levirate referred to in the Hebrew Bible). Jack Goody writes, "during the late Roman and early medieval periods, rich widows made an important contribution to the Church, which was more likely to benefit if they remained chaste and unmarried."[4]

The dowry system worked to women's advantage in enabling them to accumulate property at the death of their spouses. Legitimate offspring were also curtailed as the church over time removed the privileges of concubines and their offspring by classifying such children as illegitimate and barring them from inheriting family property. Disallowing marriage to first cousins, regulating the state of widows, and stigmatizing concubinage went hand in hand with a religion, Goody states, that was evolving from a sect to a church.

The church as it developed in Europe moved gradually from a dissonant sect to one that was characterized by a large organization with buildings, land, and personnel that would, in effect, soon be competing with family and kin groupings for control over property, inheritance, and legitimacy. The growth of the monastery became another source of church power and represented a high-status operation for the celibate. The convent, Goody observes, became a refuge for widows and daughters and was commonly in a position to attract family funds as well.

Marriage became recognized as a sacrament starting in the 13th century but not officially so until the Council of Trent about 300 years later, in the 16th century. Goody believes that the sacralization of marriage made it much more central in the theology of the church; Protestantism in many ways initiated a process of desacralization of marriage as an institution, not to mention its concern over gaining control of property and inheritance in its own right.

By curtailing the possibility of marriage, perhaps by favoring celibacy, by limiting the number of marital partners, by favoring monogamy and opposing divorce, by stigmatizing illegitimate offspring, and by not allowing priests and nuns to have families, the Roman Church got into a conflict-of-interest situation with kin groups as it struggled for control and power over materials and resources. According to Ranke-Heinemann: "In contrast to the relative moderation of the Jews, Christians worked up a whole mass of legal technicalities for prohibiting marriages that no religion hitherto had been even theoretically capable of contriving and that can be explained only by Catholic hostility to sex and pleasure."[5] Ranke-Heinemann does not, however, make the connection that Goody makes to issues of property and resource control, which would provide an economic rationale for the particular direction dominant Christian sexual morality took in the two millennia after the death of Jesus.

While polygyny was not officially recognized in the Roman Empire, it was known to exist and, in some cases, was even an approved practice. "Plural marriage was not a general feature of the Mediterranean world, certainly not of Rome; but in Rome, Greece and Israel a concubine could be taken as an additional spouse in order to provide an heir. This practice was no longer condoned. Neither were the irregular unions to which priests and laymen alike continued to enter."[6]

The church quickly reinforced tendencies already at work in the Roman Empire to establish monogamy as the religious as well as the cultural ideal. In early Christian Ireland, an examination of historical documents on the lives of saints indicates that polygyny was apparently a common model in aristocratic household. David Herlihy, for instance, noted that "the lives consistently show a tolerant attitude, not only toward bigamy, but toward all sexual relations outside of legal marriage. They describe, for example, again, without a suggestion of reproach, the illegitimate births of several other saints."[7]

The Germans' social organization, like that of the Irish Celts, composed of tribes, kindreds, and large extended families, so that kinship was central in their social lives. For this reason, it is not surprising that the households and marriages of these two "barbarian" cultures displayed some similarities.

Both the German and the Irish cultures had the bride wealth practice in which the bride and her family receives materials from the husband and his family, rather than vice versa, which was the common practice in Rome and later in Europe with the development of the dowry system. In short, the status of women, comparatively low as it was in the patriarchal social organization of barbarian cultures, certainly was not without its rewards and benefits. Aristocratic Irish women received gifts and presents from their husbands not only at the marriage but also throughout their married lives—from both their husbands and other men as well. "The wives are likely to have wielded considerable influence, power even, over decisions made within their households. They had the right to divorce their husbands and depart their households, taking their wealth with them." An examination of the lives of Irish saints reveals that women were not merely passive, sexual objects "without acquiescence or resistance among powerful males."[8] Although much is known about the rich and powerful, relatively little information is available on the common people.

AN EARLY MARRIAGE FIGHT OVER MONEY

The unfavorable view of plural marriage, which came to be subsumed under the term of bigamy, and its religious and economic parameters can be seen in a fascinating case of trans-Atlantic plural marriage that occurred in the 16th century involving the colony of Peru and its mother country, Spain. Alexandra Cook and Nobel Cook (1991) tell the story. Francisco Noguerol de Ulloa, following his mother's wishes, married in Spain a woman, Beatriz de Villasur and, shortly after, followed his dreams and went off to the New World in 1534, seeking his fortune.

He became very successful in Peru where he was given an *encomienda* with considerable opportunities for accumulating wealth in the form of tribute extracted from Indians. While living in Peru, he received letters from his sisters informing him that his wife, who he left in Spain, had died. After some time, Francisco met and fell in love with Catalina de Vergara, and they decided to marry. Part of the marriage agreement included an agreement on the size of the dowry, which was considerable. It also contained a condition that Francisco would take her back to Spain to live. Catalina wished to return to Spain to be reunited with her children from a previous marriage who lived there.

Francisco probably decided to return to Spain for family considerations as well because his mother was aging and his sisters had begged him for years to come home. At this time, however, he found out that his first wife, Beatriz, whom he had believed dead, was, in fact, alive. While he and Catalina were preparing to leave Peru, his first wife was preparing a lawsuit back in Spain, which she submitted to the Council of the Indies in Vallodalid.

Cook and Cook report that Noguerol's marriage to another women while he was still married to her shocked Doña Beatriz who "could not allow her honor as well as her family's honor to be stained. Bigamy was illegal, immoral, and sinful in the eyes of the church. Furthermore, there was the money that her father had paid as dowry, money that had helped Francisco to set forth and establish himself in the Indies."[9]

Noguerol's lawyer took up his case in his absence and lost. The court ordered Noguerol to return to Spain with all his goods to resume married life with his first wife. This decision was forthcoming, even though there was no evidence that, at the time of his second marriage, Noguerol had known that his first wife was still alive.

Legal counsel became involved with both wives because the first wife alleged that she should be compensated materially since Francisco had received half the dowry from that marriage. Dowry considerations from the second marriage had also become involved since Catalina had brought into her marriage with Francisco dowry money, some of which had come from her prior marriage. At this point, the important role of property as manifested in the dowry and its relationship to marriage should be emphasized. Who was married to whom had many implications for gaining access to property and wealth.

Noguerol, having returned to Spain, set out to collect evidence for an appeal. He brought his case to the church where he submitted evidence swearing that his original marriage was against his consent. He denied carnal copulation had taken place. He also included an explanation of why he remarried, after having been abroad for some eight years, in Peru, during which time he had been notified, by his sisters, that his wife had died. Cook and Cook explain Noguerol's actions: "He knew that he had been condemned by the Council of the Indies and fully realized the gravity of his sentence and the stigma attached to his person. Francisco's salvation depended on a swift maneuver to cleanse himself of the shameful spot on his honor. He went to Léon to throw himself at the mercy of the ecclesiastical courts" (68).

In 1557, King Philip II issued a warrant for Noguerol's arrest, sending out a search party to located him. Francisco, however, evaded arrest and moved about the countryside. Eventually, he surrendered to the authorities and was arrested.

Meanwhile, his second wife, Caterina, made a formal demand for the return of her dowry so that she could "safeguard her assets and separate her goods from her husband's property."[10] This was exactly what Beatriz was requesting also. She wanted the return of her dowry and one half of Noguerol's earnings. There were several appeals; Noguerol attempted to establish his innocence, proving evidence that his sisters had indeed lied in their correspondences to him, presumably out of love for him, thinking that this would cause him to return home. Although there are no records about the final outcome of his appeal, the last verdict decreed that he was to be fined and exiled from specific areas of Spain but was not be imprisoned. In sum, he was free.

On marriage questions, the Council of the Indies made no ruling considering that this was a matter the church should handle. It should be noted, however, that this case took place before the Council of Trent in 1563, when marriages became regulated in the Catholic Church and, for the first time, required a church ceremony and participation of a priest. When the Council of Trent concluded, marriage officially became a sacrament.

In 1588, Pope Paul IV issued a decree ratifying the marriage between Noguerol and his second wife, Caterina, in response to consideration of all circumstances surrounding their marriage. The angered first wife, Beatriz, refused to accept notification of their invalid marriage in a public setting, so she was informed privately.

Francisco went on to enjoy a successful economic life with his investments in Spain, generating a large income. After his death, Caterina, his wife, controlled large resources. Doña Beatriz, in comparison, lived in low profile following the decision against her marriage to Noguerol, never accepting the church's ruling.

MARRIAGE TODAY

If there's any one thing that this story shows, it is that marriage and economics go hand in hand. Certainly that's what Doña Beatriz knew. While it might be easy to dismiss the economic influences surrounding marriage—people tend to be giddy in love when they become engaged to one another and not likely thinking about their combined finances—economics influences marriage.

Two people, married to one another, with high incomes, which usually means they're college educated, are more likely to own a larger house and live in a financially exclusive neighborhood than those who may have stopped their educational careers when they earned their high school diplomas.

And while the latest research shows that, today, people who marry tend to have college degrees, which often provide them with the ability to find and hold better paying jobs, the latest research also shows that people who don't hold college degrees are remaining single. While that might cause society one problem—because there are fewer people marrying—the larger problem for U.S. society is that single women are giving birth because, it appears, the stigma that was once associated with birth outside of wedlock—what was once called having an illegitimate child—appears to have washed away.

The problem this trend poses is that single mothers only possessing a high school diploma don't do as well as those with college degrees. And unlike their married counterparts, they're lacking a partner, and his family resources, to help with childcare at home and sustain them through some of life's economic problems.

According to 2009 statistics, there were about 74.5 million children in the United States and about 25 percent of them, more than 18 million, are growing up in single-mother households. Single moms and their children encounter economic problems that married moms and their children usually never see. And, sometimes, single mothers with college degrees don't experience these financial problems either. As one researcher wrote, "Seven in 10 children living with a single mother are poor or low income, compared to less than a third of children living in other types of families" and that "three-fourths of all single mothers are in the labor force, and single mothers have slightly higher labor force participation rates than women in married-couple families. However, single mothers are more than twice as likely to be unemployed (13%), compared with mothers in married-couples families (5%); and the majority of employed single mothers—62 percent—are working in lower-wage retail, service, or administrative jobs that offer few benefits."[11]

Because of the jobs that they tend to find, single mothers, often lacking a college degree, are often working without health insurance. "Despite high rates of labor force participation, more than one-fourth (27%) of single mothers do not have health insurance. Among those who are insured, two-fifths are covered by public insurance programs. In contrast, 90 percent of insured mothers in married-couple families have private health insurance coverage."[12]

Indeed, as pointed out in chapter one, health insurance coverage is an important issue when looking at the economic conditions of single mothers because "children without continuous health insurance coverage are more likely to have unmet health needs and less likely to receive preventive care."[13]

It's not certain that this trend of single women giving birth is going to end anytime soon. *The New York Times* reported a "surge of births outside marriage among younger women—nearly two-thirds of children in the United States are born to mothers under 30—is both a symbol of the transforming family and a hint of coming generational change."[14]

College graduates tend to resist this trend, marrying before having children. But this approach to childbirth and marriage, the *Times* reports, could possibly spell an economic divide among families in the future. It means that marriage followed by childbirth, which always created families, regardless of the parents' educational background and economic wealth, which in prior generations was an accepted fact of life, may very well become something that's reserved for the well off. "Marriage has become a luxury good," the *Times* quoted University of Pennsylvania sociologist Frank Furstenberg as saying about the trend lines.[15]

The educational backgrounds among new mothers break down this way: "about 92 percent of college-educated women are married when they give birth, compared to 62 percent of women with some post-secondary schooling and 43 percent of women with a high school diploma or less."[16]

The rise in these nonmarital births, the *Times* reported, is due to couples living with one another—even if they're not committed to a future together. And while it use to be that one married their child's parent—even if there was an unplanned pregnancy—today, researchers are learning, that's not so much the case. Indeed, the respectability and stigma issues that surrounded unwed mothers and children born outside of wedlock 10 to 20 years ago appear not to be felt by a younger generation of women. "Today, neither of Ms. [Amber] Strader's pregnancies left her thinking she should marry to avoid stigma . . . she described her children as largely unplanned, a byproduct of relationships lacking commitment."[17]

As anyone who's likely been following attitudes toward sex over the last few decades knows, premarital sex has certainly lost its stigma, as has giving birth before marriage, but some women attending college think it remains best to have children after getting married. As the *Economist* reported a few years ago, college students think "having children out of wedlock is not wrong, but unwise."[18] Some of the new moms the *Times* interviewed said their experiences in watching their own parents' marital difficulties have made them shy about marrying.

Still, the problem that single mothers face, especially if they don't have a college education, is fewer opportunities for a high-paying job. While some couples live together without being married—because they had children with one another—one researcher notes that "children in cohabiting-partner families can benefit from economic contributions of two potential caregivers, (but) these unions tend to be less stable and have fewer economic resources compared with married couples."[19]

Children in single-mother households are "among the most vulnerable children in the country." Mather suggests that the remedy is for single mothers to "have access to education, job training, quality child care," so her earnings improve and she can ensure her "children's successful transitions to adulthood."[20]

The Pew Research Center recently showed that, unlike adults with only high school diploma, college-educated adults are more likely "to have married by the age of 30." The study showed that, in 2008, "62 percent of college-educated 30-year-olds were married or had been married, compared to 60 percent of 30-year-olds who did not have a college degree."[21]

WOMEN AND MARRIAGE

Joyce A. Joyce, a sociologist at St. Bonaventure University in Buffalo, New York, has written extensively about the financial well being of women who remain single or who are married. In her book, *Women, Marriage and Wealth: The Impact of Marital Status on the Economic Well-Being of Women Through the Life Course*, she shows a lot of data that proves "clearly the economic advantages of marriage affords women compared to any other marital status." In her examination of women, Dr. Joyce found that "despite a decline in the popularity of marriage, evidence demonstrates that many benefits accrue from being married, including: (a) greater wealth and higher wages; (b) better health and increased longevity; (c) improved intimacy and sexuality; and (d) the beneficial impact of marriage on children, including greater likelihood of completion of high school education and lowered likelihood of living in poverty."[22]

This comes about because two people, married to one another, are "partners . . . in a long-term contract" who create a "coinsurance" from shared economic and social resources; (c) economies of scale;" and they are connected to "other individuals, groups, and social institutions that provide benefits and give life meaning."[23]

Married women, Joyce shows, tend to be married to husbands in the workforce and, as a result, "have access to more income than women in other marital status groups." And while divorced women, widows and never married women may have higher lifetime earnings than married women, married women, Joyce writes, "are the most economically secure of women"[24] compared to all other women—regardless of their marital status, which explains why, more than 450 years ago, Doña Beatriz worked as hard as she did to remain Francisco Noguerol de Ulloa's wife. She knew he had assets. She also likely knew that his second wife would benefit greatly from them.

Marriage also benefits women because, as they age, the houses they tend to own contributes greatly to their financial well being. "Home values of . . . married women (are) considerably greater than those of . . . other women."[25] It's likely that married women, because they tend to have children, have purchased larger houses, likely on stronger socioeconomic communities.

THE ECONOMICS OF MARRIED MEN

One of the advantages of marriage that's been shown over the years is that married men tend to outpace single men when it comes to income. Men, after they marry, have wages that rise and the "managerial and professional effect appears to be related to receiving higher performance ratings and therefore being more likely to be promoted to higher, better-paying jobs."[26] A married man's economic advantage, because he is married, however, is now disputed, Jacobson writes, due to a variety of factors, including an increased probability of divorce; still, married men "have a 13 percent wage premium," meaning their incomes are at least 13 percent higher than those of single men.[27]

Married men often have wives who stay home and care for the couple's children. "A man who has a nonworking wife will have higher wages because his wife is free to dedicate relatively more time to furthering his career, either directly through career-related activities, or indirectly by freeing him from almost all home production obligations."[28]

SOME CHANGES TODAY

The Pew Research Center has also recently confirmed many of the most recent findings about economic status and marriage. Unlike previous generations, when it was solely women who benefited from marriage, now, more often than not, it's the husbands who do.

The Center also shows that marriage is—just like the sociologist quoted in *The New York Times* story—on its way to becoming something that's exclusive. That means the people who are marrying today, compared to more than 40 years ago are much more likely to have both a college education and a high income. Those with less education and less income aren't as likely to marry, which means there's a true economic stratification now about marriage than there had ever been before.

The other basic change in marriage, since 1970, the Pew Center reports, is that 40 years ago a husband didn't gain another breadwinner when he married. Today he does, "giving his household increased earning power that most unmarried men do not enjoy." Because married adults tend to be highly educated, "the more that adults' household incomes have risen over the past four decades . . . married adults have seen larger gains than unmarried adults." reports that "for unmarried adults at each level of education . . . men's household incomes fared worse than those of women . . . unmarried men without any post-secondary education lost ground because their real earnings decreased and they did not have a wife's wages to buffer that decline."[29]

So while there's been a change in the gender, as of late, in terms of who's benefited the most from marriage, what's clear is this—marriage works to someone's overall benefit financially.

While the percentages of adults who are married has dropped, what is being noticed, Pew reports, is that the less educated aren't marrying. In 1970, for example, more than 85 percent of high school graduate men and women, respectively, were likely to be married. That percentage has dropped significantly. Now only about 55 percent of all high school graduate women and 54 percent of all high school graduate men, Pew reports, are likely to be married. And the results, tragically, for the least educated continue. Pew reports: "Less educated Americans are not only the least likely to be currently married, but they also are more likely to be divorced."[30]

The other trend that's changing is this: Women are more likely to complete a college education than men. "Women became the majority of newly minted college graduates in the 1981–1982 school year and accounted for 57 percent of those who gained their undergraduate degrees in the 2006–2007 school year."[31] What does that mean for the future of marriage? Will a college educated woman—because her prospects for marriage are low, if she's only looking for college educated man—have to consider dating and marrying someone who doesn't match her educational credentials?

Pew gives some interesting insight into the African American community in this report, saying that a third of all "black wives were more educated than their husbands."[32] Will white wives follow the same path and marry men with less education?

RELUCTANCE TO MARRY IN ASIA

The United States and some European countries aren't the only places experiencing a decline in marriage. The *Economist* magazine reported the same tend among young adults in places in like Japan, Taiwan, and elsewhere in the region. Many of the reasons that people are holding off on marrying in Asia are the same ones that can be found in the United States—starting a career, finding the right person or there's just no interest in marrying. As the magazine reported, "almost a third of Japanese women in their early 30s are unmarried; probably half of those will always be. Over one-fifth of Taiwanese women in their late 30s are single; most will never marry. In some places, rates of non-marriage are especially striking: in Bangkok, 20% of 40–44–year old women are not married; in Tokyo, 21%; among university graduates of that age in Singapore, 27%."[33]

So far, the magazine reports, this trend hasn't affected two countries with some of the world's largest populations, China and India. Still, what does this mean for Asia if men and women aren't marrying the way they did once before? One can only speculate but the *Economist* noted that "the decline of marriage is also contributing to the collapse in the birth rate. Fertility in East Asia has fallen from 5.3 children per woman in the late 1960s to 1.6 now. In countries with the lowest marriage rates, the fertility rate is nearer 1.0. That is beginning to cause huge demographic problems, as populations age with startling speed."[34]

What this means, at least in some Asian countries, is that a younger generation, which is typically expected to support the one prior to them, through taxes so government-supported pensions are funded, will not have as many people to work to support retirees. Does this mean that a younger generation's taxes will be increased so an older generation's pension is funded—and paid?

In Asia people are waiting to marry, usually not marrying until they're around 30, older than the average age of when men and women in the United States typically marry, 28 and 26, respectively. In addition, there's some concern that demographic groups that previously married a great deal aren't marrying at all. In Japan, for example, in 1970, about 5 percent of all women between the ages of 35 and 39 had not been married. About 40 years later, nearly 20 percent of Japanese women in the same age range had not been married. This trend continues in other Asian countries, too. "In Thailand, the number of women entering their 40s without being married increased from 7 percent in 1980 to 12 percent in 2000."[35]

Like their American counterparts, women in Asia are reluctant to marry because they're far more autonomous than in the past. They tend to be educated and are holding down jobs.[36] But unlike the high school educated women in the United States, who tend to avoid marriage, Asian women, with about the same level of education, are likely to marry.

Surprisingly, the potential problem for this lack of marriage in Asia is similar to that of the United States. While women in the United States seek their educational equal when it comes to marriage, in Asia a woman is seeking to marry someone whose educational background—and income—is above theirs. That means, like in the United States, there are two demographic groups who are not likely to be married—"men with no education and women with a lot."[37]

Though economics factor into the decline in marriage in Asia and elsewhere, man does not live by bread alone. As illustrated in the Hebrew Bible's story about Abraham and Sarah, the desire for children is universal. Consider Vietnam, where polygamy was banned in 1959. Its practice persists and one of the reasons is infertility. Although the country has modern medical advances to reduce infertility, it is reported by Melissa Pashigian that

> there were . . . women . . . who asked their husband for permission to locate a second wife so the husband may have a child . . . the phenomena of second wives with which some infertile couples contend is sometimes a form of polygamous marriage but in other cases it is a form of serial marriage with the husband moving on to a new wife, leaving ambiguous his relationship to his first [supposedly infertile] wife. . . . "It is important to understand over the course of centuries polygamy has served as a socially legitimate form of de facto surrogacy in the absence of effective technological/medicinal solutions for infertility.[38]

BASIC ECONOMICS

Of course, any chapter about the economics of marriage would be remiss if it didn't include a mention of the basic financial advantages that come with being married, at least in the United States. While filing income tax forms as a couple, jointly, if both husband and wife are working, can certainly raise income and, possibly, mean a wife or husband owes taxes because they're married, as opposed to when they were single, there's also the possibility of lowering the amount of taxes that are paid through tax deductions that can be made for children and mortgage payments.

Kimberly Palmer, writing for *U.S. News & World Report*, says one of the basic advantages of being married is that "spouses can inherit the wealth of their deceased spouses without paying federal estate tax."[39] In addition, Social Security benefits go to the surviving spouse and property is much more easily shared between married partners.

MARRIAGE'S CONTEXT

Marriage is different today than it was 40 and 50 years ago because it's far more equitable for women, especially those who are college educated. But even women without college degrees are showing a considerable amount of independence: Often they're not marrying the father of their children. This means that women today have many more options than their mothers did. They're free to marry (for any reason they wish) as much as they're free to remain single (for a reason they choose).

Nevertheless, economics remains a powerful factor in marriage. Similar to earlier generations, today's marriage remains associated with deeply rooted cultural ceremonies, including engagement parties, purchasing of rings, the marriage ceremony itself and honeymoons.

As we'll see in this book, the role of economics is as much a part of plural marriage, whether it's inside or outside of the United States and the American continent, as it is in monogamous marriage.

NOTES

1. "The Flight from Marriage," *The Economist*, August 20, 2011, http://www.econ omist.com/node/21526329.

2. Stephanie Coontz, "The Future of Marriage," *Cato Unbound*, January 14, 2008, http://www.cato-unbound.org.

3. Ibid.

4. Jack Goody, *The Development of Family and Marriage and Europe* (New York: Cambridge University Press, 1983), p. 64.

5. Uta Ranke-Heinemann, *Eunuchs for the Kingdom of Heaven: Women, Sexuality and the Catholic Church* (New York: Penguin Books, 1991), p. 217.

6. Goody, *The Development of Family*, pp. 204 and 205.

7. David Herlihy, *Medieval Households* (Cambridge, MA: Harvard University Press, 1985), p. 37.

8. Ibid., pp. 36 and 40.

9. Alexandra Cook and Nobel Cook, *Good Faith and Truthful Ignorance: A Case of Transatlantic Bigamy* (Durham, NC: Duke University Press, 1991), p. 45.

10. Ibid., p. 85.

11. Mark Mather, "U.S. Children in Single-Mother Families," Population Reference Bureau, May 2010, http://www.prb.org/Publications/PolicyBriefs/singlemother families.aspx.

12. Ibid.

13. Ibid.

14. Jason DeParle and Sabrina Tavernise, "Unwed Mothers Now a Majority in Births in 20's," *The New York Times*, February 18, 2012, http://www.nytimes.com/2012/02/18/us/for-women-under-30-most-births-occur-outside-marriage.html?pagewanted=all.

15. Ibid.

16. Ibid.

17. Ibid.

18. "Marriage in America: The Frayed Knot," *The Economist*, May 24, 2007, http://www.economist.com/node/9218127.

19. Mather, "U.S. Children in Single-Mother Families."

20. Ibid.

21. "The Reversal of the College Marriage Gap," Pew Research Center, October 7, 2010, http://pewresearch.org/pubs/1756/share-married-educational-attainment.

22. Joyce A. Joyce, *Women, Marriage and Wealth: The Impact of Marital Status on the Economic Well-Being of Women Through the Life Course* (New York: Gordian Knot Books, 2007), pp. 30 and 36.

23. Ibid., pp. 36 and 37.

24. Ibid., pp. 85 and 87.

25. Ibid., p. 133.

26. Joyce P. Jacobson, "How Family Structure Affects Labor Market Outcomes," in *The Economics of Work and Family*, ed. Jean Kimmel and Emily P. Hoffman (Kalamazoo, MI: W.E. Upjohn Institute for Employment Research, 2002), p. 145.

27. Ibid., p. 145.

28. Ibid.

29. "Women, Men and the New Economics of Marriage," Pew Research Center, January 10, 2010, http://www.pewsocialtrends.org/2010/01/19/women-men-and-the-new-economics-of-marriage/.

30. Ibid.

31. Ibid.

32. Ibid.

33. "Asia's Lonely Hearts," *The Economist*, August 20, 2011, http://www.economist.com/node/21526350.

34. Ibid.

35. "The Flight from Marriage."

36. Ibid.

37. Ibid.

38. Melissa J. Pashigian, "The Womb Infertility and the Vicissitudes of Kin-Relatedness in Vietnam," *The Journal of Vietnamese Studies* vol. 4, issue 2 (2009): 34–68, esp. p. 52.

39. Kimberly Palmer, "Marriage's Financial Pros and Cons," U.S. *News & World Report*, July 2, 2008, http://money.usnews.com/money/personal-finance/articles/2008/07/02/marriages-financial-pros-and-cons.

5

The Nonmonogamous in North America

Governors Mark Sanford and Roy Romer, on opposite sides of the U.S. political divide, share something in common: both maintained romantic relationships while married.

Sanford, a South Carolina Republican, admitted in 2009 that he'd found his "soul mate" in an Argentinean woman while married to Jenny. While many of the relationship's details remain undisclosed, once it made the news, Jenny left the governor's mansion and eventually sought, and was granted, a divorce.

In a surprising development to the story, she told ABC News's Barbara Walters, during an interview for *20/20*, that when she and Mark were discussing the vows they'd use during their wedding, her betrothed refused to be sexually and romantically faithful.[1]

Romer, a Democrat and a three-term governor of Colorado, married to Bea for more than 30 years, started a relationship with B.J. Thornberry, a woman who had worked for him as his deputy chief of staff. Some of the relationship's details were reported in Denver's newspapers as well as the *Washington Post*. "Romer maintained that his relationship with Thornberry was platonic but conceded the boundaries remained murky," the *Post* reported in 1998. "These kind of things are often not black or white, they have a lot of gray in them and I think there needs to be flexibility within a family to handle that gray."[2] Romer admitted he'd told Bea and his children about this relationship.

While people might think Sanford's and Romer's actions, so far as their marriage goes, are askew, they're not the first public office holders to maintain intimate relationships with someone other than their spouses. Perhaps the most significant figure in 20th-century U.S. political life to carry on a long-term intimate relationship with someone other than his wife was President Franklin D. Roosevelt. As detailed by historian Joseph S. Persico in his book, *Franklin & Lucy: President Roosevelt, Mrs. Rutherfurd, and the Other Remarkable Women in His Life*, FDR conducted a romantic relationship with Lucy Mercer Rutherfurd for nearly 30 years and she—not the First Lady—was at his side when he died in Warm Springs, Georgia.

Sometimes a high profile woman is caught doing the same thing. There are rumors about Nikki Haley, who succeeded Sanford as South Carolina's governor, having carried on an extramarital affair.[3] Outside of the United States, the biggest case of a woman engaging in an intimate relationship with someone other than her husband involves Iris Robinson, the wife of Northern Ireland's first minister. A little more than two years ago, when she was just shy of 60 years old, Ms. Robinson admitted to an affair with an 18-year-old man. It caused her husband considerable problems, including having to temporarily leave his position while undergoing an investigation over charges of financial impropriety involving his wife's lover. He was cleared and returned to his job.[4]

Is nonmonogamy for married couples on its way to becoming the norm? Can one person be everything to their spouse, including the one who provides them with so much sexual, emotional, and economic satisfaction that they'd never stray? It's difficult to measure infidelity because, likely, few will answer a survey about such a topic honestly. That said, in the United States about 20 percent of all married women and about 30 percent of all married men will, at some point, stray from their wedding vows.[5] "When marriage was about survival and business contracts, especially for families, we decided that being monogamous was a good idea," said Robyn Trask, the executive director of Loving More, an organization based in Lovemore, Colorado, that supports and teaches the polyamorous lifestyle. "But we live longer now. Is it realistic to expect that one person is going to keep you happy (sexually and emotionally) for 60 years?"[6]

HOW MONOGAMOUS ARE WE?

Curtis R. Bergstrand and Jennifer Blevins Sinski, in their book *Swinging in America: Love, Sex, and Marriage in the 21st Century*, say the practice of recreational sex, called "swinging," started on air force bases in World War II and continued during the Korean War with what was called "wife swapping." Pilots arranged parties with other pilots and they would have sex with one another's wives.[7] "Wife swapping,"—or, to put a modern, politically acceptable term on it—"husband swapping," continues today and involves married couples engaging in sex with other married couples.

The appeal of swinging is that it allows couples to have sex outside of their marriage without becoming emotionally involved with their partners. While the number of people participating in this lifestyle is difficult to determine, some research estimates that between 2–4 percent of U.S. married couples could have experienced this lifestyle, meaning, based on information on the number of adults from the Census Bureau, between 4.7–9.4 million people have ever "swung."[8]

It should be kept in mind that these numbers are likely to change, and, quite possibly, we'll never know how many Americans have attempted this lifestyle. In an online survey of about 1,100 self-identified swingers, conducted between 1999 and 2000 by Bergstrand and Sinski, it was learned that 72 percent were "members of a church, a synagogue, or a mosque."[9] The typical swinger spent about two years in college, thinks marriage is very important, and gains a lot of satisfaction from their family.

So if your marriage is great, what's the benefit to swinging? Here is one man's view, as reported by Bergstrand and Sinski: "I think it may cut down on divorce. . . . Most problems occur because of a lack of communication. . . . In order to swing, one must communicate clearly with one's partner. Those who swing are . . . more intimate with their partner. . . . Swinging couples tend NOT to take one another for granted as non-swingers do."[10]

POLYAMORY

The polyamorous, unlike swingers, seek and maintain intimate and romantic relationships with more than one person. Usually before they engage in a sexual relationship with someone, they establish some sort of emotional intimacy with their new partner. As the polyamorous see it, their lifestyle is not just about recreational sex—it's about a relationship.[11]

It's difficult to measure how many people are polyamorous. Some might be married and have intimate relationships outside of their marriage. Others might be single and involved with others. The relationships take many different forms—some people live together, some don't, some relationships are long distance while others are local—and, according to *Newsweek* magazine, there are more than 500,000 polyamorous people in the United States.[12]

Is there an upside to being polyamorous? "Polyamory treats men and women very equally," Trask says. "Having multiple relationships changes the power dynamic. It's no longer about the dominating man." She added, "I have seen women change for the better because they're polyamorous. They become better at negotiating what they want."

She also says polyamory isn't easy. "It requires a lot of communication, work, and a willingness to go through challenging emotions, like envy and jealousy. Knowing your partner is out with someone else can make you ask the question, is she better in bed than I am."[13]

The polyamorous need to be secure in knowing who they are, she says, and understand that the relationship they have with one person is unlike the relationship they have with another.

In 2002, Trask's group sent surveys to 2,500 people who identified as polyamorous and more than 1,000 were returned. She says the surveys represented about 4,000 people in the polyamorous community.

With regard to spirituality, the polyamorous who completed the survey broke down this way:

- 28 percent identified as Christian
- 9 percent were Eastern Religions
- 30 percent were pagan
- 29 percent were atheist and/or agnostic
- 4 percent were other

An overwhelming majority of this sample group—87 percent—had been raised Christian and only 11 percent had been brought up as either atheist or agnostic.[14] "The poly community includes people who have questioned the beliefs they were raised with," said Trask.[15]

She said 4 percent of those returning surveys had a high school diploma, 26 percent had some college education, 30 percent had a college degree and 40 percent had been to graduate school or had earned a graduate degree.[16]

Bergstrand and Sinski also write that the polyamorous lifestyle provides for an extended family. They cite, as an example, the thoughts of one polyamorist who says her daughters are never without an adult—there are four of them—and each one teaches the girls very different lessons because each one brings different skills, experiences and interests to the family setting.[17]

"Polyamorous families are one way that some people are counteracting the isolation of the lone nuclear family and finding ways to provide at home caretakers for their children," writes Deborah Anapol in her book *Polyamory in the 21st Century*.[18]

There is also considerable sexual variation in the polyamorous community and Anapol describes how this variation works:

While the "mainstream" polyamory community has a decidedly heterosexual focus, it's important to recognize that all sexual minorities have played an important role in the spread of polyamorous concepts. Bisexual women in particular have been among the earliest polyamory activists and continue to maintain a high profile in the poly community. The "hot bi babe" continues to be much sought after by polyamorous heterosexual men hoping for a female-to-female-male triad, and more than half of women in committed polyamorous triads are bisexual. Bisexual men are more cautious about coming out in the polyamorous community (whether as a result of AIDS phobia or homophobia I can't say), and while lesbians and gay men are welcomed in theory, few seem to participate.[19]

Polyamory shares with polygamy, and perhaps even with swinging, a stigmatized standing in American family life. "Coming out" stories frequently shock family members.

Anthropologist Leanna Wolfe talked to women who had been mistresses, in open marriages, and even in the polyamorous community.

With regard to triads (three people in an intimate relationship), mentioned in Anapol's book, Wolfe points out that there is no precedent for them in our society, and there is considerable variability in their makeup. Wolfe notes one triad, for example, in which the partners, who are linked emotionally and socially, all express themselves sexually outside of their relationship with one another. She knows, too, of triads that are heterosexual and in which two women or two men alternate nights with the one of the men or one of the women.[20]

Other triads share the same bed each night. Under such arrangements, if there are two women who are bisexual, they may be sexual with one another as well as with the man.

Wolfe points out that triads can be "polyfidelitous" (i.e., having sex only with one another), or each member may be allowed to bring in other lovers. She suggests that a triad probably involves more relationship work than being in a dyad (two people in an intimate relationship) since many more points of view and feelings must be considered.[21]

In what some might consider a surprising development, however, when Wolfe explored the polyamorous lifestyle herself—with a man and another woman—it didn't turn out so well, at least initially.[22] She was jealous of her partner's new lover, writing that she felt "dispensable." In addition, Wolfe says, Angela, the new partner in her small group, thought Don found her attractive because he "was so unhappy with me . . . and that in a couple of months, he'd be all hers."[23] In time, however, Wolfe and Angela "forged a sister/close friend bond."[24]

SUSAN AND DAVE

In an attempt to gain additional insight into the polyamorous community, the coauthor met with a married couple involved in the polyamorous community. They live in the Boston suburbs, are in their 40s, have been married for more than 20 years and are bringing up two children. She works as an administrative assistant, and he's in the high-tech industry. Both hold college degrees.[25]

What was the advantage of becoming polyamorous? "We went from co-existing with one another to having a much more open and communicative relationship," Susan said. "Our love for one another is better than it was previously." Prior to becoming polyamorous, they said, their lives were filled with work, children and making sure their house ran smoothly. "We've become more transparent to each other whereas previously there were secrets or we just weren't communicating like we do now," Dave said.

This lifestyle, however, has been more successful for Susan than for Dave. She's had more relationships. Dave came close to having a relationship with another woman but said it didn't work out, mostly because she was going to demand a lot of his time. "How much time you give someone (your partner outside of your marriage) depends on how entwined your life is," Dave said. "We're [pointing to his wife] one another's primary relationship."

Dave also said one of the advantages of being polyamorous is that people in the lifestyle are really seeking to know others on a much more profound level. "You know, some guys have their golf buddies and some have their poker buddies. But are you really 'friends?'" he said. "When we go to dinner parties with adults we know through our children, it's not like I can really talk with the mother of one of my daughter's friends. I can't even ask her out to lunch. In the poly community, people want to get to know you on many levels," Dave added.

What about jealousy? How does Dave handle the knowledge that his wife is out with another man? "Early on, when I knew she was meeting with someone on a coffee date, I would feel sad. Sometimes I'd feel insecure," Dave said. "Over time I realized polyamory was about the concept of giving additional love and happiness and finding additional love and happiness and how could I object to that?

"It's not like that other person is giving her something she doesn't want from me. No one can be everyone's everything," Dave adds.

Both Dave and Susan, not their real names, keep their lifestyle a secret. Susan described her workplace as very conservative and not accepting of many lifestyles outside of the perceived norm, heterosexual monogamy. Dave, for that matter, said he wasn't about to reveal too many details of his private life to his coworkers.

Dave had these observations on monogamous marriage:

"The notion is that if you have an affair, then there's something you're not doing for your spouse or your spouse isn't doing for you. They're not meeting your needs or you're not meeting theirs.

"It's interesting that when you see people divorce or hear about people having affairs, we never question, as a society, whether monogamy is a good thing," he added.[26]

WHAT HAPPENS IF WE'RE LIVING LONGER?

Sonia Arrison, author of "100 Plus: How the Coming Age of Longevity Will Change Everything, From Careers and Relationships to Family and Faith," in the *Wall Street Journal* suggests that people may see relationships differently if they live longer.[27]

The U.S. Census Bureau, she writes, reports that 5.7 million Americans are at least 85 years old, and this segment of the population is expected to increase by more than 4 percent over the next 40 years. In addition, it's expected that there will be more than 600,000 centenarians by 2050.[28]

"More time to live also raises the possibility of more divorces and re-marriages—the seven-year itch turned into the 70-year itch," she wrote.[29] Indeed, as the U.S. Census Bureau reports, there are more divorces among senior citizens than in previous years.

Arrison also says that while research shows older men finder younger women attractive—because they're able to produce children—older women shouldn't despair. If scientists can figure out how older women can give birth—and both older women and older men find one another attractive because they "look less 'aged' "—then, before long, they'll be on an even footing with their younger sisters. [30]

POLYGAMY

The United States is among a number of nations where polygamy is an issue for many of its immigrant families, as we have noted. For some foreign-born U.S. residents or visa applicants, polygamy is a cultural value, religious belief and a family practice. For those aspiring to become U.S. citizens, po-lygamy is one of those cultural beliefs they must renounce.

That said, however, the practice hasn't been eliminated. In New York City, reported the *New York Times*, polygamy is under the radar. Some immigrant men have more than one wife in the city while others have one wife in New York and another (or more) in their native homeland in Africa.

Some women told the *Times* reporter, Nina Bernstein, they are bitterly upset about the fact that their polygamous marriage still existed—even after they'd left their homeland. "They said their participation was dictated by an African culture of female subjugation and linked polygamy to female genital cutting and domestic violence," wrote Bernstein.[31] This is tragic, indeed, if true; however, so far, the research on African polygyny doesn't substantiate the claim in Bernstein's article.

In 2008, National Public Radio (NPR) reported, there were between 50,000–100,000 people living in a polygamous marriage in the United States, including some black Muslims living in Philadelphia.[32]

NPR told the story of a man with two wives in a harmonious setting, including even having "family date night," when the husband and his two wives would have an outing.

Zaki, the husband in the story, thinks that polygamy is beneficial for society, especially for people living in a city, where there are few intact families.

"There are a lot of blessings in it because you're helping legitimize and build a family that's rooted in values and commitment. And the children that come out of those types of relationships only become a benefit to society at large," he was quoted as telling NPR.

The Imam in this particular story said it's often an unmarried black Muslim woman who inquires about the possibility of a married man who shares her religion, taking another wife.

Still, there are women in the black Muslim community in Philadelphia, NPR reported, who would prefer not to be part of a polygamous marriage. But the problem they face is a lack of numbers, especially among marriageable black Muslim men.

"We're dealing with brothers who are incarcerated—that is, unavailable," Aliya, a 28-year-old woman, told NPR. "And then unfortunately you have AIDS and HIV crisis, where HIV has struck the African-American community disproportionately to others. So when you look at that way, there is a shortage (of men)."[33]

While there are success stories of polygamous wives within Philadelphia's black Muslim community working together to make the family, as one said, a "well-oiled machine," NPR also reported that more than one woman in the community hoped to be the sole wife.

POLYGAMY: ALSO AN ISSUE IN EUROPE

In parts of Europe, polygamy is practiced by Muslim immigrants. Miriam Zeitzen notes, "the monogamous Christian majority in Germany is forced to tackle . . . Turkish women's rights under polygamy because Turkish immigrants to Germany may practice it" (2008, 165). In the United Kingdom, Muslims in the Midlands are openly practicing polygamy. France, too, has faced a human rights and cultural dilemma concerning plural marriage.

A *New York Times* article by Elaine Sciolino headlined, "Immigrant Polygamy Is a Factor in French Unrest, a Gaullist Says," reveals how polygamy is a hot-button political issue there (September 18, 2005). Estimates run as a high as 30,000 families in France, primarily from former French West African nations, which practice polygamy. Since 1993, second wives are banned from acquiring visas, causing some wives to enter France illegally.

Sciolino reported that social unrest in France is also blamed on these families, noting that one leading newspaper editorial stated, "it's because papa is polygamous that the son burns cars." She also writes that one government spokesman said it was not possible to draw such a close tie to urban violence. Multiple causes, this spokesman said, are at work in disadvantaged neighborhoods.

A mayor who took a more tolerant view said that polygamy alone did not create or aggravate the riots; it is more of a problem of jobs and housing. It seems that with polygamy, there is a convenient scapegoat for transferring blame for social ills that are better solved by considering other factors that could also be at work.

NATIVE AMERICANS

The Mormons were not the first people to bring plural marriage to the American landscape. Many Native American tribes—thought, based on the latest research, to start inhabiting the North American continent from Asia about 15,000 years ago—were practicing polygyny and, in some cases, polyandry long before the LDS (Mormons).[34]

While not each tribe—there were more than 500 in what's now the continental United States—practiced both plural marriage systems, some, like the Alaskan Eskimos, did. The Dogrib and YellowKnives (in Canada) practiced polygyny; the Shoshonean practiced polygyny, polyandry, and "brittle monogamy" because they frequently changed spouses; the Cheyenne were known to practice polygyny.[35]

Polyandry was practiced but not as frequently as polygyny among the Shoshone. In their high desert environment (Utah and Nevada) they lived in small bands of nuclear families (Fox 1967). Their ideal form of marriage was sister exchange where such marriages linked two nuclear families and their children together in cooperative relationships for survival. Since it was not always possible to have the right number of children of each gender, polyandry was sometimes practiced.

For example, if a family had only one daughter to exchange, she could be given as a wife to two or more sons in the other family. Economic exchanges and political ties were thus promoted by polyandrous marriage. In more complex societies, polyandry was linked to power and wealth among the Tlingit. "There was said to be a few women of high rank who had several husbands simultaneously. These secondary marriages often united persons of very unequal age" and also furthered alliances between kinship lines of nobility.[36]

The reason, in many cases, these tribes practiced plural marriage had to do with economics. In Alaska, known for its harsh winters, the men hunted while the women tended to meal preparation, butchering the catch, tanning skins, and making clothing.

One anthropology professor takes issue with how many Americans might see Native American polygyny, writing, "The pervasive Anglo-American idea that polygyny is sexually motivated on the part of the husband probably tells us more about the sexual fantasies of Anglo-American males than about the culture and values of Arabs, Africans or Native Americans."[37]

As the Native Americans saw polygyny, John H. Moore writes, it "was seen to benefit both husbands and wives.

> For men, a larger household meant that they would have more children and more relatives, with a concomitant increase in wealth and status in the community. For women, polygyny usually meant that they could maintain co-residence with their sisters as co-wives, could get daily help with child care and other household chores.[38]

Among the Cheyenne, plural marriage, as Moore points out, was tied to the "needs of the nineteenth-century trade in buffalo robes." It was labor-intensive to create one robe—each one took about 70 hours—and, thus, a large pool of workers (family members) were required to make this effort successful.[39]

Another anthropology professor, the late Jack D. Forbes, who taught for many years at the University of California at Davis and who was also a Native American, said that many Americans are short-sighted when it comes understanding the country's history, writing, "Many white writers usually forget that 'the American heritage' is a Native American heritage" that's thousands of years older than the European landings in North America.[40] Forbes says many Native American tribes recognized a variety of marital situations:

> Plural marriage was often common . . . as was the marriage of young men and women with older women and men, the age of their grandparents. In the latter case, the young partners would often marry someone younger or the same age after their older, first mate, had passed on. Couples of the same sex were recognized as legitimate in many or perhaps most tribes.[41]

Dr. Forbes continues, "It is interesting as to how some Christians and ultra-orthodox Jews believe that 'God' laid down rules in c. 2000 BCE for a few thousand desert tribesmen, refugees from a highly-organized Egypt, who were wandering around the Sinai Desert; and then made those rules binding upon all of the other hundreds of millions of human beings living elsewhere on Mother Earth (but who were not told about the Jewish rules for another 2,000 and more years!).”[42]

Forbes ends his essay with the conclusion that there is no one form of marriage. Instead, he says, “the orthodox Christian view (heterosexual monogamy) is only one such model, and one that is actually less ‘traditional’ here in North America than other, more varied forms.”[43]

NOTES

1. Rob Wallace, Katie Thomson, and Lauren Sher, “Jenny Sanford Exclusive: Husband Refused to Be Faithful in Wedding Vows,” ABCNews, February 2, 2010, http://abcnews.go.com/2020/jenny-sanford-south-carolina-gov-mark-sanford-refused/story?id=9727121#.T75gnBzwjEk.

2. Tom Kenworthy, “DNC Chief Denies Sexual Affair With Ex-Aide; Romer Says Relationship Is ‘Very Affectionate,’” *The Washington Post*, February 7, 1998, http://www.washingtonpost.com/wp-srv/politics/daily/feb98/romer020798.htm.

3. Steve Hendrix, “South Carolina Braces for Ugly Whispers,” *The Washington Post*, January 11, 2012, http://www.washingtonpost.com/local/south-carolina-braces-for-ugly-whispers/2012/01/09/gIQAEZ5pqP_story.html.

4. “Sex Scandal First Minister’s Wife Iris Robinson Cleared in Toyboy Business Deal Probe,” *Belfast Telegraph*, May 27, 2011, http://www.belfasttelegraph.co.uk/news/local-national/northern-ireland/sex-scandal-first-ministers-wife-iris-robinson-cleared-in-toyboy-business-deal-probe-16004960.html.

5. Jeanie Lerche Davis, “Cheating Wives: Women and Infidelity,” http://www.webmd.com; Sharon Jayson, “Getting Reliable Data on Infidelity Isn’t Easy,” *USA Today*, November 17, 2008, http://www.usatoday.com.

6. Robyn Trask interview by Douglas Page.

7. Curtis R. Bergstrand and Jennifer Blevins Sinski, *Swinging in America: Love, Sex, and Marriage in the 21st Century* (Santa Barbara, CA: Praeger, 2010), p. 9.

8. The Census Bureau reports that the U.S. adult population, as counted in 2010, includes over 234 million people 18 and older. Information from the Census is available at http://www.census.gov/compendia/statab/cats/population.html.

9. Bergstrand and Sinski, p. 21.

10. Ibid., p. 170.

11. Trask interview by Page.

12. Jessica Bennett, “Only You. And You. And You,” *Newsweek*, July 28, 2009, http://www.thedailybeast.com/newsweek/2009/07/28/only-you-and-you-and-you.html.

13. Trask interview by Page.

14. Survey results as provided by Trask during interview with Page.

15. Trask interview by Page.

16. Ibid.

17. Bergstrand and Sinski, *Swinging in America*, pp. 172–173.

18. Deborah Anapol, *Polyamory in the 21st Century: Love and Intimacy with Multiple Partners* (Lanham, MD: Rowman & Littlefield Publishers, 2010), p. 127.

19. Ibid., p. 61.

20. Leanna Wolfe, "Adding a Co-Wife," *Loving More Magazine* 15 (1998): 22–25.

21. Ibid.

22. Ibid.

23. Ibid.

24. Ibid.

25. The interview was conducted by Page in October 2011 in the Boston suburbs. Their names are being kept confidential and have been changed for this book.

26. All quotations in this section of the chapter come from the interview the couple had with Page.

27. Sonia Arrison, "Living to 100 and Beyond," *The Wall Street Journal*, August 27–28, 2011, http://online.wsj.com/article/SB10001424053111904875404576528841080315246.html.

28. Ibid.

29. Ibid.

30. Ibid.

31. Nina Bernstein, "In Secret, Polygamy Follows Africans to N.Y.," *The New York Times*, March 23, 2007, http://www.nytimes.com/2007/03/23/nyregion/23polygamy.html?pagewanted=all.

32. Barbara Bradley Hagerty, "Philly's Black Muslims Increasingly Turn toward Polygamy," National Public Radio, May 28, 2008, http://www.npr.org/templates/story/story.php?storyId=90886407.

33. Ibid.

34. Al Carrol, "Peopling North America," in *Native America: From Prehistory to First Contact*, ed. Rodney P. Carlisle and J. Geoffrey Golson (Santa Barbara, CA: ABC-CLIO, 2007), p. 5; Jack D. Forbes, "What is Marriage? A Native American View," May 3, 2004. It was originally published in *News from Indian Country* but is now found here: http://www.westgatehouse.com/art161.html.

35. Robert F. Spender and Jesse D. Jennings, eds., *The Native Americans: Prehistory and Ethnology of the North American Indians* (New York: Harper & Row, Publishers, 1965), pp. 164–165, esp. 141, 142. See also pp. 275 and 282.

36. Frederica de Laguna, "Tlingit," in *Handbook of North American Indians*, ed. William C. Sturtevant (Washington, DC: Smithsonian Institute, 1990).

37. John H. Moore, "The Developmental Cycle of Cheyenne Polygyny," *American Indian Quarterly* 15, no. 3 (1991): 311.

38. Ibid., p. 311.

39. Ibid., p. 312.

40. Forbes, "What is Marriage?"

41. Ibid.

42. Ibid.

43. Ibid.

6

Latter-day Saints Explained

If there's a faith that confuses the American public, it's the Church of Jesus Christ of Latter-day Saints (LDS), commonly referred to as the Mormon Church. The only other group of faithful people that might confuse Americans more is one that's part of the country's past history, the Puritans. In many ways, these two faith-based groups share common elements.

The problem mainstream Mormons face is that too often people outside of their religion only see it—and, thus, form their viewpoint—in a negative setting, when they watch video-recorded police raids on polygamous households. For that matter, too often Americans confuse the word "Puritan" as an outlook on sex.

Both faiths, like so many others created since the first splintering with Judaism, which led to Christianity, or the Protestant split with the Church of Rome, share a similar history: both the LDS and the Puritans, like those faiths created before them and many of those founded since, left established population centers, like the Jews did when they parted for the Promised Land, and each was (and the LDS remain) convinced that their religious practices and interpretations bring them closer to God than those who continue to believe in the older faiths. For the Puritans, their religious practice was about purifying Christianity. For the LDS, it's about returning to Christianity's earliest roots.

A SHORT HISTORY OF THE TWO FAITHS

The Puritans saw a flawed institution in the Church of England. Its "Catholic elements," as Rod Gragg points out in his book, *Forged in Faith: How Faith Shaped the Birth of the Nation, 1607–1776*, meaning bishops and others holding rank and power, could not be found in the Scripture and, thus, the Church of England, like the one in Rome, had lost its connection with true Christianity.[1] The Puritans also looked askance at the popes, seeing them as leaders who burdened "believers with unbiblical, man-made dogmas."[2]

The Puritans who boarded the Mayflower in 1620 in England were separatists. They'd been chased by bishops in England, lived in exile in Holland, and perceived their ocean trip to the New World as leading them to "the place where the Lord will create a new Heaven, and a new Earth in, new Churches and a new Commonwealth together."[3]

As a result of this Atlantic voyage, Massachusetts Puritans, said John Cotton, a 17th century clergyman, "had collaborated to restore the form of church government practiced by the earliest Christians—that is, not 'national' or 'Diocesan' but 'congregational.'"[4] By doing so, these early Americans created a church that dispensed with "corrupting hierarchies," giving "every congregation the privilege of self-rule and giving every minister the same rank."[5] Thus, the Puritans thought, through this experience, they could attend a church free of impurities and be closer to God.

LDS church history, beginning more than 200 years later, is similar. The LDS church started in the 1820s in New York through a series of visions that came to its founder, Joseph Smith Jr. He established many of the church's fundamental beliefs and translated the *Book of Mormon,* the LDS church's sacred text.

The 1,400-year-old text was brought to Smith's attention by Moroni, an angel, who wrote the book on gold plates in a language few understood. Moroni, according to Smith, visited him, telling him where the plates were located and instructed him to translate the text. Moroni's visit to Smith "implied the potential not only of ancient extrabiblical scripture but also of new modern scripture: a narrative of the Prophet's early visions and an extract from Moroni's words."[6]

As the new *Book of Mormon* went on sale, in 1830, many other biblical texts were also being offered to the American public. Several hundred versions of the Bible, writes Philip Barlow, were available and contained "new translations or revisions of the KJV (King James Version) containing modernizations of language, paraphrases, and alternate readings based on Greek and Hebrew manuscripts."[7]

The *Book of Mormon* was published during America's Second Great Awakening, a religious revival that was "geared toward eliciting immediate conversions to the Christian faith."[8] The revival gripped the country during the first half of the 19th century but was particularly intense during the 1820s and 1830s.[9]

The experience, as Jan Shipps, a professor of religious history, writes, had people skeptical of religious authority and, thus, weakened the "link between the story of the world told in Christian terms and the story of individual American lives."[10]

The *Book of Mormon's* initial appeal, writes Shipps, was hardly surprising. It was a "second witness to Christ" and a "reassuring document."[11] But the text was also highly questionable because it was "vulnerable to hard questions about its history and its historicity than the Old and New Testaments.[12] Regardless, one of the appeals of Mormonism, writes Shipps, was that "it put itself forward in the familiar guise of primitive Christianity," which is similar to what the Puritans thought they were doing in Massachusetts—returning to the faith's earliest practices.[13]

The book, Shipps writes, clarifies "the story of early Mormonism because it reveals the movement as one in which leader and followers were together living through . . . the stories of Israel and early Christianity."[14] She writes that "Joseph Smith's prophetic leadership, and the experience of the Saints were crucial components in the creation of Mormonism. . . . Operating together, these components brought this new religious tradition into being . . . bringing God back into the history of the Saints in such a substantial way that within Mormonism, divinity is still as real as all the other realities of everyday existence."[15]

The problem the LDS church faced, at least with other Christians—both then and now—was that some of its beliefs seem to challenge the theology. This is because much of the *Book of Mormon* is "vaguely reminiscent of certain Old Testament prophets, such as Isaiah or Ezekiel, who confidently represented God as speaking through them in the first person."[16] The LDS, as Barlow shows, believes the *Book of Mormon* is "as a companion to the Bible, written as a record of a remnant of the House of Israel."[17]

This experience—writing an entirely new, sacred text—is one of the issues that makes the LDS stand out compared to many other Christian faiths and why some consider it a cult. The many strands of Christianity may disagree about the interpretation of the Bible but, with some exceptions, they're all looking at the same text.

Smith and his earliest followers left New York and, after a few stops, settled in Illinois, where many viewed them as "isolationists . . . and . . . a dangerous threat to the social order."[18] In 1844, rumor spread in their Illinois town that Smith was running for president of the United States and soon after, he was jailed and then killed by the locals.

The LDS's leadership was then assumed by Brigham Young, who led his followers to the Utah territory, where their goal was "to create a religious community . . . away from the jurisdiction and discrimination of the United States."[19] Their idea—creating a new religious community—is similar to what the Puritans said they were going to accomplish by sailing for the New World in 1620.

Salt Lake City soon became the new spiritual center for the LDS faith and, in time, under Young's guidance, dominated Utah's economy, society, and cultural practices. Before Utah became a U.S. territory, Jan Shipps writes, the Mormon Church "had its own diplomatic department."[20] The LDS gradually spread throughout the American West and Southwest, reaching California, Arizona, Idaho, Wyoming, even Mexico and Canada.

As the Mormons see God, Richard Abanes (2002) writes in his book, *One Nation Under Gods: A History of the Mormon Church,* "He's polygamous and He has a wife, sometimes referred to as the 'Heavenly Mother.'" Coexisting with these two deities was a limitless amount of cosmic spirit matter known as "intelligence," out of which Elohim (the Heavenly Father) and Heavenly Mother made countless bore their image, but had resident within them the potential for godhood, an attribute of Heavenly Father and Mother.[21]

The first children, Abanes writes, were Adam and Eve.

> They arrived in order to do what all of us are supposed to do—i.e., travel along the route of eternal progression toward godhood. As gods, we in turn will be able to have our own spirit babies, who will then populate other worlds as they progress toward godhood, all the while giving us the kind of worship bestowed on Elohim (the Heavenly Father), the god of this planet.[22]

Indeed, the Heavenly Father who oversees earth, as the Mormons believe, "progressed toward godhood in a similar manner," writes Abanes. "He is a man just like us, albeit an exalted, glorified, and perfected man, but nevertheless a man with 'a body of flesh and bones.'"[23]

Abanes goes on to show that the *Book of Mormon* doesn't endorse polygamy, referring to Jacob 1:15, which states, "and now it came to pass that the people of Nephi . . . began to grow hard in their hearts, and indulge themselves somewhat in wicked practices, such as like unto David of old desiring many wives and concubines."[24]

POLYGAMY

Plural marriage was one of Smith's visions. Polygamy, as Smith revealed, was a component of a new and everlasting covenant whereby marriage would last into eternity, sometimes referred to as a "celestial realm" or even "celestial marriage" and did not end with a spouse's death. While there was resistance to plural marriage in the beginning, LDS men and women, in time, largely accepted the practice, although only a minority of them actually entered into plural unions.

While the LDS no longer accept plural marriage today, the faith still believes that marriages formed on earth will continue into death, which, unlike most Christian faiths, believe a married couple is locked in matrimony until they "are parted by death." LDS members also believe that family units formed on earth will be linked in the afterlife and will rule universes of their own.

This is one of the reasons that Salt Lake City maintains in-depth databases for people conducting genealogical studies. If someone converts to the LDS faith, his or her ancestors can be converted, too, in what's referred to as "post-mortem baptism," the *Economist* reported.[25]

One of the first defenses of polygamy came from William Henry Hooper, a congressional delegate from Utah just prior to the Civil War.[26] He pointed out that it was based on the belief that a man had the right lawfully and religiously to do so.

The Hebrew Bible sanctioned polygamy, Hooper said, because it was practiced by some of Judaism's first leaders, including Abraham, Jacob, David, and Solomon. This, as pointed out by Abanes (2002), convinced Smith "and his successors to believe that having many wives was commanded by God."[27] But, Abanes also writes, "Nowhere in the Bible does . . . God sanction, let alone command, polygamy."[28]

Hooper said the United States couldn't prevent LDS members from practicing polygamy because to do so was unconstitutional, citing the First Amendment, which prohibited, he said, Congress from interfering with people's "free exercise" of religion.

He also noted that LDS communities were "quiet, orderly, and Christian. . . . Our towns are without gambling-halls, drinking saloons or brothels, while from end to end of our Territory the innocent can walk unharmed at all hours"[29]

PUBLIC REACTION TO PLURAL MARRIAGE

Stephanie Forbes said that polygamy "was not openly practiced in the Mormon Church until 1852, when the Church preached and encouraged its followers to marry additional wives."[30] She says it wasn't until shortly after one of the church's leading men, Apostle Orson Pratt, defended polygamy in speech that antipolygamy sentiment spread in the United States. Resistance to polygamy grew, she said, when Utah initiated actions to obtain statehood.

Lawrence Foster believes that the existence of polygamy posed a cultural threat to many Americans because it was so vastly different from the Victorian family ideal, primarily monogamy and sexual restraint, which had been established in the country. "Throughout this period, a new genre of anti-polygamy novels and 'true stories of life under polygamy' developed, primarily by people who had never been near Utah. . . . This anti-polygamy literature is very similar to anti-Catholic and anti-foreign writings of the antebellum period. It relies heavily on stereotyped characters and seems to constitute a . . . Victorian pornography."[31]

Forbes (2003) confirms this, saying "Congress's distaste for both the Mormons and the practice of polygamy became evident when it moved to outlaw polygamy in the territories in 1860 with a House Report on anti-polygamy."[32]

One congressman, John McClernand of Illinois, used language that anyone involved in the fight over same-gender marriage today might recognize, saying plural marriage is "a reproach to Christian civilization; and deserves to be blotted out."[33] He argued for Mormons to be "made subservient to the standard of Christian morality, as well as the legal authority of the Constitution."[34]

In spite of the obstacles in Congress, the Mormon Church wanted Utah to become part of the United States as a state, Forbes writes, so it would fall under U.S. law, and, thus, the U.S. Constitution. The congressional debates on polygamy in the 19th century revealed a number of reasons why the wider public opposed it. Polygamy was seen, by some people, as a violation of natural law, God-given monogamy. It was also perceived as akin to slavery because some slave-state governors, in an attempt to show their political support for local autonomy or state's rights, supported plural marriage in Utah, thinking it might help them maintain slavery. The issue was very much misunderstood by the general public since false information was widely circulated in popular literature.

As the debate continued in the second half of the 19th century, internal forces began to operate against this custom so that LDS theology was reorganized to disavow polygamy. Not only did many women oppose the practice, perhaps even silently, but so did Joseph Smith III, the son of the faith's founder, who later came to disavow polygamy and to deny that his father ever encouraged or practiced plural marriage.

Smith III organized a separate Mormon church, known as the Reorganized Church of Jesus Christ of Latter-day Saints, with headquarters in Illinois; his mother, Emma, the wife of Joseph Smith Jr., the founder, denied polygamy had ever been practiced by the saints. They, as well as others, blamed Brigham Young for having institutionalized the practice of polygamy.[35] Smith III made four trips to Utah before 1890 during which he made every attempt to denounce polygamy and to promote the antipolygamy viewpoint of his church.

In the 1880s, as the Utah territory advanced toward statehood, Congress passed two laws to stamp out polygamy. The first one, the Edmunds Act, made "convicted polygamists ineligible for public office . . . and deemed 'unlawful cohabitation' a criminal offense."[36] When that law proved ineffective, Congress passed the Edmunds-Tucker Act, which was far more stringent, forcing "plural wives to testify against their husbands . . . and provided a mechanism for the government to acquire property" from the Mormon Church.[37]

Finally, in May 1890, the U.S. Supreme Court upheld the laws Congress had passed, forcing the church's president, Wilford Woodruff, to outlaw polygamy. When Utah then announced that it would no longer support plural marriage, its application for statehood was accepted and it joined the country as a state in 1896.

THE LDS TODAY

One of the reasons that the Mormon faith is so scrutinized, writes Jan Shipps, is because the religion is no longer seen as an odd faith practiced in only one section of the country. LDS temples and members can be found across the United States.

In addition, two of their members, Mitt Romney and Jon Huntsman, are high-profile political figures because they sought their party's nomination for the presidency of the United States. If either man were elected president, they, like former president John F. Kennedy, a Catholic, before them, would become the first member of their faith to win the White House.

The LDS is one of the fastest growing faiths in the world, primarily because all LDS men are considered to be priests and must devote, ideally, at least two years to missionary activity either in the United States or elsewhere around the world. According to the National Council of Churches's 2010 *Yearbook of American and Canadian Churches*, the LDS has nearly 6 million members in both countries and nearly 14 million worldwide. That's up from 11 million around the globe, the *Economist* magazine reported, and an increase of about 1 million in the United States, and could reach 50 million worldwide in the next 30 years.[38]

In spite of their impressive numbers, Catholicism remains the single largest faith in the United States, with more than 68 million members, followed by the Southern Baptist Convention with just over 16 million members, the NCC *2010 Yearbook* reports.[39]

The world's top faith, however, is Islam, with 1.6 billion followers. Catholicism comes in second with just over 1 billion.

ISOLATION AMONG THE LDS AND THE FUNDAMENTALISTS

To gain a better understanding of how the Latter-day Saints might think others in the United States see them, as well as how their Fundamentalist cousins might think they're perceived by the wider American society, we should make an attempt to consider their viewpoint. The LDS hold a belief in a celestial life; the Fundamentalists have the same belief and also believe that it's achieved through plural marriage. This point of view held by anyone in either strand of the LDS faith is contrary to the Abrahamic faiths, which hold that life after death includes heaven,—not an existence among the stars, as the LDS see it, where one is living with everyone they had in their family on earth.

We should also keep in mind that history provides many examples of people holding religious beliefs or carrying out religious practices that are contrary to the majority or a country's citizenry and suffering for it greatly, including being jailed, tortured and even to put to death.

So is it any surprise, then, that people who are monogamously married, or who grew up in a monogamous culture, sometimes view those who practice plural marriage very narrowly, only seeing polygyny as a sexual system, not one that involves the love, responsibility, and commitment of marriage?

Those committed to their faith, writes Winnifred Fallers Sullivan, in her book *The Impossibility of Religious Freedom* (2005), can be seen to be very different from the society in which they live. "To be religious is, in some sense, to be obedient to a rule outside of oneself and one's government,"[40] Sullivan writes. While religion can be seen to challenge the rule of law, Sullivan writes, she also notes that for someone to be religious, they cannot be free—they are required to restrict their actions to the rules of their religion—because they are faithful.[41] As a result, faithful people, especially if they are in the minority, can be easily misunderstood, maybe even feared. She goes on to say:

> Religion is also different in that, as usually understood today, it divides rather than brings together the human community. When religion was historically differentiated from politics, science, and so forth, it also became optional. Modern humanity . . . was rhetorically divided between those with faith and those without.
>
> In an effort to end violence, in deference to the supposed virtue promoted by religious education, and from a failure to imagine a society without religion, religion was given legal privileges. Increasingly, however, those privileges are seen to violate the higher American principle of equality.[42]

Perhaps in the attempt to make the United States a country that's available for any religion, we have also sustained an unpredicted consequence—people are less faithful than 200 years ago and, as a result, hold little understanding of basic Christian beliefs, let alone those beliefs from other Christian denominations.

Scott Anderson, in his article in *National Geographic*, talked about some of the isolation that's experienced within Fundamentalist Latter-day Saint communities. He visited FLDS communities that, to say the least, are remote and mentions how he was given permission to gain insight into their lifestyle.

> To spend time in Hildale and Colorado City is to come away with a more nuanced view. That view is revealed gradually, however, due to the insular

nature of the community. Many of the oversize homes are tucked behind high walls, both to give children a safe place to play and to shield families from gawking Gentiles, as non-Mormons are known. Most residents avoid contact with strangers. *National Geographic* was given access to the community only on the approval of the church leadership, in consultation with the imprisoned Warren Jeffs.[43]

It's not hard to get the impression that, from reading the above paragraph, that Fundamentalist Latter-day Saints want little to do with people who hold differing religious beliefs. Putting aside any possible legal issues that might entangle them, it is clear they are living far outside of either midsize or large, or even diverse population centers. As a result, the only people who truly know them—and their lifestyle—are people who share their approach to faith and life.

Anderson also described the shock that likely any previously isolated Fundamentalist Latter-day Saint must endure if they ever leave their community:

Walking away means leaving behind everything: the community, one's sense of security, even one's own family. Carolyn Jessop, the plural wife of Merril Jessop who did leave the FLDS, likens entering the outside world to "stepping out onto another planet. I was completely unprepared, because I had absolutely no life skills. Most women in the FLDS don't even know how to balance a checkbook, let alone apply for a job, so contemplating how you're going to navigate in the outside world is extremely daunting."[44]

Perhaps this is one more reason to decriminalize plural marriage. It would allow Fundamentalist Latter-day Saints to live in a wider society; and their family members would be far less likely to only know people who share their faith and, thus, they would gain experience in interacting with others who do not share their religious preferences.

ARE MEMBERS OF THE LDS FAITH CHRISTIAN?

There's often this question, what are Mormons? What do they really believe in? Do they pray to the same God I do? Maybe we should consider, Shipps says, that the earliest Christians thought, that by accepting Jesus Christ, that they were being better Jews. The short answer is to say, based on our limited knowledge, yes, members of the LDS, and even the FLDS, are Christians. They may not be Christian like many others but their faith is based on accepting Jesus Christ as God's only son. So, clearly, that makes them Christian.

The best answer, however, comes from Shipps. She goes through various disagreements between Christians and Mormons but ends her essay on this note:

> In the fullness of time, a decision will be made in a higher court as to whether the Holy Catholic church that evolved from the apostolic church described in the New Testament managed to stay Christian; whether the Protestants, including the Anglicans, who separated from the Roman church maintained their status as Christians; whether the Methodists who separated from the Anglicans continued to be Christian; and whether the new Christian movements that evolved in the United States in the nineteenth century—Mormonism, Seventh-day Adventism, Christian Science—are authentically Christian . . . I withhold judgment, counting within the definition of Christian any church . . . movement, liberal or conservative coalition, or new religious tradition that gathers persons . . . in the name of Christ . . . creates a community wherein women and men may . . . take up the cross to follow him.[45]

NOTES

1. Rod Gragg, *Forged in Faith: How Faith Shaped the Birth of the Nation, 1607–1776* (New York: Howard Books, 2010), p. 44.

2. Ibid., p. 43.

3. Philip F. Gura, *A Glimpse of a Sion's Glory: Puritan Radicalism in New England, 1620–1660* (Middletown, CT: Wesleyan University Press, 1984), p. 12.

4. David D. Hall, *A Reforming People: Puritanism and the Transformation of Public Life in New England* (New York: Alfred A. Knopf, 2011), p. 97.

5. Ibid., p. 97.

6. Philip L. Barlow, *Mormons and The Bible: The Place of the Latter-day Saints in American Religion* (New York: Oxford University Press, 1991), p. 19.

7. Ibid., p. 47.

8. Barry Hankins, *The Second Great Awakening and the Transcendentalists* (Westport, CT: Greenwood Press, 2004), p. 5.

9. Ibid., p. 4.

10. Jan Shipps, *Mormonism: The Story of a New Religious Tradition* (Chicago: University of Illinois Press, 1985), p. 36.

11. Ibid.

12. Ibid., pp. 36 and 37.

13. Ibid., p. 34.

14. Ibid., p. 38.

15. Ibid., p. 39.

16. Barlow, *Mormons and The Bible*, p. 24.

17. Ibid., p. 27.

18. Laura E. Woodworth-Ney, *Women in the American West* (Santa Barbara, CA: ABC-CLIO, 2008), p. 149.

19. Ibid., p. 150.

20. Shipps, *Mormonism*, p. 124.

21. Richard Abanes, *One Nation Under Gods: A History of the Mormon Church* (New York: Four Walls Eight Widows, 2002), p. 285.

22. Ibid., p. 286.

23. Ibid.

24. Ibid., p. 308.

25. "The Church of the West," *The Economist*, February 7, 2002, http://www. economist.com/node/976398.

26. Marion Mills Miller, *Great Debates in American History*, vol. 8 (New York: Current Literature Publishing Company, 1913), p. 444.

27. Abanes, *One Nation under Gods*, p. 305.

28. Ibid.

29. Miller, *Great Debates in American History*, p. 449.

30. Stephanie Forbes, "Why Have Just One?: An Evaluation of the Anti-Polygamy Laws under the Establishment Clause," *Houston Law Review* (April 3, 2003): p. 1521.

31. Lawrence Foster, *Religion and Sexuality: Three American Communal Experiments of the Nineteenth Century* (New York: Oxford University Press, 1981), p. 221.

32. Forbes, "Why Have Just One?," p. 1521.

33. Ibid., p. 1522.

34. Ibid., p. 1522.

35. Linda King Newell and Valeen Tippets Avery, *Mormon Enigma* (Chicago: University of Illinois Press, 1994).

36. Forbes, "Why Have Just One?," p. 1524.

37. Ibid.

38. "The Church of the West."

39. NCC, *2010 Yearbook*, http://archive.wfn.org/2010/02/msg00100.html.

40. Winnifred Fallers Sullivan, *The Impossibility of Religious Freedom* (Princeton, NJ: Princeton University Press, 2005), p. 156.

41. Ibid.

42. Ibid., pp. 156 and 157.

43. Scott Anderson, "The Polygamists: An Exclusive Look Inside the FLDS," *National Geographic*, February 2010, http://ngm.nationalgeographic.com/2010/02/polygamists/anderson-text.

44. Anderson, "The Polygamists."

45. Jan Shipps, "Is Mormonism Christian? Reflections on a Complicated Question," in *Mormon & Mormonism: An Introduction to an American World Religion*, ed. Eric A. Eliason (Chicago: University of Illinois Press, 2001), p. 97.

7

Living in Polygyny Today

If any one picture of polygyny as practiced in the United States comes through—as brought forth by anthropologists and even by polygamists themselves—it's this: the stress, anxiety, and issues can frequently be multiplied by the number of wives a man marries. This system of marriage, like monogamy, is far from perfect. The worst-case scenario includes sister-wives hating one another, husbands failing to live up to their end of the bargain, and abusive behavior. The best-case scenario is far different: sister-wives like one another, sometimes forging deep and meaningful relationships with each other, children are loved, and husbands are excellent providers for their wives and offspring. Like their monogamous counterparts, plural marriages are a mixed bag. Some work. Some don't. It depends.

LDS HISTORIC POLYGYNY

Jessie Embry (1987) using materials gathered between 1976 and 1982, at Brigham Young University, conducted a study using oral historians to interview 250 children from church-sanctioned polygynous marriages in which the parents were married before 1904.

The project also included a control group: they interviewed 150 children from monogamous families who had grown up during the same time and whose parents had also been married prior to 1904.

The study also reviewed autobiographies, diaries, and other materials available from LDS Church archives and the Brigham Young University manuscript collections, including the lives of approximately 200 plural husbands, 400 plural wives and 150 monogamous husbands and wives.

Embry discovered some unique martial responsibilities were associated with polygyny. Her data revealed that many husbands actually saw all of their

wives regularly. Of the 156 families studied, 47 percent had a regular daily or weekly visiting schedule with only 8 percent reporting no such routine. Another 24 percent visited once every three days, once a month, or visited at general conference or harvest time.

Embry says that, through these regular visits, husbands were probably made cognizant of their wives physical and emotional needs. This is supported by the fact that 60 percent of the wives in his study lived in the same community as their husbands and co-wives. Embry also found that plural husbands divided their supplies and financial resources among all of their wives.

Although jealousy was evident, most husbands tried to ease this by not carrying stories from one wife to another and by avoiding any behavior that might bring about jealousy. There were occasions when one wife would emerge as a husband's favorite, which could lead to bad feelings among the other wives.

The picture that emerges from Embry's study of the literature and her own research is one in which neither polygamy nor monogamy dictates harmonious marital relationships. Rather, individual personalities have much more influence. The abilities of the participants to get along and treat one another fairly are far more crucial to marital satisfaction than the form the marriage takes.

Concerning childrearing practices, Embry's research supports the notion that Mormon members were not unlike their counterparts in the wider American society with wives, by and large, caring for the home as well as the children. Fathers were distant, if not absent, from the daily dynamics of the household. Embry notes that just like other 19th-century children, the majority of children she studied, from both monogamous and plural families, felt especially close to their mothers.

Nineteenth-century LDS women were similar to those of other frontier women of that era. Richard Van Wagoner (1986) reports that only 12 percent of women in 19th and early 20th century LDS homes ever worked outside of their homes after marrying. About 36 percent of LDS women supplemented their family's household income by taking in boarders or selling quilts or foodstuffs.

Plural wives tended to consider polygyny much as their husbands did: It was a practical way to provide marriage and, most importantly, motherhood to women who would have otherwise remained single in a societal and cultural system based on monogamy. Nevertheless, Van Wagoner found polygyny was practiced by only 20–40 percent of LDS families, mirroring demographic statistics from other polygamous societies around the world, where monogamy is the real or most frequent marital form practiced.

Polygamy was not without problems. For example, many first wives were known to have quietly suffered their polygamous state. Some complained of

difficulties in raising children in a house filled with other wives and their children. Brigham Young's second wife was reported to have said, "God will be very cruel if he does not give us poor women adequate compensation for the trials we have endured in polygamy."[1]

Another woman told a friend that she loathed polygamy but feared saying anything negative because she was old and did not want to be turned out of her home. Still another wife stated that to be a successful polygynous wife, a woman must regard her husband indifferently, with reverence rather than love, which is a false sentiment that should have no existence in polygyny.[2]

The most famous opponent was the "19th wife" who, as part of a public crusade, wrote a book with biting testimony titled, *The 19th Wife, Featuring One Lady's Account of Plural Marriage and its Woes Being the Chronicle of Personal Experience of Ann Eliza Young—19th and Rebel Wife of the Leader of the Utah Saints and Prophet of the Mormon Church, Brigham Young, Written by Herself*.[3]

Despite the negative feelings, many plural wives had more favorable reactions to polygamy. In some cases, a first wife would even encourage her reluctant husband to take another wife for religious reasons, so that they could both reach an exalted state in the afterlife or, for more practical concerns—economics and labor sharing.

In addition, female support networks among co-wives were especially evident in crisis situations, such as childbirth, economic hardship, and bereavement. Lawrence Foster (1981) cited one study that showed that nearly one-third of all polygynous marriages included at least a pair of sisters. This practice, called sororal polygyny, generally promoted harmony among co-wives.

Foster also provides some interesting insights into the relationship between women's work and plural marriage. Polygyny may have helped free some women from the constraints of the homemaker so they could take part in other work by necessity or by choice. In their lives in early Utah, polygynous women were involved in farming, retailing and the medical profession; they also participated in various helping activities through the Relief Society and developed and published a newspaper, the *Women's Exponent*.

FLDS POLYGAMY

In spite of state and federal laws outlawing polygamy and the LDS Church's beliefs and policies, which also no longer tolerate polygamy, there remain pockets of FLDS (Fundamentalist Latter-day Saints) believers who continue to practice plural marriage.

While it's impossible to determine a definite number, it is estimated that there are between 30,000–50,000 polygynists in the United States today,[4] maybe even as many as 100,000, according to a *New York Times* report in 2006.[5]

From time to time, agents from the Federal Bureau of Investigation and state police raid polygynist families. The biggest one, recently, was in April 2008, when Texas authorities raided an FLDS community (Eldorado Yearning for Zion), headed by Warren Jeffs, resulting in his arrest as well as that of his wives; their more than 400 children were placed in foster care, which also included a 14-year-old girl who was forced to "marry" Jeffs.[6]

Still, in spite of the attention polygynist families received because of this raid, and even from television shows such as *Sister Wives* and *Big Love*, plural marriage continues. FLDS communities practicing plural marriage are scattered throughout the western states. One FLDS community, called Short Creek, in Colorado City, Arizona, which is near the Utah border, is a good example of how these communities continue today.

It was settled in the early 1930s in an area that's particularly difficult to reach, isolated by desert cliffs and sandstone environs, with entry possible only from the north along a single highway.

When he visited Colorado City, Ken Driggs, (1991), a criminal defense attorney and a Mormon, who's written extensively about FLDS communities, said individuals do not necessarily select their marital partners based on romantic love. While an individual's feelings are considered, the parents and the community's religious leaders, who are believed to be guided by divine inspiration, arrange marriages.[7]

Large families are considered the ideal since having children is the primary reason for marriage. Driggs states, "The stereotype of the meek and submissive (Short Creek) plural wife is simply off the mark in my experience. Most of their young people today seem to understand that there are other lives to be lived if they wish."[8]

In a *New York Times* article in 1991, reporter Dirk Johnson provided yet another glimpse into the Colorado City community. Johnson described a favorable view of a polygamous woman who believes that polygamy is an ideal way for a woman to have both a career and children.

This particular wife, a lawyer and one of nine wives, told Johnson, "In our family, the woman can help each other care for the children. Women in monogamous relationships don't have that luxury. As I see it, if this lifestyle didn't already exist, it would have to be invented to accommodate career women."[9]

In a nearby town, in Cain County, Utah, where polygamy is the norm, Johnson tells about the town's mayor with his nine wives and 20 children. Like the lawyer he quoted, most of the mayor's wives have careers, including one as a graphic designer and another as a real estate broker.

SISTER-WIVES

Janet Bennion, an anthropologist at Lyndon State College in Vermont, developed a model in 2004 called "desert patriarchy" to explain how LDS institutions evolved in America as an adaptation to frontier conditions posing severe challenges for survival. Community cooperation is crucial under such circumstances.

Plural marriage binds women together as "sister-wives" in the interest of economic cooperation and promotes female solidarity. Bennion, who grew up in a polygamous family, writes, "women's solidarity is stronger in the presence of alienating patriarchal control . . . as a challenging force."[10]

Citing her own ethnographic research, she states that the women "see themselves as fortunate in having a large group of sister-wives and female friends . . . with whom they pray and work and laugh and cry . . . intense and passionate relationships—the female network."[11] Bennion also notes that there's often an emotional distance between a polygamous husband and his wives, which seems to mirror the relationship of a father to a child.

Bennion (c.f. 1998, 2004, 2011) has compared both LDS and FLDS women on issues such as women's roles, childrearing, and relations among wives. In general, she notes, the lives of LDS women revolve more around their husbands than other FLDS women. Fundamentalist women are empowered more fully in female networks, domestic child-care routines and work outside of the home.

Bennion attributes this difference to three reasons: (1), the frontier-like existence in the communities; (2), religious ideology that emphasizes an important role for a goddess symbol; and, (3), a polygyny in which co-wives cooperate in their domestic duties.[12]

Through her five years of ethnographic research, Bennion observed that "women are attracted to Mormon polygynous fundamentalism because they experience extreme deprivation in the mainstream . . . women are seeking alternative forms of sex, marriage, and family in response to the decline of the nuclear family and the growing poverty of the mother-child unit."[13]

These women developed cooperative networks among themselves because their husband was rarely home. Bennion found that 35 percent of the men work in another state during the winter. In essence, she says, women are often required to bring up their children by themselves, teach them in the community private school and budget their own incomes. Bennion writes: "Women develop a strong interdependence with each other that creates a large repertoire of domestic and mechanical skills . . . 'If one wife can't fix it, the other can' is a commonly spoken concept. Few monogamous women experience this type of shared skilled."[14]

Bennion illustrated how each wife, in a polygamous family setting, brings their own unique talents to the group. Two of the wives, she wrote, were focused on working around the house and tending to the children while the other three wives were working outside the home, one in real estate, another as a lawyer and another in operations management.

Female cooperation extends even to courtship, where a wife, along with her husband, will actively woo a prospective new wife for the family. During the wedding, all the wives join hands with the couple, thus sealing their relationship with each other for an eternity. FLDS weddings are described by Bennion:

> Women voice satisfaction in the "Law of Sarah" ceremony, which covenants women to each other for eternity. Ideally, the first wife agrees to link the second wife not only to her husband but also to herself in this life and the next. Through this eternal bond, women are encouraged to work together economically, socially and spiritually and, in some rare cases, sexually. These bonds are enhanced through the common feature of women courting other women as future co-wives.[15]

Female solidarity in plural marriage even provides a powerful antidote to correcting the behavior of some husbands:

> When faced with a challenge, such as a husband who get "out of line," women may unite in opposition against him. For instance, one woman said that her husband wasn't spending enough time with her son and that he also forgot her birthday. The other wives joined her in "boycotting" their husband, barring him from access to food and sex for a week. . . . Within polygamy, they argue, one can gain respite from their husband and engage in individual pursuits.[16]

Each wife frequently has her own home or, if there's one house, her own room or set of rooms. This dwelling or this space, depending on the living conditions, is for the wife and her children.

Bennion observed a high frequency of co-mothering in the FLDS communities, so much so that young children often do not distinguish their biological mother from other women in a polygamous family. Children are considered "gifts from God" and mothers speak with pride about the group's offspring. Because of the help given by co-wives, each mother is able to devote herself completely to her infant's care during the early months of life, and because a mother spends most of her time with her children, she often prefers their company to that of her husband.

Bennion also found that the quality of parenting depends on co-wife relations, which is often influenced by the number of children per wife. She reports, moreover, instances where many first and second wives got along well until their husband married a third wife, thereby "putting a wrench in the works."[17]

Irwin Altman and Joseph Ginat note that, for the wives, "the home is an important place to express themselves . . . for husbands, the home is a place to visit . . . a site to house their family and a place to which they make little emotional commitment and . . . exert little control."[18]

Altman and Ginat observed that childcare is also a key area for conflict and cooperation among plural families. In one instance of cooperation, one wife cared for 18 children while her sister-wives worked outside the home. Wives sometimes become upset about how other wives treat their children. And, in one case, one of eight wives expressed concern over difficulties among them regarding disciplinary strategies that were fair to all children.

Most people in FLDS communities live out their childhood years in a patriarchal family with obligations. Scott Anderson, in his 2010 cover story for *National Geographic* magazine, noted that FLDS is striving to be as a self-sufficient as possible, writing, "members, even young children, are expected to be help with the chores—sewing, picking, canning, throughout the year."[19]

One daughter from a polygynist marriage described her walks with her father while growing up. As reported by Jankowiak and Allen:

> The love of the father is found, too, in the remarks of a woman in her mid-thirties, who recalled that, as a young girl, she would go on walks with her father who never failed to explain the importance of living God's law (i.e. polygamy). she declared, with an emotional timbre in her voice, that through "his kindness and love, I am a better person."[20]

Jankowiak and Allen also told the story of one son from a polygynist family who said he'd learned the importance of the family sharing a meal together:

> That his father always stressed the importance of eating, at the very least, one meal a week together as a family. "Dad always said," he added, "the family that eats together, stays together." He dwelled on his father's enlightenment and how he, too, as a father, wanted to continue what was, for him, a memorable family tradition.[21]

ABUSE

Bennion is well aware that polygamy is not without abuse of women and children. She notes that monogamy, too, is not without its blemishes. As she states:

> I challenge the IHR [International Health Regulations] assumptions and the existing media-driven paradigm that polygamy uniformly "violates women's

rights to equality within marriage and the family." It is essential to examine the full land variable impact of polygamous family life on the health and well-being of women and children based on satisfaction levels, sexuality, economic activities, living arrangements, leisure and autonomy, financial stability, socialization and the presence or absence of abuse.[22]

For those who suffer abuse, Bennion believes that it is not polygamy, per se, that's the problem but, instead, specific circumstances combined with polygamy. Other contributing factors, Bennion writes, can include: "(1), father absence or low father parental investment, (2), isolated rural environment or circumscription, (3) absence of a strong female network (4), overcrowding in the household, and (5), male supremacist ideology."[23]

One argument, which we'll look at later, to decriminalize and even legalize polygyny, is that it will allow an abused plural wife to seek help and protection, either from the local police or an attorney, without putting herself at risk legally as well as her entire family, perhaps even her children. Because of today's laws against plural marriage, as one legal scholar notes, many cases of abuse among the FDLS are likely going unreported.

Of course, the same thing is happening with women in monogamous marriages, too, because, as the National Coalition against Domestic Violence reported, in 2007, about 1.3 million women are assaulted annually—that's about 25,000 each week—by their intimate partner.[24]

And those are just the ones we know about.

DIVORCE

The LDS historically have had very strong feelings about divorce and, early on, the FLDS Church was officially opposed to it. Many statements by Brigham Young, for instance, along with those of other leaders, railed against divorce. Some early FLDS pamphlets pointed out that the only ground for divorce was fornication.

Women were given the primary initiative in ending a marital bond. Foster reports that, since it was mainly up to the woman to end a marriage, it was difficult for a man to divorce his wife, if she was opposed. A divorced woman, however, could easily remarry, giving her the opportunity to practice what amounted to serial polygamy.

Richard Van Wagoner (1986) points out that LDS men were under a lifetime moral obligation to care for their ex-wives during the heyday of polygyny. We might conclude that conflict within LDS families, though difficult to ascertain on purely quantitative grounds, was probably no more, or even less, than that found within contemporary American families.

In fact, a widely cited pioneering study by Kimball Young (1954) reports that most of the polygynist families that he rated in his research could be categorized as successful. For example, Young found that half of 110 family cases were highly successful and marked by unusual harmony or were reasonably successful. An additional 25 percent were moderately successful, with some conflict. The remaining experienced considerable conflict and marital difficulties, including in some cases separation or divorce.

Divorce among the FLDS communities appears to be higher than in the historic LDS community, but lower than the national average. Bennion, for example, writes, "even though the Harker [an FLDS community] divorce rate is 35%, it is still much lower than the national rate."[25] Marital conflict is lessened, Bennion believes, because sister-wives are a built-in support group. Bennion writes, "at the first hint of trouble, a Harker woman talks about it with her sister-wives."[26]

Historic LDS and contemporary FLDS divorce and conflict patterns suggest a cautious model for America, one for serious study by those, like the authors of this book, who cautiously suggest plural marriage might be an antidote, albeit to a small degree, to divorce.

Similar challenging experiences among all married Americans, including FLDS believers, contribute to marital stress. The cause of this anxiety can include a lack of money. Thus, based on what we know, so far, the type of marital institution—polygamous or monogamous—doesn't itself alone determine a marriage's success or failure.

It's all about the people and varying circumstances. In fact, legalizing, or at least decriminalizing, plural marriage might increase the prospects for domestic harmony and put an end to legal maneuvers to conceal a plural marriage and, in some circumstances, reduce the power of some polygamist men who, in secrecy, flaunt their control over their wives and children.

CAN A POLYGAMOUS HUSBAND LOVE HIS WIVES EQUALLY?

William Jankowiak, an anthropologist at the University of Nevada at Las Vegas, who we cite earlier, doesn't think so. His opinion is based on his own anthropological study of the FLDS in the United States.

"There's a favorite wife in every family," he said in an interview with the coauthor of this book.[27] "She can change over time but there's always a favorite wife." He added, "That's not to say that the husband didn't enjoy sexuality with another wife. There's affection for her. But the deep, intimate bond is reserved for one wife."

The problem some husbands encounter—in their obligation to visit each wife—is what Jankowiak describes as a "shifted emotional loyalty," which prevents them from being comfortable, right from the beginning, with the next wife.

Jankowiak also says that, based on his research, usually the first wife is often disappointed when a second wife comes along. The level of education that the wives achieved, as well as their age, can also be a factor in how well they get along.

"If the first wife in a polygamous setting is young, she's living some high school romantic fantasy," he said.

"I've been struck by when co-wives are college educated and over 35, they seem to get along much better," Jankowiak said. "They're educated professionals. They're use to working with others, and they're not lost in a youthful romantic fantasy."

"They know what they want out of marriage. They know there are many types of marriage—they may have even been previously married—but they're willing to embrace polygamy. They're more comfortable compromising, they can manage their own emotions when things don't go well and that's something you can't do well as a 20-year-old wife," he added.

He also said that two wives, who share the same age, can grow old together well in a long term polygamous marriage. But if the husband decides to marry a younger woman, it can cause tension, with the two older wives shunning the younger wife.

Some women, Jankowiak says, enter into plural marriages hoping to become the favorite wife. "If you become the favorite wife, you tend to receive more benefits from the husband plus you receive support from the other wives," Jankowiak said.

So how does a polygamous man persuade a woman to enter into a plural marriage? "Everyone is going to work together, they say," said Jankowiak. "It's a nice sell. It sounds good and it doesn't seem like bizarre sexuality. They're not selling a sexual system but a family system."

One of the telling points about how the wives' feelings for one another are found in each wife's bedroom, Jankowiak says. "There's never a picture of any other wife on the wall. They're connected through the husband, never through the other wives," he said.

Do polygamous families get along well with one another? "If the man makes a lot of money, there's not the insecurity of a lack of resources," Jankowiak said. "When there's not enough money, economics becomes a big issue.

"Only a wealthy man can really afford it," he adds.

And what's the typical polygamous man like? "They're not sexual hedonists," Jankowiak said. "They're devout and true to their faith. It's authentic.

"This is not an easy life. The men have a lot of demands placed on them. And if they've had a lot of children, because of their marriages, they learn it's just impossible to be a daddy to every single kid."[28]

THE DARGERS

In an example of polygynists fighting for their right to live as they wish—and taking some legal risks to do so—Joe Darger and his three wives, Alina, Vicki, and Valerie, wrote a book titled *Love Times Three* (2011), which details the life they lead in a Salt Lake City suburb. The Dargers, who are FLDS, admit that, "plural marriage isn't easy," writing:

> It's a lifestyle that requires of each woman a constant gentle empathy for her sister wives and a respect for boundaries and fairness. We face the same struggles that monogamous wives do, but those trying times are often magnified because there are multiple partners whose perspectives and feelings have to be considered. It starts with the husband and his character, but what really makes success possible? It's that woman who's agreed to take the journey with you, your sister wife.[29]

Joe runs a successful business. His family, which includes 24 children, lives in a 6,000 square-foot home, with 10 bedrooms, 5 bathrooms, and 2 laundry rooms.

Each of the wives, like Joe, is given their own voice in the book. Each details some of their most trying times of living together. The last woman to join the family, Valerie, in fact, is the twin sister of Vicki, Joe's only legal wife, so sororal polygyny is practiced.

She came to the family after divorcing her first polygamist husband. Valerie says her first marriage came to an end because her husband had a gambling problem.

Each of Joe's wives write about their many ups and downs in their lives together. And Joe says having three wives is far from easy:

> Living this lifestyle requires me to focus on fundamental gospel principles and work to overcome the slothful, selfish, jealous, lustful and prideful aspects of my character. I can't be controlling or manipulative, behaviors that have doomed many plural marriages. And I've learned the hard way that I have to keep my temper in check.[30]

While many people might see Joe as engaging in plural sexuality, he sees his relationships with his wives very differently. It's an obligation to "sustain three healthy monogamous, but interwoven, marriages."[31]

NOTES

1. Richard Van Wagoner, *Mormon Polygamy: A History* (Salt Lake City, UT: Signature Books, 1986), p. 101.

2. Ibid., pp. 101–102.

3. Ann Eliza Young, *The 19th Wife Featuring, One Lady's Account of Plural Marriage and its Woes Being the Chronicle of Personal Experience of Ann Eliza Young—19th and Rebel Wife of the Leader of the Utah Saints and Prophet of the Mormon Church, Brigham Young Written by Herself* (New York: Easton & Co., 1875).

4. James Brook, "Utah Struggles with Revival of Polygamy," *The New York Times,* August 23, 1998, http://www.nytimes.com/1998/08/23/world/utah-struggles-with-a-revival-of-polygamy.html?pagewanted=all&src=pm.

5. Felicia R. Lee, "*Big Love:* Real Polygamists Look at HBO Polygamists and Find Sex," *The New York Times,* March 28, 2006, http://www.nytimes.com/2006/03/28/arts/television/28poly.html?_r=1&pagewanted=all.

6. Ben Winslow, "Foster Care for Jeffs' Apparent Child Bride," *Deseret News,* August 20, 2008, http://www.deseretnews.com/article/700252061/Foster-care-for-Jeffs-apparent-child-bride.html.

7. Ken Driggs, "Twentieth Century Polygamy and Fundamentalist Mormons in Southern Utah," *Dialogue, Journal of Mormon Thought* (winter 1991), pp. 44–58, esp. p. 55.

8. Ibid., p. 56.

9. Dirk Johnson, "Polygamists Emerge From Secrecy, Seeking not just Peace but Respect," *The New York Times,* April 9, 1991, http://www.nytimes.com/1991/04/09/us/polygamists-emerge-from-secrecy-seeking-not-just-peace-but-respect.html?pagewanted=all&src=pm.

10. Janet Bennion, *Desert Patriarchy: Mormon and Mennonite Communities in the Chihuahua Valley* (Tucson: University of Arizona Press, 2004), p. 7.

11. Ibid., p. 190.

12. Janet Bennion, *Women of Principle: Female Networking in Contemporary Mormon Polygamy* (New York: Oxford University Press, 1998). Dr. Bennion provides an in-depth ethnographic study about how the wives in FLDS polygamous marriages work together.

13. Ibid., p. 6.

14. Janet Bennion, "The Many Faces of Polygamy: An Analysis of the Variability in Modern Mormon Fundamentalism in the Intermountain West," in *Modern Polygamy in the United States: Historical, Cultural and Legal Issues,* ed. Cardell Jacobson and Laura Burto (New York: Oxford University Press, 2011), p. 173.

15. Ibid., p. 172.

16. Ibid.

17. Bennion, *Women of Principle,* p. 141.

18. Irwin Altman and Joseph Ginat, *Polygamous Families in Contemporary Society* (New York: Cambridge University Press, 1996), p. 272.

19. Scott Anderson, "The Polgyamists," *National Geographic,* February 2010, http://ngm.nationalgeographic.com/2010/02/polygamists/anderson-text/4.

20. William Jankowiak and Emilie Allen, "Adoring the Father: Religion and Charisma in an American Polygamous Community," in *Anthropology and Theology: God, Icons, and God-talk,* ed. Walter Randolph Adams and Frank Salamone, pp. 293–313 (Lanham, MD: University Press of America, 2000), p. 301.

21. Ibid.

22. Bennion, "The Many Faces of Polygamy," p. 166.

23. Ibid.

24. National Coalition Against Domestic Violence, "Domestic Violence Facts, July 2007," http://www.ncadv.org.

25. Bennion, *Women of Principle*, p. 154.

26. Bennion, *Women of Principle*, p. 139.

27. Jankowiak interview by Douglas Page.

28. All the comments in this section come from an interview of William Jankowiak by Page.

29. Joe Darger, Alina Darger, Vickie Darger, and Valerie Darger, *Love Times Three: Our True Story of a Polygamous Marriage* (New York: HarperOne, 2011), p. 159.

30. Ibid., p. 189.

31. Ibid., p. 190.

8

The Family Reinvented:
Early Euro-American Feminists

The traditional, ideal American family, which is being contested, is the nuclear family composed of a husband, wife, and children residing together, with the husband as sole breadwinner and the wife performing the roles of homemaker and childcare provider. For many Americans, albeit fewer today than in the past, this family form was seen as endowed by biology, God-given, even natural.

It was thought women were, by nature, better suited to nurturing children than men. Gender relations were structured around this "essential" difference between men and women, having implications for how society is organized in the workplace, the place of worship, the community, as well as within the family. This cultural ideal, overall, worked against women who wanted to work outside the home or, in an earlier time, become full citizens with voting rights.

Initiated in the 1960s, early feminism was a powerful, theoretical, and ideological movement, challenging the philosophy that the "natural order" of things was for men to work and women to remain at home or, perhaps, hold jobs that suited them, like teaching. Once women became the center of attention, it was revealed that their ambitions had been concealed and their aspirations, with rare exception, had been repressed.

Due to the success of feminist ideology, today there is an appreciation of the diversity of women's roles, even for those women who choose to remain at home and engaged in traditional family roles (cf. Alma Gottlieb 2004). At the same time, women of color often reject the label of feminism in favor of "womanism," a viewpoint which includes, in theory, not only gender, but race and class too. Later, we will see how recent feminists and "womanists" appraise the practice of polygamy in, for example, the FLDS and African American communities.

In a key piece of feminist literature, Sanford Dornbusch and Myra Strober (1988) recognize a diversity of family forms. They emphasize their concern with "families" rather than with "the family," seeing this distinction as a "major part of the reconciliation between feminism and family rights and responsibilities" in that feminists have reiterated the reality that "the traditional model of family relations does not apply to the bulk of contemporary families."[1] These authors point out that the central concern of feminists is autonomy for women and the building of political agendas that recognize, as paramount, that freedom of choice will enhance female autonomy.

At the same time, feminist thinking need not hold that there are no differences between men and women, although these differences often arise through childrearing practices rather than being inherent in biology. Sarah Ruddick (1989), for example, suggests that women develop certain capacities for nurturing tendencies through their roles in childrearing. This results in what she calls "maternal thinking." One implication of Ruddick's view might be to involve men even more in childrearing so they, too, can develop nurturing styles for bringing up children and infants.

The relationship between women and children has been a stickler in much feminist discourse. The natural order assumption, which places women in the home, emphasizing the exclusive importance of motherhood, has often been used as a rationale to hold women back in the workplace and, thus, inhibited their freedom; because of this issue, women might resist any attempt to link their needs, aspirations, and goals directly with that of child rearing.

Dornbusch and Strober, in examining the writings on the family by both traditionalists and feminists, are surprised at the scarcity of attention given by either to children's needs. Instead, conceptions about children's needs are filtered through assumptions about acceptable gender relations to which children are expected to conform. "Children's needs seem all too readily subsumed by the eagerness to win acceptance for a particular preferred arrangement of men's and women's place in adult society."[2]

Of course, it is the intention of the present book to advocate a continued rethinking of the family form but with a simultaneous eye on the needs of women, children and men. Dornbusch and Strober indicate that the overriding concern of feminists, one that's still strong today, is autonomy for women and even though most feminists recognize other important goals as well, such as community.[3]

LEANNA WOLFE: A FAMILY PIONEER

The writings and experience of anthropologist Leanna Wolfe document how some Euro-American women pursued autonomy and community in a cultural world influenced by feminism. In her anthropological fieldwork, Wolfe interviewed women who had been mistresses, in committed triads, in open marriages, and who lived in communes. She has conducted field work overseas to better understand how polygyny works and, eventually, resolve jealousies and other dilemmas she encountered in her own polyamorous family, mentioned earlier (Wolfe 2006).

Wolfe (1993) writes about the growing phenomenon of professional, largely middle-class women who have opted out of traditional life style restrictions, including the assumption that a woman must marry in order to achieve self-fulfillment, in pursuit of a more personally fulfilling career. Wolfe, in rethinking the American family situation, argues that many women must accept a social reinvention of their very identity. Given the dramatic social changes of recent years, many women will simply never marry, she says.

Wolfe suggested that society stop looking at marriage as a measure of the ultimate female fulfillment. She challenged women who have never married to think of themselves as whole and complete human beings in spite of the absence of marriage. Although Wolfe cherishes the human desire for intimacy, including the deep sexual and emotional needs that may be satisfied in marriage, she believes these needs can also be satisfied outside of marriage.

The pursuit of community while living autonomously has led Wolfe to advocate what she calls a "family of choice.' The "family of choice" is self-constructed and includes close friends, former lovers and spouses, coworkers, current and former housemates, and romantic partners. Much as immigrants relied on the extended family, Wolfe believes the current generation, and ones in the future, will rely on an "expanded" family, which may not be exclusively consanguineal. Gay and lesbian families have, in fact, opted for a family of choice model, one that could serve as a model for all Americans (Weston 1991).

Wolfe's attitudes are grounded not only in her personal experiences but also in direct observation as well. For instance, she has considered the difficulty single adults encounter in attempting to find self-satisfying love. To illustrate this point, she offers the example of a woman named Donna, whom she describes as an intelligent, somewhat rigid, high-tech-instrument sales executive. Donna's search for someone to marry inspired Wolfe's interest in the question of single women who may never marry.

Donna, 43, had spent the last 10 years doing everything she could to meet that special guy. She purchased self-help books, attended singles workshops, answered personal ads and met other single men at mixers. She even attempted to modify her appearance by coloring her hair and lying about her age. And what may be fairly typical as well, she intentionally adopted a more passive and receptive personality in hopes of being attractive to men.

Wolfe sets out five common strategies she believes women practice in pursuit of marriage:

1. Play the numbers game in an attempt to find a suitable partner;
2. Modify the body through diets, surgery, makeup, and the like;
3. Practice courtship manipulation strategies such as playing hard-to-get;
4. Become financially self-sufficient, which helps to reduce feelings of desperation by fostering independence from the traditional reasons that women need a provider in their family; and
5. Become a "new traditionalist" by learning or relearning how to become passive, so that traditional men will provide them with affection.[4]

These strategies may result in success but at what cost? Wolfe warns they will not help build honest relationships with good communication and emotional closeness. Rather than orienting one's life around the pursuit of happiness through marriage in the traditional sense of the term, Wolfe advocates withdrawal from the dating game and the cessation of self-blame.

She says women should feel satisfied with their accomplishments and be comfortable with their lives. She emphasizes that once marriage is no longer considered the ultimate measure of female fulfillment or male achievement, a woman is free to pursue life's many alternatives.

Wolfe's resolution for the fact that many women will never marry is for them to consider, as we have said, an extended "family of choice," which she prophetically believed may be the future family model.

The second resolution Wolfe offers to the marriage dilemma is to point out that being single should not be stigmatized since it is becoming commonplace in American society. Wolfe writes that years ago being single would have been considered strange; now being single is thoroughly acceptable. This change was reaffirmed by many of the people she interviewed for her book.

Another change is that now, more than before, single women include many who are physically attractive and financially independent, with no need to exchange sex or homemaking services for economic support. Their mere existence is a challenge to the traditional female/male dynamics and the functions of marriage. Thus, many women assume the responsibilities of adulthood through their own efforts rather than through their husband's accomplishments.

Owing in part to changing demography and to an increased cultural tolerance, many single people feel they to need rely on no one but themselves. As Wolfe points out, "family culture" is being displaced by the "culture of individual achievement" in which energies are directed away from relationships that don't last to a perhaps more enduring happiness derived from what one creates and owns. Of course, part of what is to be created in the culture of individual achievement is a new family style or form that Wolfe believes would include extended families of choice.

For the vast majority of women who do desire to marry, either because of loneliness or the ticking of the "biological clock," the extended family of choice is an interesting alternative. Wolfe believes that the expanded (elsewhere she uses the word "extended") family of choice is far superior to that of the exclusive nuclear family ideal in which one person is expected to fulfill all of their partner's needs. In order to set out to construct expanded families of choice, she says it is necessary to attack a number of myths, namely:

1. That humans mate for life.
2. That men marry as a mark of maturity and can support women and children.
3. That the nuclear family is the most effective and viable way to raise children.
4. That women will tolerate anything to keep "the family" intact.[5]

Wolfe's argument is that all humans have family-type needs, including desires for social and emotional support, physical touching, and sexual expression, as well as a longing to feel important and be a member of a group in which they feel wanted.

Another kind of attempt to build expanded families as described by Wolfe concerns group living arrangements and communal sexual practices. The Kerista tribe in San Francisco is an example. Wolfe, who has been a radio talk show hostess, interviewed a Kerista woman who "raved about the benefits of her fourteen-way group marriage."[6] On a rotating schedule, she slept with a different man each night of the week. What she liked about this arrangement was the variety since each of them was enjoyable and each brought out different aspects of her.

Contrasting this positive assessment, two male informants said they despised "soup kitchen sex" and that they had been forced to sleep with women for whom they felt no attraction. They indicated that every person was pressured to have sex every night for the good of the group, and people who did not do so were shunned.[7] The Kerista fell apart over such feelings.

Wolfe also looked into other communal arrangements, such as a movement founded 25 years ago at More University. This community had three More houses in the San Francisco Bay area as well as one in Hawaii. Any given More house has three types of people. On the bottom floor are formerly homeless guests who are fed, sheltered, and clothed so that they can regain their dignity and control over their lives. These homeless guests rarely take part in the family sexual activities of the community. The second category apparently comprises people who have internalized the More jargon and have come to seek pleasurable social interaction. The third group is more professional, usually former yuppies who display a materially rich life. The More subculture includes such practices as shared parenting and the construction of age-mate sibling relationships. There are also charitable activities and feed-the-hungry projects.[8]

Although Wolfe accepts the idea of family diversity, her personal preference in is an "expanded family of choice," which, for her, will not include marital ties, though it might for others. For example, she tells of a Los Angeles sexologist whom she believes has found something many people seek. While this woman lives with her husband, for the past 25 years they have both been deeply committed to a network of people who have chosen to love one another for the rest of their lives. The caring, trusting relationships they have with one another is illustrated by her arrangement for one member of the group, an attractive widow, to stay with her husband while she was hospitalized so that he would be comfortable and well cared for. She saw no reason why he should be home alone. Wolfe points out that when members of the network become widowed, they move in with and often marry other survivors. This situation shows that the network itself is lifelong and permanent, transcending the individual or couple.[9]

Wolfe herself, has faced the dilemma experienced by many women who seek not to take part in traditional marriage-that is, the decision whether to have a baby.[10] Either through family pressure or some "biological clock" tendency, women in their 30s frequently describe an anxiety over having a child. For Wolfe, this meant that should she actualize her desire to have a child, she would have to do so in a nonconventional fashion. For her, wanting a child has become focused around the construction of a suitable environment for raising a child. Her preference for such an environment coincides with what she thinks is best for herself—namely, an expanded family of choice. By staying outside of conventional marriage, she also seeks to avoid the risk of trauma for the child associated with divorce while trying to build a more enduring community.

CO-PARENTING

For women opting for an expanded family choice, Wolfe (1993) notes the issue of co-parenting. A co-parent is someone who would be willing to enter into a communal parenting relationship. A man who would become a co-parent in Wolfe's model must sign a co-parenting statement of intent that contains very explicit guidelines. The father must be actively involved in the pregnancy period and maintain personal contact. He must also be present at the birth in a supporting and loving way, although other intimate friends, perhaps even unknown to him, may also be there.

The mother would provide personal assistance or arrange for others to provide for assistance, such as cooking, cleaning, or bathing, during the first three months after birth. The co-parents would not expect to share a residence, although they may decide to do so. Any shared residence would most likely include other partners and other children. It is significant also that the mother and father enter into their co-parenting agreement without the expectation of becoming husband and wife.

In Wolfe's model, the father must be active in the child's life and, ideally, live in the same geographical area so he can visit the child several times a week. Later, the father may take the child, perhaps to his residence, on a regular basis. If, however, the father lives at a distance, he must play an active role by calling or visiting whenever possible. So that a professional woman, for example, can continue to pursue her career and professional interests, the father, when he is financially able, should help pay for regular day care services.

CENSUS BUREAU STATISTICS

While many Americans may have never heard of Leanna Wolfe, it appears, based on the data from the U.S. Census Bureau, that many are living exactly as she proposed. In 2010, the Census Bureau reported that there were nearly 5.8 million single male households, meaning there is no woman in the house. Nearly half of these single male households, almost 2.8 million, were bringing up children by themselves. The Census Bureau also reported in 2010 that there were over 15 million single female households, with about 8.4 million of them bringing up children.[11]

Over the last few decades unmarried births have contributed greatly to single parent households. Government researchers learned that there were about 360,800 births to unwed mothers in 1969, an increase of 6.3 percent from the previous year.[12] Throughout the 1960s, in fact, the United States averaged just over a 5 percent annual increase in births among unmarried women.

By the time the first edition of this book was published in 1994, the government reports that there were nearly 1.29 million births to unmarried women,[13] an increase of nearly 400 percent from about the time Kilbride was embarking on his teaching career. In the most recent statistics available, from 2009, there were just under 1.7 million births to unmarried women, a slight decrease from 2008, when the country saw 1.726 million births to unmarried women.[14]

While some might see a trend worth celebrating, it is impossible to conclude that the latest decrease spells a future of a continuing decline in the number of out-of-wedlock births. Since 1940, government reports show, there have only been three other years when the numbers of these births dropped: 1942, 1995, and 1997.[15] There's even some data that suggests that the number of births to unwed mothers in 2010 continued to drop, too.[16] Otherwise, the statistics show, the numbers of births among unmarried women continue upward.

In fact, what's surprising—and perhaps this is why few have taken notice of the trend—is that while the numbers of these births have increased by more than 600 percent since 1960, the average yearly increase has remained small, 2.3 percent in one decade to as much as 5.3 percent in another.[17] This might explain why no one, with perhaps the exception of a few demographers and others looking at the numbers, has cried out that there's an epidemic in the numbers of children born to unmarried mothers.

In 2008, according to information provided by the Census Bureau, more than 40 percent of all births in the United States were to unwed mothers. In 1980, less than 20 percent of all births were to unwed mothers, so the number has been increasing over the last 30 years. While 40 percent might seem high, the percentage of births among unwed mothers in the United States is less than what some other countries have experienced, at least in the Western world. Denmark, France, the Netherlands, and Sweden have seen higher percentages of births to unmarried women. Germany has one of the lowest percentages of births among unwed mothers, just over 30 percent in 2008.[18]

Too often the issue with births to unwed mothers is that both the mother and the child suffer dire economic circumstances, especially if the mother lacks a college degree or family support, which would enable her to continue her education so she can advance herself financially. Certainly there are cases of college-educated women, wealthy women, or women with strong family support who remain single, giving birth and not suffering the same consequences as economically challenged women. We're not here to provide judgment one way the other about single mothers. We're just stating the facts as we've come to know them.

The living arrangements of children have changed. With just over 74 million children in the United States today, a majority of them (68.6%)[19] live with married parents while nearly 30 percent live with only one parent, an increase from 1970, when 11 percent of all children lived with only their mother. In 1991, the number of children living with one parent increased to 24 percent. The Census Bureau says that in 1990, there were just over 1.1 million single father households and nearly 6.6 million single mother households.

The latest Census figures show that 50 million children are growing up in married households while just over 23 million are growing up with parents who are have either "never married" or who are "separated, divorced or widowed."[20]

How will children in single-parent households, once they're adults, view marriage? If they're boys being brought up by a man, or girls being brought up by a woman, are they developing an appreciation and understanding for the gender not present in their house? We can only speculate.

Perhaps the biggest surprise in the latest Census Bureau data is the status of traditional married households, where both mom and dad live together and each has a biological connection to the children in the house. In 2006, there were just over 24 million of those households. In 2010, there were about 23.5 million, meaning that traditional married households with children are falling.[21]

Between 2006 and 2010, single female households grew from about 13.9 million to more than 15 million. Single male households remained fairly steady.[22]

As for births, there were just over 1.5 million unmarried women who had given birth, according to information the Census Bureau received in 2010. Unmarried women, according to the Census Bureau are women who were divorced, widowed, or single at the time they had their baby. In 2006, just under 1.4 million unwed women had given birth.[23]

SIMILARITIES BETWEEN DIFFERENT COMMUNITIES IN THE UNITED STATES

It might be easy for some people to look at the trends on unmarried births in the United States and dismiss it as something that's only happening within minority communities. But in some of the most recent information about births to unwed mothers, provided by the Centers for Disease Control and Prevention in 2010, which looked at the trend of births to unmarried women by race and ethnicity over the course of nearly 40 years, they discovered a surprising number of similarities, prompting one knowledgeable observer on relationship trends to make the following comment in an interview with Page:

> "What's been happening in the black community is ahead of the white community by 20 to 30 years," said University of Iowa Law Professor Adrien Wing, who happens to be African American. "There are many more households headed by white women, but what's been happening in the black community—black women never marrying or having multiple relationships instead—will be experienced by white people in a few decades if not sooner."[24]

The Centers reports that in 1970 5.5 percent of all births among white women were to unmarried ones. That number increased to nearly 35 percent by 2007. Nearly 38 percent of all births among blacks were to unmarried black women in 1970 and that number increased, in 2007, to more than 71 percent.[25]

Births to unmarried Hispanic mothers were not measured by the Centers until 1980, when it was reported that more than 23 percent of all births among them were to unmarried women. In 2007, the Centers reported, more than 50 percent of all births among Hispanics were to unmarried women.[26] Unmarried births to Asians and Pacific Islanders were not measured until 1980, too, when it was reported that 7.3 percent of all births among them were to unmarried women, with that percentage increasing to nearly 17 percent in 2007.[27]

Finally, the latest information about births to unmarried women shows the number of births decreasing, since 1970, among women younger than 20 years old but increasing, since 1970, to women older than 25. More than 50 percent of all births in 1970 were to women under the age of 20. By 2007, that had dropped to about 23 percent. Whereas just over 18 percent of all births to unmarried women in 1970 were to those over 25, by 2007, that percentage had increased to nearly 40 percent of all births to women older than 25.[28]

MAN-SHARING

Audrey Chapman describes in her early research how women engaged in a "hen session" with her and other women, admitting their suspicions that they had been sharing husbands with other women. Later in her work as a human relations trainer and counselor, she discovered "the man-sharing seminars I conduct in Washington and elsewhere have been comprised of women of all ages, ethnic groups and professions."[29] While a number of them expressed bitterness, others tried to examine the situation and evaluate their position. These women concluded that being without a man or having to share a man with another woman may be the price one has to pay for a professional degree and career.

One woman reported that she had originally decided not to share another woman's man, but when she moved to Washington, DC, where the ratio of men to women was about 1:7, she saw that women were competing for men who refused to make any commitment. At first, Chapman opposed man-sharing, but a number of her respondents in her capacity as professional trainer and counselor said things like, "Wake up. Sometimes if you don't share another woman's man, you don't have any" or "Most of us are sharing anyway. What difference does it make?"[30] Chapman eventually realized that, given these affairs which border on polygamy, it was important that American women be given a set of guidelines or rules to make their situation more workable and emotionally satisfying.

Chapman held her first workshop, "Man-Sharing: Dilemma or Choice," in the spring of 1983. She had expected only 50 to attend but was surprised when 110 women, most of whom had been or were involved in some form of man-sharing, showed up. Her goal was to help women who felt helpless and oppressed in their dealings with men so that they could better cope with man-sharing.

Chapman points out that the women came to her seminars for a variety of reasons. Some were involved with single men who refused to make any commitments, others were recently separated or divorced, still others were involved with married men. She points out that the man-sharing seminars she conducted were attended by women of all ages, from all ethnic groups, and all professions.

Women commonly reported that they had sought out a monogamous relationship only to find out that they were not in one, a discovery that led to a variety of negative feelings. Chapman decided to write her book in order to ease their suffering and to help them feel less anger and guilt. She also wanted to point out that, while she did not advocate man-sharing as a permanent way of life, because it is a social condition that often results from little choice, it needed to be dealt with in a pragmatic way rather than simply be condemned.

Chapman offers a typology of married and single men involved with women who share. The male sharers are classified as, for example, the "charmer," the "hit-and-run man," "El Jocko," the "married man," and "Charlie the clinger." The married man type is typically paranoid that any signs of his cheating behavior might get home to his family. Women in these relationships are in a second-class status, Chapman states, and should never fall victim to the hope or intention that this man will ever leave his wife because most never do so. The married man sometimes takes on the guise of the sugar daddy; this type is economically privileged and is able to "offer you the world on a silver platter. He is the embodiment of Shirley Temple's Good Ship Lollipop."[31] The "new male" is "a consummate cook, a sensitive lover and friend, a ready helpmate, and a professional confidant."[32] This new male is frightened to death of commitment, however. As part of his master plan for how a relationship should develop, he has a built-in means of flight when he begins sensing that the relationship may become too serious. Being highly intelligent, he gives lip service to women's equality and male liberation.

Chapman also offers a typology of women, who, though still resisting multiple relationships and preferring monogamy, feel that sharing is the only way to proceed. Among these types are the "liberated Lily" whose goal is to be independent and answer to no one; the "fabulous Fanny" who spends enormous amounts of money and time keeping her body up to perfection and who has many men; the "Cinderella Cindy" who spends a lot of her me-time fantasizing about the perfect man; the "panicked Polly" who has been around for many years and fears that the right man has alluded her grasp; "bored Betsy" who after some years of marriage has discovered that passion has faded, so she wants a little excitement and may cautiously give into another man; and "Daisy dilemma" who wants a relationship this week but by next week may have changed her mind.[33]

Not surprisingly, given our cultural context, reactions to Chapman's book and views are frequently hostile. She explains that when women agree to share several men, the idea is usually considered deviant, especially by American men who usually expect their women to be exclusively theirs. In addition, the term *man-sharing* has engendered many strong negative emotions, more so from women than from men. Chapman has even received hate mail from women accusing her of setting up abusive situations for women and giving men the right to share them.

Curiously, Chapman, though not disapproving of polygamy in some other cultures, frowns on openly recognized plural relationships in America. Even so, she estimates that the number of de facto polygamous families in this country may in fact be large if we include men and women with semi-polygamous lifestyles of the sort described in her book. Unlike Wolfe, who favors community and cultural reform, Chapman directs our attention instead to the survival of women in an individualistic, competitive world where dyadic relationships and monogamous ideals reign supreme.

Chapman is not so much concerned with building family and, thereby, viewing man-sharing in the context of family dynamics. Her book has no separate treatment of children and how children would relate to the man-sharing strategies of women who desire children. She is not promoting a new family option whereby children's place in any family structure is a crucial concern. There is some reference to support groups of men who wish to become involved with women for the purpose of providing father figures in single-parent households. Nevertheless, Chapman's material is provocative, informative, and very much in the mainstream of American cultural values. Man-sharing represents one pragmatic approach to dealing with the family crisis at issue in the United States.

NOTES

1. Sanford Dornbusch and Myra Strober, *Feminism, Children and the New Families* (New York: Guilford Press, 1988), p. 4.

2. Ibid., p. 37.

3. Ibid., p. 44.

4. Leanne Wolfe, *Women Who May Never Marry* (Atlanta: Longstreet Press, 1993), p. 60.

5. Ibid., p. 168.

6. Ibid., p. 60.

7. Ibid., pp. 172 and 173.

8. Leanne Wolfe, *Exploring Non-monogamy*, unpublished manuscript.

9. Ibid.

10. Wolfe, *Women Who May Never Marry*, pp. 45–57.

11. "Family Type by Presence and Age of Own Children, 2010," United States Census Bureau, http://factfinder2.census.gov/faces/tableservices/jsf/pages/product view.xhtml?pid=ACS_10_1YR_B11003&prodType=table.

12. "Table 1–17. Number and Percent of Births to Unmarried Women, by Race and Hispanic Origin: United States, 1940–94," Centers for Disease Control and Prevention, National Health Statistics, U.S. Department of Health and Human Services, http://www.cdc.gov/nhs/data/statab/t941x17.pdf.

13. "Births: Final Data for 2009," National Vital Statistics Reports, November 3, 2011, Centers for Disease Control, National Center for Health Statistics, U.S. Department of Health and Human Services, http://www.cdc.gov/nchs/data/nvsr/nvsr60/nvsr60_01.pdf.

14. Ibid.

15. "Table 1–17."; "Births: Final Data for 2009."

16. "Selected Social Characteristics in the United States, 2010 American Community Survey 1-Year Estimates," United States Census Bureau, http://paulryan.house.gov/UploadedFiles/U.S._Census_Bureau_-_Social_Characteristics_-_2006-2010_American_Community_Survey_5-Year_Estimates.pdf.

17. The data on the numbers of births to unmarried mothers comes from two sources previously cited, "Table 1–17. Number and Percent of Births to Unmarried Women, by Race and Hispanic Origin: United States, 1940–94" and "Births: Final Data for 2009."

18. "Table 1335. Births to Unmarried Women by Country: 1980 to 2008," http://www.census.gov/compendia/statab/2012/tables/12s1337.pdf.

19. "Living Arrangements of Children: 2009," United States Census Bureau, June 2011, http://www.census.gov/prod/2011pubs/p70-126.pdf.

20. Table D1. "Characteristics of Children Under 18 and their Designated Parents: 2009," United States Census Bureau, http://www.census.gov/hhes/socdemo/children/data/sipp/well2009/tables.html.

21. "Family Type by Presence and Age of Own Children, 2010," United States Census Bureau, http://www.census.gov/population/www/socdemo/hh-fam/cps2010.html.

22. Ibid.

23. "Women 15 to 50 Years who had a Birth in the Past 12 Months by Marital Status and Age, 2010, American Community Survey," United States Census Bureau, http://factfinder2.census.gov/faces/tableservices/jsf/pages/productview.xhtml?pid=ACS_09_1YR_B13002&prodType=table.

24. Douglas Page interview with Adrien Wing, University of Iowa Law School professor.

25. U.S. Department of Health and Human Services, Centers for Disease Control and Prevention, and the National Center for Health Statistics, "Table 7. Nonmarital Childbearing, by Detailed Race and Hispanic Origin of Mother, and Maternal

Age: United States, Selected Years 1970–2007, *Health, United States, 2010, with Special Feature on Death and Dying,* http://www.cdc.gov/nchs/data/hus/hus10.pdf#007.

    26. Ibid.

    27. Ibid.

    28. Ibid.

    29. Audrey Chapman, *Man Sharing* (New York: William Morrow, 1986), p. 17.

    30. Ibid., p. 16.

    31. Ibid., p. 115.

    32. Ibid., p. 117.

    33. Ibid., pp. 118–121.

9

African American Marriage Crisis

Many observers believe that family patterns and gender relations in the African American population are in a crisis state. Longstanding forces of racism and poverty continue to negatively impact black families. The inordinate rise of teenage pregnancies within this population as well as male-absent households and other signs of perceived crisis in the black family structure are well documented.

This pattern of family life, however, must be understood in the historical context of a very strong family tradition in the African American community, one in which extended families, a desire for children, and a strong sense of male and female cooperation in family life is to be found (cf. Stack 1974; Aschenbrenner 1983; Billingsley 1993; Hudson-Weems 2006). This pre-slavery, African-derived tradition is a backdrop against which informal polygamous practices and extended family grandparental participation in family life can be best understood.

The African American male's economic status is hit particularly hard, historically speaking, by racism and slavery, and in modern times, especially by racism. Nathan and Julia Hare (1989) report on one study at the University of Chicago that predicted that, at present rates, in the not too distant future, a majority "of black males will be either unemployed, in jail, on dope, or dead; with obvious consequences for their women, children and for society in general."[1]

Since that time, more than 20 years ago, that prediction has proven prophetic. The term "incarceration generation" currently marks African American children, and increasingly Hispanic children, too, because they're often growing up with at least one or both parents either presently or previously in jail (cf. Siegal 2011).

The incarceration generation brings about well-described troubled child-hoods, particularly among African American children. Erik Eckholm reports in the *New York Times* in 2009, that among children born in 1990, 1 in 4 black children, by the time they turned 14, had a father in prison. Children of parents who are high school dropouts have an increased risk of having a father in prison, up to 50 percent more for black children compared to 1 in 14 for the children of white parents who are also high school dropouts.

Eckholm writes, "Recent studies indicate that having an incarcerated parent doubles the chance that a child will be at least temporarily homeless and measurably increases the likelihood of physically aggressive behavior, social isolation, depression, and problems in school."[2]

Jane Siegel's book *Disrupted Childhoods* notes that the reason the United States has the highest incarceration rate in the world is due to the 1980s-era "war on drugs," which included longer prison terms. Though these policies affect all, they disproportionally impacted poorer segments of American society.

"Prisoners are disproportionally young compared to the general population with half of adult prisoners under the age of 35, so it is not surprising that the majority of them are parents to minor children."[3]

She documents negative consequences for children of the incarcerated so as to conclude that incarceration is, among other causes, associated with a child's antisocial and, later on, potentially criminal behavior. She also notes that in 2007 the U.S. Justice Department estimated that 1.7 million children had a parent in prison, up from about 76,000 in 1991.

The issue of incarceration in the context of a demographic crisis is causing a gender imbalance between black men and women as potential spouses. Increasingly, what's being seen is that African American women, striving to marry and bring up children, see a very small pool of eligible African American men—ones who are employed and not in prison—from whom to consider as potential spouses. This dearth of black men is leading some black women to engage in a variety of relationships with men—who are sometimes already in committed relationships—upon which the larger, white society appears to frown.

One scholar, seeing the small number of marriageable black men is telling her students, especially women, as they advance toward 40 years old, and beyond, they may need to consider plural marriage as an option—especially if they hope to have children and not grow old alone.[4]

CRISIS POLYGYNY

The African American community's family crisis has prompted a number of African Americans to discuss the issue of man-sharing as a viable option for some women who are either experiencing informal polygynous conditions or who are finding the search for a single, eligible man problematic. This situation is resulting in a number of African American women to engage in some kind of informal polygyny—they're dating or having children with an attached man—or they're considering becoming intimately involved with such a man.

Joseph Scott (1989) in a pioneering study described in the Hares' book, learned, based on his data, that polygyny begins with a willingness of single and married men and women to enter into and maintain affairs outside of their marriage. He believes that these relationships, though not numerated in Census Bureau figures, are not uncommon.

His own data, resulting from 22 in-depth interviews, shows that extramarital, polygynous families frequently start when a married man begins an outside family with a single, never-married woman. Typically, he says, this single woman will have been forced into single parenthood as a teenager and out of her mother's home before she turns 20 and, as a result, finds herself seeking out a "sponsor."

This sponsor often turns out to be an already-married man who is willing to help in exchange for sexual companionship, something that she also desires as well as help for her children. Interview data show that a woman in this position also want their sponsor to be a good role model for her children and to provide protection from those men who are out to exploit her.

Scott's informants state that married men often have positive qualifications and, therefore, are the mostly highly desired mate for the never-married mother. These women usually prefer married men over single ones because married men are "more family-oriented and more willing to have part-time relationships."[5]

By the same token, married men interested in extramarital affairs are likely to find willing partners in single, never-married women with children, particularly those living on their own. Scott also discovered in his research that young women involved with a sponsor sometimes become pregnant.

This new relationship—that of being a parent to a child they both share—adds parental obligations. This additional commitment transforms an extramarital affair into an extramarital family so that a de facto polygynous family is now in evidence.

Scott also notes that wives rarely approve of these polygynous arrangements. Perhaps this is because motherhood came to most of these wives after they were married. But, short of divorce, these first wives have little choice than to accept an existing, extramarital relationship.

Some wives ignore the situation as long as the husband maintains his responsibilities to his primary home. Should he not, then he must end his relationship with the outside family. Scott believes that such conflict may help explain that married African Americans are six times as likely as whites to separate.

Scott concludes his study by distinguishing between what he calls extra-marital polygyny with consensual polygyny, which is sanctioned by the community. He believes that consensual polygyny could be a temporary answer to a shortage of African American men. In contrast, he says, extramarital polygyny, which is generally forced on legal wives, is in his view, divisive and produces conflicts in the family and, thus, the black community. He also reminds us that this situation comes about because of the shortage of marriageable African American men.

HOW DID THIS HAPPEN?

Any conversation about African American families starts with a history that many might prefer to forget—slavery. While this is a book about polygyny, it's important to provide an overview of slavery's effects on African American family life, some of which continue to this very day, as well as the culture that many slaves experienced in Africa.

Experts say that immigrants, even those forced to the country against their will like Africans, retain their culture to some extent, which alters their host country, in this case the United States. The preeminent immigrant scholar in the United States, the late Oscar Handlin, said as much back in the 1950s, writing that African Americans, like other immigrants groups, would impact the country—in spite of their history as slaves:

> In a more subtle sense, the most valuable contribution of the immigrants, old and new, was always to remind Americans of the motto on the great seal, E Pluribus Unum, From Many One. Their adjustment involved the achievement of unity—and yet the preservation of diversities—in American society. . . . A point-by-point examination of the social and cultural characteristics of the American Negroes leads to the identical conclusion as with regard to immigrants.[6]

French author Alexis de Tocqueville, who observed the country in the 1830s, wrote in his book *Democracy in America*, that Africans—especially because they were enslaved—had the potential to force the United States into making some difficult choices:

> the destiny of the Negroes is in some measure interwoven with that of the Europeans. These two races are fastened to each other without intermingling; and they are alike unable to separate entirely or to combine. . . . Christianity suppressed slavery, but the Christians of the sixteenth century re-established

it, as an exception, indeed, to their social system, and restricted to one of the races of mankind; but the wound thus inflicted upon humanity . . . was far more difficult to cure.[7]

Indeed, the story of the African American experience before the Civil War and since is that they've influenced all areas of American life—business, religion, politics, the arts, science, diplomacy, government, the presidency, and the military. What future impact will African Americans bring to the United States? We may not answer this question in its entirety in this chapter, let alone this book, but the next area of life they may influence is one that most would likely have never expected—the shape of the American family.

OVERVIEW OF SLAVERY

The African slave trade started with the Portuguese. They, and other Europeans, traded with African leaders who purchased some of the day's leading consumer products, including textiles, iron, pewter dishes, silk sashes, hats, guns and ammunition, even brandy, as well as other items.[8]

In the slave trade's early days of the 17th century, African leaders had a surplus of slaves from the wars they had carried out against their neighbors on the continent. As time went on, these African leaders "realized the profit-making potential in kidnapping men, women, or children by continuing to fight old enemies or starting wars with new ones."[9]

While the exact number of Africans sent as slaves remains debated, the latest estimate is that about 12 million crossed the Atlantic Ocean[10]—to destinations in Latin and South America and the Caribbean—but only about 500,000 arrived on U.S. shores.[11] By the time the Civil War broke out in April 1861, there were nearly 4 million slaves, constituting about 13 percent of the U.S. population, according to the 1860 Census.

Slaves lived in a variety of conditions. Large plantations, found mostly in the Deep South, saw slaves often working as field hands, while southern Appalachian owners had their slaves working both as tradesmen as well as in the fields.

If a slave was lucky, by the odd standards of this "Peculiar Institution," they remained with one owner, and the owner's children, their entire life. This allowed the slave the opportunity for a long-lasting marriage to another slave and some influence on the upbringing of his children. Too often, however, this was not the case. Slaves were sold because their owners wanted or needed cash, or they had their fill of their property's personality. Young black men and women, and even black children, especially if they were sold without their mother, commanded a high price.[12]

Many slave owners even practiced a cruel form of polygyny: they had children with both their wives and their female slaves. As Henry Wiencek points out, Virginius Dabney, a newspaper editor in Virginia, described life in the antebellum South this way:

> In summer the head of the household and his wife and children whiled away
> many a long hour together on the verandah . . . while during the winter months
> they gathered in close communion about the family fireside . . . this idyllic
> picture was in many instances marred by the fact that while the planter was
> rearing a large brood [sic] of children in the "big house," he was rearing another
> brood of mulattoes in the slave quarters.[13]

Children from the unions of slave owners and slave women, as was determined by a law started in Virginia and often put into practice by other colonies, "mandated that the children of a black female, regardless of the color or condition of their father, had to take the status of the mother."[14]

There are suggestions, by some historians, that by raping and impregnating a slave woman, the owner was doing two things: First, he was attempting to control his property, if not outright degrade her; and, second, he was providing himself with another slave he didn't have to purchase—but could possibly sell for a premium.[15]

This was in addition to all the other indignities slaves suffered, including being whipped, forced to work in difficult and harsh conditions, not provided with time to look after their children, even if they were sick, separated from their families, and, in childhood, learning to conform to slavery by taking orders from their playmates—often the masters' white children.

Both Wilma A. Dunaway and Wiencek describe a crude and merciless form of daycare that existed for some slave children: an elderly slave cared for the children while their parents worked. Sometimes, Wiencek writes, the parents "would come back . . . to find their two-year-old gone forever"—sold to a slave trader![16] In spite of what many slaveholders said publicly—that they didn't want to break up slave families—the truth is that they rarely considered the feelings of their captives.

Rarely were slave men and women allowed a religious ceremony when they married; as Dr. Dunaway writes, "Despite their own family ideals, Appalachian masters and mistresses constructed an ethnocentric ideology grounded in the assumptions that slaves did not construct permanent marriages, did not establish strong emotional ties to their children, or did not value extended kinship networks."[17] As such, slave marriages were never recorded in the county court house but, perhaps, if the slaves were lucky, by the master himself.

Even if a child lived with both his slave mother and father, the owner often denied any "acknowledgement of the father's role—biologically, emotionally, socially or materially."[18] The child's identification was through their mother. Since owners rarely considered slave marriages legitimate, there were instances of polygyny among those held in bondage—with the consent of the owners. Former slave Israel Massie told of how he found many wives among his fellow slaves:

> Ef I liked ya, I just go an' tell masrster I wanted ya an' he give his consent . . . Ef I see another gal over dar on another plantation, I'd go an' say to de gal's marster, 'I want Jinny fer a wife' . . . I got two wives now . . . Do ya kno' women den didn't think hard of each other? Got along fine together.[19]

The result of these polygynous family situations was that it increased female-dominated households among slaves. Slave adults had no legal claim over their children—they were considered the master's property—and slave fathers, in particular, "retained no legitimate right to command visitation privileges nor to maintain linkages with their children."[20]

As both European slave traders and their African accomplices advanced slavery on the continent, David Brion Davis writes, they preferred captured men, not women, which only reduced the numbers of men for marriage. This resulted in a "preponderance of women in many West African societies," which "helped to increase polygyny and more rapid reproduction."[21]

It's possible that polygyny survived among slaves in the United States because of their native land's tradition of oral story telling. As a result of this tradition, Harold Courlander writes, "it is abundantly evident that many tangible elements of African ways, customs, attitudes, values and view of life survived the Atlantic crossing."[22]

Joseph Holloway (1990), in his book *Africanisms in American Culture*, documents many African derived American cultural practices. The American West, for example, had significant numbers of black cowboys and an African-derived grazing pattern. Other contributions to U.S. culture include language (the southern speech dialect with African tonal language influences). Foods such as Southern cooking and soul food are now standard American fare. Musical creativity includes the banjo, an African-derived instrument and its role in bluegrass music. Gospel and jazz, to name but two other examples, are noteworthy. Holloway, in fact, believes what makes Euro-Americans distinct from Europeans is primarily the cultural creativity of African Americans.

THE CIVIL WAR'S CONCLUSION AND AFRICAN AMERICAN MIGRATION

With the Civil War's end, newly freed black men and women didn't publicly continue polygyny. "Former slaves hoping to legitimize their domestic world through acquisition of a marriage license had to publicly abandon polygyny," writes Brenda Stevenson.[23]

For the first 50 years after the Civil War, many African Americans remained primarily in the rural South. But in the late 19th century, starting after 1880, and into the first decades of the 20th century, as the South began to industrialize, African Americans began to leave their rural surroundings for jobs in the "sawmills, coal mines, lumber and turpentine camps, and railroad construction sites."[24]

In those same years following the Civil War, African Americans were also migrating from the South to the North, as Andrew Billingsley writes, and this migration pattern began impacting racial attitudes among white settlers in northern cities. By 1910, he writes, "the black ghetto began to take hold. . . . And by 1910 blacks were rigidly segregated in separate neighborhoods."[25]

As for African American family units, Williams writes, most were marked by two parents and were "relatively stable units" through the end of World War II.[26] While African Americans were experiencing tremendous amounts of racial discrimination and difficulty advancing themselves economically and politically between the end of the Civil War through the end of World War II, "ex-slaves held on to their families and their religion," Dr. Billingsley writes.[27]

After World War II, life for African Americans changed dramatically. They were increasingly living in urban areas throughout the country. And because they were often in ghettos—which are short on jobs—African American men, as well as women, found themselves without work, and it impacted their family life. As Williams writes, "Without decent work, men simply do not settle down to raise families; and when there is not enough money to meet familial needs, couples, even if one or both are working, find it difficult to stay together."[28]

CENSUS NUMBERS

African American women started outnumbering African American men with the 1840 U.S. Census. The difference continued to increase and in 2010, when the last Census was conducted, there were 1.8 million more African American women than men, about 20.3 million to about 18.5 million.[29]

A closer look at the latest Census numbers shows that there are 500,000 more African American women than men between 20 and 44, the prime marrying and child rearing ages. The latest Census figures count about 6.6 million African American men between those ages to 7.2 million African American women in the same age range.[30]

One of the reasons for this numerical difference, writes Williams, is that black men, more so than black women, are homicide victims. "The homicide rate combined with the disproportionate number of deaths of black males from cancer, heart disorders, strokes, cirrhosis of the liver, and countless accidental causes means a black male life expectancy almost ten years shorter than the United States average," Williams writes.[31]

Also reducing the number of marriageable African American men is the fact that about 600,000 of them are in jail, which, according to the latest numbers from the Bureau of Justice Statistics, is about 38 percent of the prison population in the United States.[32]

The Census Bureau numbers from 2010 also show that African American families and household arrangements are usually at odds compared to the Caucasian population[33]:

- While just over 6 million African Americans own a house or a condominium, 7.6 million rent. In comparison, 63 million Caucasians own housing and 26 million rent. About 6.2 million Latinos own a house or a condominium but just over 7 million rent.
- When married and unmarried households are tallied up, there are more unmarried households among African Americans than there are married ones, 5 million to 3.8 million. In comparison, there are 46 million married households to 30.5 million unmarried households among Caucasians; 6.4 million married households among Latinos to 2.9 million unmarried households among them; and there are 2.7 million married Asian households to 1.19 million unmarried households among Asians.
- When marriages are added up among these groups, we see more "never married" African Americans than "now married," about 14.5 million to 8.7 million. Among Caucasians, 97.8 million report being married, while about 53 million report being never married. With Latinos, 14.8 million reported being never married, to 15.9 million report being married. Among Asians, nearly 7 million report being married while about 3.8 million say they're never married.[34]

WHAT'S A WOMAN TO DO?

Ralph Richard Banks, a Stanford University law professor, shows in his book *Is Marriage for White People? How the African American Marriage Decline Effects Everyone*, that African American women are now outpacing African American men in education and income and, as a result, are not very likely to marry.[35] Since African American women tend to refrain from dating and marrying anyone but black men, Banks suggests they're doing themselves, as well as African Americans as a whole, a disservice.

Banks says the scarcity of marriageable black men makes the ones that are desirable—who are educated and hold a job—quite powerful, especially in their relationships with black women. "One important source of power is the set of options that each party has outside of the relationship," he writes. "The better one's options outside of the relationship, the more power one has within it. . . . Because black men, successful ones in particular, are scare and black women are not, black men wield greater power as they negotiate relationships with black women," he adds.[36]

Thus, Banks proposes that black women do just like black men—date and marry outside of the race; in other words, African American women should date and marry white men. If there's any hesitation by black women to dating and marrying white men, Banks says, it may be due to them seeing a white men's heritage as a racist, maybe even as a slave owner.[37]

If African American women can overcome their perceptions, Banks says, black men may begin to realize that their "sisters" have the same options and the same power they do. As a result, black men will begin taking a second look at black women.[38]

The most comprehensive survey of dating and lifestyle habits among African American women appears to suggest, however, that Banks' solutions to dating, and eventually marriage, are difficult to implement. A survey of more than 800 black women, conducted by the *Washington Post* and the Kaiser Family Foundation, reported that they are "less likely than other women to receive messages of interest from men of other races." In addition, researchers discovered, the lack of interest in black women is because of a "social hierarchy that still undervalues them and unflattering stereotypes of black women—loud, aggressive—that remain in popular culture."[39]

"Some minority men will prefer the top group, the historically forbidden group (white women)," said University of Iowa Law School Professor Adrien Wing, who's written about polygamy, in an interview with the book's coauthor. In her many years of teaching, she's witnessed the dating patterns of young black men and young black women. She says she's seen black women go out of their way to attract a black man. "Women are fighting for them. You have [black] guys who wouldn't be a good catch but one [black] woman is doing his homework, another is lending him her car, another is cooking for him and yet another is doing his laundry," Wing said during the interview. "I encourage black women to think outside the box. You can't look for a Barack Obama. Even if his wife were to pass away or they would divorce, this kind of man would be snatched up immediately. They're not going to be on the market for long. "I encourage interracial dating and dating and marrying someone who doesn't have a college degree," she added.[40]

The arguments made by both Banks and Wing have some merit, based on the latest survey from the Pew Research Center. In a study titled "Marrying Out," the Pew Research Center reported that nearly 15 percent of all new marriages in the United States in 2008 were interracial. In particular, the study reported, 22 percent of "all black male newlyweds in 2009 married outside their race, compared with just 9 percent of black female newlyweds."[41]

The report went onto to say, "White-Hispanic couples accounted for about 4-in-10 (41%) of such new marriages; white-Asian couples made up 15%; and white-black couples made up 11%."[42] The study also reports that "of the 3.8 million adults who married in 2008, 9% of whites, 16% of blacks, 26% of Hispanics and 31% of Asians married someone whose race or ethnicity was different from their own. For whites these shares are more than double what they had been in 1980 and for blacks they are nearly triple."[43]

THE PROTESTS OF ONE AFRICAN AMERICAN FEMALE

In 2010, the U.S. Census Bureau reported that nearly 67 percent of all births in the African American community were to single women. Of the 638,440 black women who gave birth, 210,983 were married; the remaining 427,457 were single.[44] All told, the Census Bureau reports, about 5.8 million African American children are living in a single parent household compared to nearly 3.7 million African American children living in a married couple household.[45]

As Niara Sudarkasa sees it, numbers like these, when viewed by the white majority in the United States, might be seen as tragic because children, when born out of wedlock, are considered illegitimate or are being brought up, it's implied, by an unstable single mother. As Sudarkasa sees it, nothing could be further from the truth: "there are many mature Black women who are heading families today by necessity or by choice. To characterize their families as 'unstable' or 'pathological' simply because they do not conform to the nuclear family ideal . . . is unfounded and irresponsible."[46]

The other issue, often discussed when it comes to the well-being of children in single mother households is the lack of a father. Here, again, Sudarkasa sees the situation differently:

> discussions of family stability that focus only on the roles of husband and wife or father and mother overlook the stability and support that traditionally have been provided by a nucleus of consanguineal relatives in African American households headed by women. The instability of the marital bond cannot be taken as an infallible barometer of family instability among African Americans because they have maintained the African commitment to 'blood' kin

and have used those bonds of kinship as building blocks for a significant proportion of their households and families.[47]

The thrust of her book is that African American families have been viewed, for about a century, through the prism of the (white) nuclear family, which is seen, by most social commentators, as the only valid family system in the United States. She says African American families have historically borrowed from the African homeland in creating extended families: "Black families in the U.S. have conceptualized these institutions as aberrant forms of the nuclear family rather than as readaptions of the African extended families out of which they evolved. The conditions of 'the slave plantation' made it impossible for Blacks to form African-type extended family households."[48]

In other words, as Dr. Sudarkasa sees it, African Americans are denied their heritage's family structure because they're culturally Americans with no African-derived ethnic heritage. The structure they're forced to live with—nuclear and monogamous—is completely at odds with family patterns their ancestors, potentially even their extended families, knew in Africa.

AFRICANA WOMANISM

Clenora Hudson-Weems (2006) has developed an ideological position known as "Africana womanism," a position that adds an ethnic dimension to a critique of feminism as advocated by both black and white feminists. She believes that her term "Africana Womanism" has grown out of a need to recognize that women from Africa have a common struggle against racism, as well as historical and cultural commonalities that serve to set them apart from other women in the United States and elsewhere.

Although gender may be an appropriate issue worthy of central concern among feminists, for African American women the issues of racism, class oppression, and ethnic-cultural difference are also of prime importance. Black men and black women share a common, African-derived ethnic heritage, and the experience of racial exploitation sets them both apart from white women and white men. Indeed, crisis polygamy is itself a direct response, as noted previously, to racial factors affecting primarily black men.

Hudson-Weems (2006) names 18 values or features that collectively define the Africana woman as a distinct, culturally specific person. For instance, she notes that the Africana woman is, among other features, family centered, united with men in the struggle against racism, spiritual, male-compatible, respectful of elders, mothering, and nurturing.

The Africana womanism ideology needs to take into account the male counterpart, whom Hudson-Weems sees as linked to women in culturally appropriate ways. Thus, she presents 18 concomitant features that characterize the Africana man. These include: respect for women, respect for elders, a nonthreatening attitude to his companion, ambition, fathering, family centeredness, and commitment to struggle.[49]

Hudson-Weems derives these values for men and women from an original African cosmology and suggests that the current situation in which Africana men and women find themselves is not to be understood in terms of following their traditions but rather in terms of the impact of foreign religious and political ideologies in which female subjugation is inherent. Hudson-Weems urges men and women of all ethnic groups to combine in the struggle against these forces of the modern world where patriarchal institutions and racist and sexist norms prevail.

Hudson-Weems's ideology neither denies nor endorses man-sharing, but it does invite us to consider a cultural dimension when evaluating this practice. For example, as already mentioned, the importance of children is a very central norm in the African American experience. Carol Stack (1974) describes the joy of children as "give me a little sugar" in reference to adults' delight in passing around and holding their own and other people's children. Joyce Aschenbrenner (1983) reports a similar focus.

The material overall on African American family life clearly shows that Hudson-Weems is correct in her claim that strong family values, for both men and women, are an extremely important cultural heritage and a potential future model for the upbringing of children who are so highly valued. Given Hudson-Weems' concern for African derivation, the material on polygamy from Africa in this book is most relevant to her ideology and for those who would apply it to the man-sharing debate in this country, both within and outside the African American community.

CORRECTING WHAT'S GONE WRONG— POLYGYNY'S DEBATE

In at least that last 20 years, there's been a strong debate within the African American community about the best way to repair family life. African American families, as we've seen, have suffered from a variety of negative influences including slavery, when black families were broken apart by slave masters; economic deprivation; racism and, since the first part of the 19th century, which has only grown exponentially since then, a demographic problem: there are more African American women than men.

As a result of the demographic issue especially, some African Americans think plural marriage should be a viable option in spite of how the U.S.'s larger society—the one that lives outside the LDS faith—view polygyny, often dismissing it as nothing more than a sex system.

Professor Kilbride witnessed some of this debate in 1993, when he attended a panel discussion at Temple University in Philadelphia, hosted by the Delaware Valley Association of Black Psychologists, titled, "Man-Sharing: African American Male/Female Relationships in the Nineties." Kilbride observed the meeting, with the hopes that he might be able to interview some of its participants at a later date.[50]

The panel included a counselor from a neighboring university, two psychologists, and a university archivist familiar with the literature on polygyny. Two were male and two were female. There was a very lively moderator and several officers of the association offered opening and closing remarks. The first speaker was a young woman who said that she and her friends had shared a man at one time or another. She was understanding but not enthusiastic about man-sharing. Another panelist, a man, said that while he wasn't against polygyny, he was not its advocate either. He said his wife told him he was "crazy" not to condemn it—which revealed, as has been seen often, a gender bias against the idea.

He had two points: First, he said, it is very Western to link polygyny only with sex and see it as unethical in terms of sexual morality. Second, he said, to overcome the stigma of polygyny, society needs to become more accepting of multiple relationships and understand that people have the capacity to love more than one person simultaneously.

Another speaker, a woman psychologist, did not see man-sharing as an alternative, arguing that it would not address a woman's emotional requirements, commitment needs, and desire for parenting help. She thought that man-sharing would only increase sexuality transmitted diseases among African Americans as well as the number of children in households headed by women.

And, as a pragmatic matter, she asked who would be responsible for teaching people conditioned to living in dyads how to live in triads. She felt, overall, that polygyny would cause more problems than it would solve. Her short-term intimate partner solutions to man shortage faced in the African American community included lesbianism and interracial, heterosexual relationships.

The final speaker, a male archivist, who had lived in Nigeria, provided many cross-cultural examples in which polygyny builds and unites families. A man from Ghana, and another man from Nigeria, both in the audience, made comments along these lines, too. The archivist wasn't advocating polygyny, but he didn't think it should be banned either, particularly in a society that tolerates both prostitution and extramarital affairs. His biggest concern about man-sharing was that it had the potential to release men of any familial responsibility.

Kilbride's overall impression of this meeting was that the women tended to oppose man-sharing whereas the men tended to approve of it. One woman commented that people needed to learn from Africa, where polygyny is practiced responsibly. One man said society's moral level needed to be raised because there was no reason to expect men to act better if polygyny came about without an improvement in sexual behavior.

In her closing remarks, the president of the association said that she did not want to endorse or oppose polygyny. She said her experience in Nigeria made her identity as an African more salient and suggested that African Americans explore their African roots and their own reverence for God.

POLYGYNY'S ACCEPTANCE

Patricia Dixon-Spear, a professor in the African American Studies Department at Georgia State University, has served the same scholarly role for African American polygyny that Janet Bennion has for the FLDS. Dr. Dixon-Spear's work as an insider to the culture provides superb ethnographic material, especially rich in a woman's viewpoint.

Dixon-Spear (2009) says the argument against polygyny is ill founded—because it assumes it's all about male domination—and suggests that women, especially in the African American community, will achieve greater equality in the United States if both plural marriage and monogamy live side-by-side.

Another part of her argument goes very much against some of the country's leading feminists from the 1960s. Dr. Dixon-Spear writes, "Because the Greco-Roman and European-American forms of patriarchy are often used as the basis of feminist analysis, the social structures and practices of peoples in other cultures throughout the world are often inadequately examined."[51]

In other words, she's suggesting that if you're white—and not a Mormon—your European, Judeo-Christian background as well as other cultural influences, some which date back to the Ancient Greeks and Romans, prevent you from seeing the benefits of polygyny.

As a result of her research, Dixon-Spear advocates for polygyny as an option for African Americans. She writes, "African Americans can turn to Africa for social structures that are more natural for us, and more conducive for our social reality." The question that Dixon-Spear seeks to answer is that if "men cannot engage in such relationships without participation of women, how can they be structured in ways that are more advantageous for everyone involved?"[52] Polygyny's benefits, she says, include the following:

[it] can eliminate the potential for dishonesty and deceit . . . as the basis for relationship formation, provide a larger pool of men for women to select from,

avoid women being reduced to their sexuality, potentially hold men account-
able to all women with whom they enter into sexual relationships, and provide
a mechanism for women and men to work together to build our relationships,
families and communities.[53]

Her research took place among three African American communities, each
differing in its rationale for polygyny. She writes about polygyny in the Ausar
Auset Society, among African Hebrew Israelites, and among American
Muslims.

The Ausar Auset Society, founded in 1973, provides an African tradition–
based model for life in North America. Headquartered in New York City,
there are 50 chapters in various countries. Each community operates its own
social center, school, and food stores. Polygyny is accepted based on indigenous African cultural and spiritual beliefs.[54]

Since women outnumber men, one advantage of polygyny is to insure that
all women will benefit from family life. Polygyny works well for most women
and a major benefit is childcare help. Dixon-Spear also notes that a big factor
in polygyny's success or failure is how husbands treat their wives.[55]

Polygyny isn't perfect, Dixon-Spear reports. Sister-wives disagree over
parenting styles and jealously among the women can exist.[56] The professor
writes, "One wife pointed out that . . . his first wife is his wife" but when his
first wife and her husband took care of her in sickness, she happily concluded
it was a "family affair," and she was a valued member of the family after all.[57]

Life without legal standing, however, adds to marital strain in any marriage, polygynous or not. The legal issues for the Ausar Auset Society, like
with the FLDS, includes property, taxes, and health insurance, where only
the husband and the first wife have benefits as a legally recognized couple.

The African Hebrew Israelites is a community of African Americans who
have been living in Israel since 1969. This community claims it is descended
from Abraham and lives a biblical way of life, which includes polygyny. Israel tolerates polygyny in this community, although only one wife is legally
recognized.

Dixon-Spear recorded many advantages with polygyny from the women
she interviewed. Positive attributes included a sense of family from sister-
wives and their children, a family for wives without children, childcare help
for mothers and other household responsibilities, and assistance in providing
emotional and physical needs for their husband.[58]

Similar to FLDS women, women in this community reported that polygyny's advantages also included sister-wives at home caring for the children
while other sister wives worked outside the home. Sister-wife bonding also
marked the community, with one woman telling Dixon-Spear, it is "great
having a friend that you can talk and laugh with."[59] There is some jealousy

among the women. But Dixon-Spear reports that prayer helps many women deal with jealousy. One co-wife said, "when I want to be with him and I can't, that's when I pray because . . . thoughts . . . I am really shocked to know I am having."[60]

Polygyny among American Muslims, Dixon-Spear writes, is problematic when it's examined against the Ausar Auset Society and the African Hebrew Israelites. Part of the problem American Muslims face, similar to the Ausar Auset Society, is that they practice polygyny in a country where it's illegal but also where there's little cultural understanding of plural marriage.

She writes that the Muslim community differs from the other two communities, saying, "there is little or no support for polygyny, there is a general unacceptance of it by women, and the women live in separate residences."[61]

Dixon-Spear's overall message in this comparative study concerning women's views is that plural marriage's quality can be summarized as "it depends." Success depends not only on personal characteristics of the spouses—just as it does with monogamous marriage—but also on cultural, political and the religious framework shaping its practices in a particular location.

This book's coauthor reached out to Dixon-Spear for a follow-up interview, inquiring about her research and her experiences teaching young college students about the possibility of plural marriage. Before researching her book, the professor said, she was opposed to polygyny but changed her mind as she learned more about the practice and compared it to African American family life. "It makes a lot of sense to me, particularly after I look at a lot of black communities where the marriage rate is very low," she said. "African American men are marginalized in the opportunity structure, making it difficult for African American women to find eligible men. "There are a lot of single mothers. Older [black] women are more open to it [polygyny]," she added.[62]

When asked how her students react to the prospect of polygyny, she said, "I can see from their facial expressions that they're really pissed off about it. Part of this is because there is a perception that men are unfaithful. . . . But once I explain to them [her students] the demographics and get them to imagine being 40 [years old], alone, not married and wanting a family, they begin to make the shift. They become more open to it," she added.[63]

The question that remains unanswered—and may never be answered—is whether polygyny will ever become culturally accepted in a Eurocentric society like the United States. Moreover, slavery and post–Civil War attitudes and actions by segments of the country's white majority took a toll on African Americans. Blacks were forced to do something no other immigrant group had to do—come here against their will and then, once their freedom was granted, as some African American writers have said, forced to uphold U.S. cultural standards in family life.

Through his many years of studying the immigrant experience in the United States, the great lesson Oscar Handlin taught is that immigrants are more than just numbers on a ship or in an airplane. They're a cultural influence. Each immigrant group, regardless of its origin or method by which it came to America's shores shapes the politics, culture, religion, economics, outlook, and perceptions of U.S. society. Perhaps African Americans will make plural marriage an accepted marital practice in the United States.

NOTES

1. Nathan Hare and Julia Hare, eds., *Crisis in Black Sexual Politics* (San Francisco: Black Think Tank, 1989) p. 26.

2. Erik Eckholm, "With Higher Numbers of Prisoners Comes a Tide of Troubled Children," *The New York Times*, July 5, 2009, p. 13.

3. Jane Siegel, *Disrupted Childhoods: Children of Women in Prison* (Piscataway, NJ: Rutgers University Press, 2011), p. 3.

4. Page interview with Patricia Dixon-Spear.

5. Joseph Scott, "The Sociology of the Other Woman: Man-Sharing," *Crisis in Black Sexual Politics*, ed. Nathan Hare and Julia Hare (San Francisco: Black Think Tank, 1989), p. 107.

6. Oscar Handlin, *Race and Nationality in American Life* (Boston: Little, Brown, and, Company, 1957) pp. 205 and 206.

7. Alexis de Tocquville, *Democracy in America*, vol. 1, ed. Phillips Bradley (New York: Vintage Books, 1945), pp. 370 and 371. This famous book was first published in 1835.

8. Wilma King, *African American Childhoods: Historical Perspectives from Slavery* (New York: Palgrave MacMillian, 2005) p. 14.

9. Ibid.

10. Ronald Segal, *The Black Diaspora: Five Centuries of the Black Experience Outside Africa* (New York: Farrer, Straus and Giroux, 1995), p. 4.

11. David Davis Brion, *Inhuman Bondage: The Rise and Fall of Slavery in the New World* (New York: Oxford University Press, 2006), p. 106.

12. Wilma A. Dunaway, *The African-American Family in Slavery and Emancipation* (Cambridge: Cambridge University Press, 2003), p. 68.

13. Henry Wiencek, *An Imperfect God: George Washington, His Slaves and the Creation of America* (New York: Farrar, Straus, and Giroux, 2003), p. 280.

14. Brenda E. Stevenson, "Black Family Structure in Colonial and Antebellum Virginia: Amending the Revisionist Perspective," in *The Decline in Marriage Among African Americans*, ed. M. Belinda Tucker and Claudia Mitchell-Kernan (New York: Russell Sage Foundation, 1995), p. 38.

15. This assertion is made by Nell Irvin Painter, Angela Davis, and Barbara Omelade.

16. Wiencek, *An Imperfect God*, p. 184.

17. Dunaway, *The African-American Family*, p. 53.

18. Stevenson, "Black Family Structure in Colonial and Antebellum Virginia," p. 38.

19. Ibid., p. 50.

20. Dunaway, *The African-American Family*, p. 64.

21. Davis Brion, *Inhuman Bondage*, p. 100.

22. Harold Courlander, *A Treasury of Afro-American Folklore* (New York: Crown Publishers, 1976), p. 9.

23. Stevenson, "Black Family Structure in Colonial and Antebellum Virginia," p. 51.

24. Michael W. Williams, "Polygamy and the Declining Male to Female Ratio in Black Communities: A Social Inquiry," in *Black Families: Interdisciplinary Perspectives*, ed. Harold E. Cheatham and James B. Stewart (New Brunswick, NJ: Transaction Publishers, 1990) p. 177.

25. Andrew Billingsley, *Climbing Jacob's Ladder: The Enduring Legacy of African-American Families* (New York: Simon & Schuster, 1993), p. 124.

26. Williams, "Polygamy and the Declining Male to Female Ratio in Black Communities," p. 181.

27. Billingsley, *Climbing Jacob's Ladder*, p. 127.

28. Williams, "Polygamy and the Declining Male to Female Ratio in Black Communities," p. 183.

29. U.S. Census Bureau, "Sex By Age (Black or African American Alone) 2010 American Community Survey 1 year estimates," http://factfinder2.census.gov/faces/tableservices/jsf/pages/productview.xhtml?pid=ACS_10_1YR_B01001B&prodType=table.

30. Ibid.

31. Williams, "Polygamy and the Declining Male to Female Ratio in Black Communities," p. 174.

32. U.S. Department of Justice, Bureau of Justice Statistics, "Prisoners in 2008," December 2009, http://bjs.ojp.usdoj.gov/content/pub/ascii/p08.txt.

33. It should be noted that the Census Bureau continues to use the term "Caucasian" when describing ethnic differences in the population.

34. U.S. Census Bureau, "American Community Survey, 2010," http://factfinder2.census.gov/faces/nav/jsf/pages/searchresults.xhtml?ref=top&refresh=t.

35. Ralph Richard Banks, *Is Marriage for White People? How the African American Marriage Decline Affects Everyone* (New York: Dutton, 2011), p. 45.

36. Ibid., p. 180.

37. Ibid., p. 152.

38. Ibid., p. 181.

39. Krissah Thompson, "Survey Paints Portrait of Black Women in America," *The Washington Post*, January 22, 2012, http://www.washingtonpost.com/politics/survey-paints-portrait-of-black-women-in-america/2011/12/22/gIQAvxFcJQ_story.html.

40. Page interview with Adrien Wing.

41. Paul Taylor, "Marrying Out: One in Seven New U.S. Marriages is Interracial and Interethnic," Pew Research Center, June 15, 2010, http://pewresearch.org/pubs/1616/american-marriage-interracial-interethnic.

42. Ibid.

43. Ibid.

44. "Women 15–50 Years who had a Birth in the Past 12 Months by Marital Status (Black or African American Alone, 2006—2010 American Community Survey 5-Year Estimates," U.S. Census Bureau, http://factfinder2.census.gov/faces/tableser vices/jsf/pages/productview.xhtml?pid=ACS_10_1YR_B13002B&prodType=table.

45. "Living Arrangements of Children Under 18/1 and Marital Status of Parents by Age, Sex, Race and Hispanic Origin and Selected Characteristics of the Child for All Children: 2011," U.S. Census Bureau, http://www.census.gov/hhes/families/data/cps2010.html.

46. Niara Sudarkasa, *The Strength of Our Mothers: African & African American Women & Families: Essays and Speeches* (Trenton, NJ: Africa World Press, 1996), p. 38.

47. Ibid., p. 27.

48. Ibid., p. 7.

49. Clenora Hudson-Weems, "Africana Womanism: Black Feminism, African Feminism, Womanism," in *Black Studies: From the Pyramids and Pan Africanism and Beyond*, ed. William "Nick" Nelson Jr. (New York: McGraw-Hill, 2006), p. 180.

50. These are the observations of Kilbride from attending about man-sharing, hosted by the Delaware Valley Association of Black Psychologists, 1993.

51. Patricia Dixon-Spear, *We Want for Our Sisters What We Want for Ourselves: African American Women Who Practice Polygyny by Consent* (Baltimore, MD: Imprint Editions, 2009), p. xxxi.

52. Ibid., p. xxviii.

53. Ibid., p. xix.

54. Ibid., p. 263.

55. Ibid., p. 267.

56. Ibid., p. 159.

57. Ibid., p. 155.

58. Ibid., p. 167.

59. Ibid., p. 131.

60. Ibid., p. 134.

61. Ibid., p. 268.

62. Page interview of Dixon-Spear.

63. Ibid.

10

Polygyny's Purgatory

If the United States never changed a law—just kept the ones since George Washington was inaugurated president—life would look far differently than it does today. Only men would vote. Women would have few, if any, legal rights. Blacks would be enslaved. There wouldn't be a Bill of Rights. The voting age would be 21. Indeed, if U.S. culture and society remained what they were in the 1780s, it is very likely women would be relegated to handling housework and divorce would be almost out of the question.

But life changes. Women vote, 18-year-olds acquired voting rights in 1971, and African Americans are no longer held in bondage. And whites and blacks are even marrying one another. One legal scholar writes that U.S. immigration law—which prohibits polygamy—may be closely examined because the country recently issued special visas to Iraqis, some of whom may practice plural marriage, to settle in the United States.

Arguing the merits of same-gender marriage, *Atlantic Monthly* contributor Andrew Sullivan said this about one of society's oldest institutions: "if marriage were the same today as it has been for 2,000 years, it would be possible to marry a 12-year-old you had never met, to own a wife as property and dispose of her at will, or to imprison a person who married someone of a different race. And it would be impossible to get a divorce."[1] Sullivan goes on to write that failure to allow changes in an institution that dates back to ancient Mesopotamia and ancient Greece is akin to saying, "New York's senators are men and have always been men,"[2] and, thus, a woman should never be elected to the United States Senate. Advancing that line of thinking, you could also say:

- Since people have never had the right to divorce, they don't need that right today.
- Since women have never voted, women don't need to vote now.

- Since Africans have always been enslaved in the United States, they should remain enslaved.
- Since women have always tended to household chores, they should carry on with their domestic duties today because they're better suited to it.
- Since marriage has always been between two people of the opposite gender, there's no reason to modify it now.
- Since Judeo-Christian and Roman-Greco-influenced societies have always preferred monogamy, there's no room for polygyny in the United States today.
- Since monarchs have always been empowered by the Divine right to rule, no one else has political authority—now or ever.

The issue of the laws reflecting the times in which people live can be a challenge. Some of this is playing out in the debate about same-gender marriage. But one of the first examples the United States experienced—where it's laws didn't necessarily measure up to modern times—was in its obscenity rules.

AN OVERVIEW OF THE CHANGING
LAWS ON OBSCENITY

Until the middle of the 20th century, U.S. obscenity laws were based on a legal ruling in Great Britain from 1868. Britain's Hicklin decision, as it was called, was still influencing American laws in 1956, when Samuel Roth was convicted of distributing *Lady Chatterley's Lover* and *Fanny Hill* through the mail. Laws from the 19th and at least the early part of the 20th centuries assumed that the government had "a legitimate and paternalistic interest in preventing moral harm to its citizens"[3] and, thus, books were considered pornographic if they contained one paragraph considered lewd.[4]

As Gay Talese writes in his book, *Thy Neighbor's Wife*, the Hicklin decision stated, "the test of obscenity is whether the tendency of the matter charged as obscenity is to deprave and corrupt those whose minds are open to such immoral influences and into whose hands a publication of this sort may fall."[5]

Jerome Frank, a federal appeals court judge, who heard the Roth case, saw the issue this way: while "he did concede that sexual literature was often stimulating . . . the same could be said for perfume and dozens of other commercial products that were sent through the mail and were displayed in stores; and while photographs of nude women undoubtedly aroused men, men could as easily be aroused by newspaper advertisements showing women in bathing suits and lingerie."

So while there were print ads in newspapers in the 19th century, when the Hicklin decision came down, the advertising industry, as well as women's clothing styles, had changed considerably since 1868. Thus, as Judge Frank saw it, the obscenity laws needed to catch up with the times—nearly 90 years after Hicklin. Frank recommended that the Supreme Court review the Roth case and update the legal interpretation of obscenity:

> To vest a few fallible men—prosecutors, judges, jurors (and the United States Postmaster General)—with vast powers of literary or artistic censorship, is to convert them into what J.S. Mill [John Stewart Mill] called a "moral police" is to make them despotic arbiters of literary products. If one day they ban mediocre books as obscene, another day they may do likewise to a work of genius.[6]

As the 20th century progressed, the obscenity laws changed through a series of Supreme Court rulings. In the Roth case, the Supreme Court ruled that Hicklin was unconstitutional and that the new test of obscenity was determined on "whether to the average person, applying contemporary community standards, the dominant theme of the material taken as a whole appeals to the prurient interest."[7]

The last ruling—as far as print and filmed media is concerned—from the Supreme Court on obscenity was in 1987, when the court determined that obscenity was based on whether the average person would find the material, as a whole, obscene or determine that there was something in the book, movie, or magazine, however morally challenging, that was of socially redeeming value.[8]

The Supreme Court has even ruled on obscenity as it applies to the Internet. It is difficult to regulate the Internet since a website developed in one country can be seen in another. Still, First Amendment rights on the Internet have been upheld, but the Supreme Court has also upheld the constitutionality of the Child Internet Protection Act, which requires schools and public libraries to "include technology protection measures to block or filter Internet access to pictures that are: (1) obscene; (2) child pornography; (3), harmful to minors."[9]

While laws defining free speech and obscenity have changed over the course of the 20th century and even in the 21st—for the better, we might add—it's likely, if the past is prologue, these laws will be challenged again. The only thing that appears to remain certain is the ban on child pornography will continue.

PLURAL MARRIAGE IN THE UNITED STATES

Today, whether you watch it on television, read some of the latest books, or follow Utah's leading newspapers, people are living in polygynous marriages. Whether it's reality television star Kody Brown and his wives or Joe Darger and his wives, these people—fundamentalist Mormons—are, by today's standards, living outside of society's legal boundaries, putting their lifestyle out in the open and by doing so, challenging U.S. law, and certainly the country's cultural norms, that the only type of marriage that should be recognized is monogamous—gay, lesbian, or straight.

"They're coming out of the closet and saying we're not going to allow society to stigmatize us," one Salt Lake City civil rights attorney told the book's coauthor about people like Brown and Darger, who are making themselves public figures. "As they see it, God told them to do this [plural marriage]. . . . "They're saying, 'We're tax-paying citizens, we live normal lives, we're your next door neighbor,'" he added.[10]

It's clear that by using the media, whether it's television or book publishing, the Browns and the Dargers are seeking to gain acceptance, however reluctant, for their lifestyle and religious practices. If they're successful and polygyny is legalized, it wouldn't be the first time in the country's history that marriage laws were changed so they're fair, equitable and fit the times in which people live.

INTERRACIAL MARRIAGE

More than 100 years after the Civil War ended, the country's antimiscegenation laws were overturned. In 1967 the Supreme Court ruled in *Loving vs. Virginia*, that Virginia's ban on interracial marriage was unconstitutional, ending the legal restrictions across the country to prevent Caucasians and African Americans from marrying one another.

In June 1958, Mildred Jeter, an African American woman, and Richard Loving, a white man, were married in Washington DC. They returned to Virginia—where they were from—and were arrested in July for violating the state's laws prohibiting interracial marriage. The judge suspended their sentence, telling the Lovings he would do so on the basis that they would no longer live in Virginia. The couple returned to Washington and eventually hired an attorney to take up their cause.

At issue was Virginia's Racial Integrity Act of 1924, which the Supreme Court said in its ruling on the *Loving* case, involved the "absolute prohibition of a 'white person' marrying other than another 'white person.'"[11] Virginia's Supreme Court of Appeals upheld the laws against the Lovings, saying the court "concluded that the State's legitimate purposes were to 'preserve the racial integrity of its citizens' and to prevent 'the corruption of blood,' 'a mongrel breed of citizens,' and 'the obliteration of racial pride,' obviously an endorsement of the doctrine of White Supremacy."[12]

The case moved through a variety of courts until it was finally brought to the U.S. Supreme Court. The court noted in its ruling that Virginia's miscegenation laws applied equally "to whites and Negroes in the sense that members of each race are punished to the same degree." The court also said:

> Thus, the State contends that, because its miscegenation statutes punish equally both the white and the Negro participants in an interracial marriage, these statutes, despite their reliance on racial classifications, do not constitute an invidious discrimination based upon race. The second argument advanced by the State assumes the validity of its equal application theory. The argument is that, if the Equal Protection Clause does not outlaw miscegenation statutes because of their reliance on racial classifications, the question of constitutionality would thus become whether there was any rational basis for a State to treat interracial marriages differently from other marriages. On this question, the State argues, this Court should defer to the wisdom of the state legislature in adopting its policy of discouraging interracial marriages.[13]

The court overturned Virginia's miscegenation laws, as well as those of 15 other states, saying, "The mere 'equal application' of a statute containing racial classifications is enough to remove the classifications from the Fourteenth Amendment's proscription of all invidious racial discriminations."[14] The court also said, "We do not accept the State's contention that these statutes should be upheld if there is any possible basis for concluding that they serve a rational basis."[15]

The Supreme Court's ruling was that Virginia's interracial marriage laws violated the Constitution's Fourteenth Amendment and, specifically, its Equal Protection Clause as well as the Due Process Clause. The court wrote:

> We have consistently denied the constitutionality of measures which restrict the rights of citizens on account of race. There can be no doubt that restricting the freedom to marry solely because of racial classifications violates the central meaning of the Equal Protection Clause. . . . These statutes also deprive the Lovings of liberty without due Process of law in violation of the Due Process Clause of the Fourteenth Amendment. The freedom to marry has long been recognized as one of the vital personal rights essential to the orderly pursuit of happiness by free men.[16]

The Pew Research study cited in chapter 9, titled "The Rise of Intermarriage," (2012) about the numbers of interracial marriages in the United States also suggests that the country is becoming far more tolerant with blacks and whites marrying one another. More than 60 percent of those surveyed in the 2010 study said they would not be disturbed if a "if a family member told them they were going to marry someone from any of three major race/ethnic groups other than their own."[17] Another Pew Research study indicates about two-thirds of whites (64%) feel, "They would be fine with a member of their family marrying a black person, an additional 27 percent would be bothered, but would accept it." Among blacks, 80 percent would accept such marriages and 16 percent would accept it but be bothered by it.[18]

Today same-gender marriage is in the headlines. As of the writing of this book, six states—Connecticut, Iowa, Massachusetts, New Hampshire, New York, and Vermont—allow same-gender marriage as does Washington DC. A federal judge struck down California's Proposition 8, which was approved by the state's voters and did not allow same-gender marriage. It's thought that this ruling will be appealed and, eventually, decided by the U.S. Supreme Court.[19]

THE LEGALITY OF PLURAL MARRIAGE

The first—and only—time the Supreme Court weighed in on polygynous marriage was in January 1879, with the *Reynolds* decision. Writing for the court, Chief Justice Morrison Waite said, "polygamy has always been odious among the northern and western nations of Europe, and, until the establishment of the Mormon Church, was almost exclusively a feature of the life of Asiatic and of African people," and his logic followed:

> At common law, the second marriage was always void (2 Kent, Com. 79), and from the earliest history of England polygamy has been treated as an offence to society. . . . By the statute of 1 James I. (c.11), the offence, if committed in England and Wales, was made punishable in the civil courts, and the penalty was death . . . we think it may safely be said there never has been a time in any State of the Union when polygamy has not been an offence against society, cognizable by the civil courts and punishable with more or less severity.[20]

While the Constitution permits religious freedom, as Chief Justice Waite saw it, there are restrictions to religious practice, especially as it pertained to marriage:

> it is impossible to believe that the constitutional guaranty of religious freedom was intended to prohibit legislation in respect to this most important feature of social life. Marriage, while from its very nature a sacred obligation, is nevertheless, in most civilized nations, a civil contract, and usually regulated by law. Upon it society may be said to be built, and out of its fruits spring social relations and social obligations and duties, with which government is necessarily required to deal.[21]

Waite supports his opinion by citing expert testimony from Professor Francis Lieber, a political analyst: "Professor Lieber says, polygamy leads to the patriarchal principle, and which, when applied to large communities, fetters the people in stationary despotism, while that principle cannot long exist in connection with monogamy."[22] Waite goes on to say that Congress is well within its rights in passing laws that prohibit polygyny: "the statute immediately under consideration is within the legislative power of Congress. It is constitutional and valid as prescribing a rule of action for all those residing in the Territories, and in places over which the United States have exclusive control."[23]

Finally, Waite explains why polygamy is not allowed as a religious practice in the United States:

> Suppose one believed that human sacrifices were a necessary part of religious worship, would it be seriously contended that the civil government under which he lived could not interfere to prevent a sacrifice? Or if a wife religiously believed it was her duty to burn herself upon the funeral pile of her dead husband, would it be beyond the power of the civil government to prevent her belief into practice?[24]

With this ruling, plural marriage was outlawed. The LDS Church would later give up its fight, determining in 1890 that plural marriage would no longer be practiced by its members.

JEFFERSON AND MADISON VS. REYNOLDS— RELIGION AND LEGALITY

There's no shortage of criticism of the *Reynolds* decision. One legal scholar, Jeremy M. Miller, who makes it clear he's not a Mormon, wrote that "polygamy, as practiced by the early Mormons was not obscene, untraditional, dirty, or a threat to society." He went on to write: "the practice is, of course, questionable morally; but it is not questionable 'religiously.' It should have been allowed in the Mormon community because it was an integral part of the Mormon religion. That it categorically was *not* a questionable religious practice makes the *Reynolds* decision seem *even more* aberrant."[25]

Miller says that the world's major religions, with the exception of Christianity, accept polygyny. And in what appears to be an attempt to slap down Waite's thoughts on polygamy in Africa, Miller says, based on what he's studied, plural marriage has not made women subservient. He finishes off his description of African polygamy by comparing it to the morals of many Americans: "In our own society the divorce rate is pathetically high, premarital sex abounds, and adultery is commonplace. Are we so much better than the Africans there studied?"[26]

The crux of Miller's argument against the Reynolds ruling has to do with how the country's Founding Fathers, especially Thomas Jefferson and James Madison, viewed religion. Jefferson took up religion's cause because he thought government had no role in spiritual matters. Madison wrote about religion in The Federalist Papers, a series of documents to support the newly written U.S. Constitution in 1787. Miller writes, "Madison . . . warned about one part of society attacking less powerful parts. He specifically cited the need for protecting the freedom of religion." Jefferson also supported free-dom of religion, Miller writes, because if "men's minds are free" they'll "reach the truth" and society will continue to evolve.[27] The third president also supported the separation of church and state. Miller describes Jefferson's thoughts about religion:

> What Jefferson truly feared was that the free exercise of religion would be impinged, not that a religion would be helped [in apparent opposition to the First Amendment's establishment clause]. . . . It is my tangential contention that the sole purpose and really only virtue of the establishment clause was to insure that the free exercise of religion be protected . . . Jefferson, in fact, was far more concerned with protecting the free exercise of religion.[28]

Miller takes issue with Waite's notion that polygamy's existence within a Western society, like the United States, is problematic for the majority, who would likely continue to practice monogamous marriage, saying it should be tolerated because, when practiced voluntarily, plural marriage "does not cause death or injury."[29]

Miller also points out an interesting nuance about a difference between people practicing polygamy and those who might be described as retaining rather loose morals, especially as it pertains to sexual behavior:

> In polygamy, the husband and particular wife make a permanent commitment to each other. And in the case of the Mormons, they believed their plural marriages to be moral and religious. Thus, in gross absurdity, if *Reynolds* is *still* good law, one can behave in the same way in two circumstances but in one (polygamy) the action is illegal, and in the other (promiscuity) the action is ignored by the law.[30]

There's also an issue about exercising religious beliefs. As Miller shows, critical to religion is exercising ceremonies because it's more than just thoughts or beliefs. It's also about living and practicing the religion. "Were Christianity and Judaism confined merely to their intellectual thought and beliefs, then unarguably their full expression would be clearly shackled," Miller writes.[31]

Finally, Waite argued that polygamy "leads to tyranny." But Miller has an answer for this, too, saying, "religious tolerance fights tyranny. It does not encourage it."[32]

A COURT RULING ON THE EXERCISE OF RELIGION

Keith Sealing, in a lengthy article about polygyny's legal status, writes about one Supreme Court case, likely forgotten, that did more to advance plural marriage's legal recognition than its opponents and, perhaps even its proponents, may realize. In 1993, in the case *Church of the Lukumi Babalu Aye vs. City of Hialeah*, the Supreme Court ruled that the church's religious practice of animal sacrifice could not be thwarted by the City of Hialeah (Florida). Justice Kennedy stated that "petitioners' assertion that animal sacrifice is an integral part of their religion 'cannot be deemed bizarre or incredible.'"[33] As Sealing writes:

> Thus, to translate Justice Kennedy's opening argument into an argument against the anti-polygamy statutes: Mormonism or Mormon Fundamentalism is a religion; polygamy merits First Amendment consideration despite being abhorrent to some; and the fact that polygamy is an integral part of these religions is credible.[34]

Furthermore, Justice Kennedy wrote for the Court, "If the object of the law is to infringe upon or restrict practices because of the religious motivation, the law is not neutral."[35] Sealing appears to conclude that since state laws, like the one in Utah and other southwestern states, prohibiting polygyny are really aimed at the LDS faith, they are, therefore, unconstitutional, meaning plural marriage is constitutional and, therefore, a protected practice under the law.

CHINESE IMMIGRATION

Between 1848 and 1852, about 20,000 Chinese immigrants sailed for the United States, attracted to the country because of the discovery of gold in California. At the time the Chinese were arriving in the United States—and they were a polygynous people, often bringing their second wives as well as their concubines with them—there was also debate in Washington about ways to manage the polygynous Mormons in the Utah territory.

As two legal scholars point out, the country's laws and immigration rules were very much influenced by the reaction to the Chinese, often holding racist overtones. And in a twist that perhaps some didn't expect, today's U.S. immigration laws—shaped by racism—are even sexist, putting power in the hands of polygamous men.

Martha Ertman, a research professor at the University of Maryland's School of Law writes that the problem much of the non-Mormon, white majority in the 19th century had with polygyny is that it was being done by whites—in violation of their racial identity. "According to this view," writes

Ertman, "polygamy was natural for people of Color, but unnatural for White Americans. . . . When Whites engaged in this unnatural practice, antipolygamists contended, they produced a 'peculiar race.' . . . This racialization requires us to ask whether the polygamy ban today continues to import those white supremacist values."[36] Antipolgynists, Professor Ertman shows, were against plural marriage because they saw whites living like Asians and Blacks: "Whites following practices attributed to Asians and Blacks undermined the premises justifying white supremacy. The links between race and Mormon polygamy in many nineteenth century Americans' minds were both tight and complex."[37]

Some of America's racist views against the Chinese in the 19th century included a fear that they might even conquer the West. In February 1879, one Senator, supporting a bill that would limit the number of Chinese on any ship bound for the United States, "framed the issue as a racial contest for dominance of the American West: 'either the Anglo-Saxon race will possess the Pacific slope or the Mongolians will possess it.'"[38]

Ertman also shows the low level of discourse against Mormons by one U.S. government employee assigned to the Utah territory. Benjamin Ferris, in an 1854 report to Congress, wrote "polygamy belongs now to the indolent and opium-eating Turks and Asiatic, the miserable Africans, the North American savages, and the latter-day saints." If polygamy were allowed to continue unabated, Ferris reported, the consequences for Americans could be severe, with a "rapid degeneracy of races."[39]

This racial fear in the 19th century influenced the country's perception of polygamous Mormons, essentially seeing them as barbaric and foreign—a people whose practices needed to be stopped or they'd ruin the country. As Ertman shows, much of this thinking not only influenced the laws written by Congress but also the Supreme Court's ruling against polygyny in 1879.

Ertman also writes about the debate on marriage. The antipolygamists claimed that no reasonable woman would ever enter into a plural marriage. Here again, Ertman shows, the antipolygamists are saying that monogamy is the preferred form of marriage among civilized—read white—people.

Claire Smearman, writing in the *Berkeley Journal of International Law*, reviews how the United States's views on polygyny have influenced the country's immigration laws. Writing in 2009, Smearman says that because the country is offering a special visa to Iraqi nationals who worked for the United States while it was in their homeland, these laws should be examined because some new immigrants and their families will be polygamous.

Current immigration law, she writes, doesn't allow a second wife to immigrate to the United States with her husband and his first wife. In fact, much of today's immigration law, says Smearman, is based on immigration restrictions the country introduced in the 19th century. These laws, the author notes, were racist in outlook, placing prohibitions on people from Asia coming to the United States as well as returning to the country even if they were legal U.S. residents. In addition to the racism, much of the impetus behind these laws, Smearman shows, is a fear of polygamy infecting U.S. culture and marital practices.

Because U.S. immigration law today forbids polygamists from entering the United States, Smearman writes, the result of this policy is likely something few people would expect: it allows a polygamist husband to decide which wife he'll sponsor for entrance into the United States. Smearman writes that "U.S. immigration policy for spouse-based categories empowers a husband in a polygamous marriage to choose which wife he will sponsor for immigration . . . a second or subsequent wife cannot confer or receive status for any family category." This gender discrimination, Smearman writes, is based on "a legacy of centuries-old doctrine of coverture, under which a woman's legal existence merged with that of her husband upon marriage."[40]

Just like domestic marriage laws were changed, enabling whites and black to marry one another, as well as other people from other ethnicities to marry one another, the question that remains answered is whether the United States will change its immigration laws so they also fit the times in which people live. Will they become more beneficial to both genders? Will they stop being influenced by racism and the country's prohibition against polygyny? We don't know. But the next case to be examined just might provide constitutional reasons to reexamine U.S. immigration laws.

LAWRENCE VS. TEXAS, 2003

In 1998, in an apartment outside of Houston, Texas, two men, John Geddes Lawrence and Tyron Garner, were arrested by a Harris County Sheriff. The charge? They were violating the state's antisodomy laws against gay people.

Sodomy, as Slate.com points out, has changed over the years. The term has been used to describe sexual conduct between two men, and it's also been used to describe any kind of sexual conduct between men and women that does not lead—or carry the risk of—pregnancy:

> the majority of anti-sodomy laws, both today and in the past, apply to both heterosexual and homosexual acts. Although we now understand those acts in the main to encompass oral and anal sex, the historians (from the University of Chicago) point out in their brief (to the Supreme Court on behalf of Lawrence and Garner) that at different times 'sodomy' has been defined to include bestiality, mutual masturbation, sex in the wrong position, sex without procreative intent, male-male, and male-female sex, though only rarely female-female.[41]

Slate's reporter, Kristin Eliasberg, wrote that Colonial America made sodomy illegal not only due to the Bible's writings on the topic but also because it had an interest in making sure the New World was populated. "In Ezekiel, the sin of the Sodomites is described as inhospitality. In later theology, sodomy became associated with unnatural sex acts in general but was interpreted broadly and never limited to homosexual sex; in fact it included all forms of non-procreative sex."[42]

In the Supreme Court's *Lawrence* ruling, the justices supporting the 6–3 decision explained that laws against sodomy were to protect children from adults and to have a criminal charge for someone who didn't commit rape as it's usually defined, forcible penetration of a woman's vagina:

> One purpose of these prohibitions was to ensure there would be no lack of coverage if a predator committed a sexual assault that did not constitute rape as defined by the criminal law. Thus the model sodomy indictments presented in the 19th century treatise . . . addressed predatory acts of an adult man against a minor girl or a minor boy . . . 19th century sodomy prosecutions typically involved relations between men and minor girls or minor boys, relations between adults involving force, relations between adults implicating disparity in status, or relations between men and animals.[43]

The Supreme Court stated in *Lawrence* that the case, "does not involve minors . . . persons who might be injured or coerced, or who are situated in relationships where consent might not easily be refused." The case involves "two adults who, with full and mutual consent from each other, engaged in sexual practices common to a homosexual lifestyle."[44]

After a series of lower court rulings, the *Lawrence* case made its way to the Supreme Court in 2002. At issue was whether Texas law restricting homosexual sex violated the Constitution's Fourteenth Amendment, which includes the Equal Protection and Due Process Clauses. The question was this: If a man and woman can legally engage in non-procreative sex with one another, why can't two people sharing the same gender engage in the same kind of sexual activity?

The court ruled in June 2003 on behalf of the men, making antisodomy laws as they applied to same-gender couples in the United States null and void; in addition, the ruling threw out antisodomy laws as they applied to opposite gender couples.[45] As the justices supporting the decision saw it, they were upholding the Fourteenth Amendment's Due Process Clause, meaning if heterosexuals can engage in sexual activity that doesn't include the risk of pregnancy so can people who are gay and lesbian.

With this ruling, some legal scholars say, there's potential to either decriminalize or make polygyny legal. In particular, one legal scholar wrote, "the Court not only declared the Texas statute . . . unconstitutional, it went further to state that the real issue was the ability of individuals to define their own relationships without the threat of being branded 'criminals.'"[46]

Indeed, the court's ruling on *Lawrence* referenced an earlier decision, titled *Bowers v. Hardwick,* which upheld Georgia's antisodomy laws. With *Lawrence,* the Supreme Court overturned that decision, saying, "the laws involved in Bowers and here [Texas's antisodomy laws]are, to be sure, statutes that purport to do no more than prohibit a particular sexual act."[47]

As the court saw *Bowers,* and also *Lawrence,* "their penalties and purposes, though have far more reaching consequences, touching upon the most private human conduct, sexual behavior, and in the most private of places, the home. The statues [Georgia's and Texas's antisodomy laws] do seek to control a personal relationship that, whether or not entitled to formal recognition in the law, is within the liberty of persons to choose without being punished as criminals." The Court went on to say:

> This, as a general rule, should counsel against attempts by the State, or a court, to define the meaning of the relationship or to set its boundaries absent injury to a person or abuse of an institution the law protects . . . adults may choose to enter upon this relationship in the confines of their homes and their own private lives and still retain their dignity as free persons. When sexuality finds overt expression in intimate contact with another person, the conduct can be but one element in a personal bond that is more enduring.[48]

This line of thinking by the Supreme Court's majority led one justice, Antonin Scalia, to dissent, writing that the court's decision is with significant ramifications:

> State laws against bigamy, same-sex marriage, adult incest, prostitution, masturbation, adultery, fornication, bestiality, and obscenity. . . . Every single one of these laws is called into question by today's decision. . . . Not once does it [the ruling on Lawrence v. Texas] describe homosexual sodomy as a "fundamental right" or a "fundamental liberty interest" . . . having failed to establish that the right to homosexual sodomy is "deeply rooted in this Nation's history and tradition" the [ruling] concludes that the application of Texas's statute . . . fails the rational-basis test.[49]

Elizabeth Emens, a Columbia University law professor, writes, "after Lawrence, some have speculated that anti-polygamy laws are ripe for a challenge."[50]

Of course, to challenge the constitutional validity of a law, first you need a case. And as some legal scholars have written, and as two Salt Lake City attorneys told the coauthor of this book, that doesn't appear to be in the making anytime soon. But there is a case in Texas that, once it's adjudicated in the Lone Star State, might test the Reynolds decision.

Meantime, the legal stalemate the United States appears to be in is articulated by Shayma M. Sigman this way: "this disconnect extends to modern treatment of polygymists, which criminalizes the practice, yet neither enforces the criminal statues nor allows polygamists to formalize their family status legally."[51]

Another argument against the *Reynolds* decision, writes Sigman, is on behalf of women:

> The societal decision to remove the choice of polygyny from women was and is paternalistic. Both in nineteenth century America and today, some adult women prefer polygyny. Some reasons are strictly religious, e.g., to be saved from damnation or obtain privilege of celestial eternity, whereas others are more pragmatic, e.g., to obtain the support of sororal networks or provide for children. Yet without offering a counter-balancing explanation regarding the psychology of the choice, prohibiting polygamy infantilizes women, declaring them incapable of providing consent and foreclosing true choice by criminalizing one of their options for family living.[52]

When monogamists look at polygynists, they typically see—because they're not viewing the practices within plural marriage at all times—abuse. But Sigman has an answer to that, too. "There is no evidence that polygamy per se creates abuse or neglect. Having sister wives can be a support network. The status of senior wives versus junior wives and the relationships among these women vary between cultures. In fact, by banding together, women sometimes wield more power to change their husband's problematic behavior. Yet sometimes co-wives are perpetrators."[53]

Anthropologist Janet Bennion, in an interview with this book's coauthor, for an article about changing families in *Bay State Parent* magazine, had this to say about abuse among fundamentalist Mormons practicing plural marriage:

> In all my years working with the Allred Group [a branch of the Mormon faith] I've never heard of a man beating his wife(s). Yet, there can be other forms of abuse, such as financial deprivation, emotional abuse, and underage marriage [of course this is more common in FLDS and Kingston groups]. Here in Vermont [she's a professor at Lyndon State College] I just heard that we have the second rate of men killing women . . . and this is a monogamist state. So, to address your question, I think monogamy fosters violence against women more so than polygamy per se, does.[54]

The biggest problem for people practicing polygyny, currently, Shayna Sigman writes, is that there can be large age differences between a new wife and a husband and, in addition, polygamy isn't always fair to young men because, often, they don't have the financial resources to afford multiple wives. In some cases, they're even kicked out of their FLDS community.

UTAH'S LEGAL PRACTICES

"Laws against polygamy have been around since before statehood [for Utah]," a Salt Lake City civil rights attorney told the coauthor of this book. "The current practice is not to prosecute anyone who engages in polygamy. There's been a couple of high-profile prosecutions but those fellows have been prosecuted not just for polygamy. They came with other baggage. Tom Green has been in the news. He and his family were milking the welfare system and he also married his underage stepdaughter. Then there's Rodney Holm. He married the underage sister of his legal wife. In both these cases, the prosecution wasn't straight up for polygamy (with a consenting adult woman)," he added. The refusal to prosecute someone only on the charge of polygamy, the civil rights attorney said, has been the practice of Utah's attorney general for the last 25 years.

"If you had a case of consenting adults, who didn't have a criminal record, who weren't engaged in statutory rape, or someone who wasn't trying to marry an underage woman and they were practicing polygamy for deeply held religious reasons and it was cleanly presented like that, then there's a good chance the Reynolds Decision [of 1879] would be overturned," he said.[55]

Indeed, this civil rights attorney may see his wish come true but in Texas— not Utah. Wendell Loy Nielsen, age 71, a former president of the FLDS and a former cohort of Warren Jeffs, is married to three women, between the ages of 43 and 66. He faces bigamy charges in Texas. He's not been charged with marrying a minor.

Originally, Nielsen was going to accept a plea bargain on the charges and accept a sentence of 10 years probation. But once he learned that the conditions of his probation included "staying away from playgrounds, not having contact with people under 17 and participating in a cognitive behavioral therapy program," he withdrew his plea, against the advice of his attorney, David Botsford.[56]

This case appears to have all the makings of a case that this civil rights attorney discussed: it's a clean polygyny case that could very well wind up in the Supreme Court, with the potential of overturning the *Reynolds* decision. The trial is scheduled to start in January 2012.

"I've told [Utah Attorney General] Mark Shurtleff that he's afraid to prosecute someone just on polygamy charges because of that fear, and he said, 'Yeah, we will.' But his chief deputy, Kirk Torgensen, who was standing there, right next to him, said 'No we won't,'" the civil rights attorney told this book's coauthor.[57]

Paul Murphy, a spokesman for Shurtleff, says it's difficult to prosecute someone strictly on polygamy charges because the victims are usually reluctant to come forward. He also says Utah's laws against adultery, fornication, and polygyny are usually defended by county prosecutors, not the state attorney general.

"It becomes an issue of choices and resources," Murphy said. "There's no climate to enforce these laws against adultery, fornication and sodomy—although given the Lawrence ruling sodomy would hard to prosecute." Also, "there's no pressure from the [state] legislature to fill our jails with polygynists and our foster homes with the children of polygynists," he added.[58]

Murphy also says that Shurtleff has increased the penalties for marrying underage girls, those under the age of 18, in a polygynist setting. It's now a 2nd degree felony, meaning the penalty, if convicted, is between 1–15 years in prison. It had previously been a 3rd degree felony, with a penalty between of up to 5 years in prison. He says that, with the exception of some FLDS groups, there's been widespread acceptance of this potential penalty among polygynists in Utah.[59]

Rod Parker, another Salt Lake City civil rights attorney, in an interview with this book's coauthor, described this legal stalemate this way: "The problem with it is that when you have a law on the books and you rely on the prosecution when to enforce it and not to enforce it, it's kind of arbitrary. . . . It creates an environment ripe for abuse by the prosecution."[60]

As for the *Reynolds* decision, both Parker and a civil rights attorney who spoke to the book's coauthor, as might be expected, take issue with the ruling.

"You'd never see a decision like that today. It can't stand up against modern constitutional analysis. The language about polygamy only being done by Asians and Africans, that kind of stuff is archaic," Parker said.

"There's little or no legal analysis on that decision. It's essentially a hysterical opinion—only people in the deepest, darkest parts of Africa and Asia practice polygamy. It's an embarrassment to the Judiciary today," the civil rights attorney said.

"But Reynolds is still good law on one point. The idea the Court was trying to get at is that you cannot allow all religious practices," Parker said. "Reynolds is valid when it comes to human sacrifice or even drug use. But on polygamy it's different."

"Life changes. Society changed. Our expectations have changed. Our tolerance for gay marriage and shacking up has changed. The laws, in some cases, haven't changed," Parker added.[61]

To be sure, Parker thinks the charges of statutory rape should be prosecuted. "Warren Jeffs is in prison for having sex with minors. He richly deserves it," Parker said.

NOTES

1. Andrew Sullivan, "State of the Union," *The New Republic*, May 8, 2000, http://www.tnr.com/print/article/politics/state-the-union-0.

2. Ibid.

3. Matthew Benjamin, "Possessing Pollution," *New York University Review of Law and Social Change*, November 30, 2007, p. 737.

4. Gay Talese, *Thy Neighbor's Wife* (New York: Doubleday and Company, 1980), p. 111.

5. Ibid., p. 107.

6. Ibid.

7. Margaret C. Jasper, *The Law of Obscenity and Pornography* (New York: Oxford University Press, 2009), p. 6.

8. Ibid., p. 8.

9. Ibid., p. 24.

10. Douglas Page interview with a Salt Lake City civil rights attorney, November 29, 2011, who wishes to remain unnamed.

11. *Loving v. Virginia*, Supreme Court ruling, June 12, 1967.

12. Ibid.

13. Ibid.

14. Ibid.

15. Ibid.

16. Ibid.

17. "Marrying Out: One in Seven New U.S. Marriages is Interracial and Interethnic," Pew Research Center, June 15, 2010, http://pewresearch.org/pubs/1616/american-marriage-interracial-interethnic

18. "Blacks Upbeat about Black Progress Prospects," January 12, 2010, http://pewresearch.org/pubs/1459/year-after-obama-election-black-public-opinion.

19. "Judge Overturns California's Ban on Same-Sex Marriage," August 5, 2010, http://www.cnn.com/2010/US/08/04/california.same.sex.ruling/index.html?hpt=T1.

20. *Reynolds v. U.S.*, 98 U.S. 145(1878) retrieved http://www.laws.findlaw.com/is/145.html.

21. Ibid.

22. Ibid.

23. Ibid.

24. Ibid.

25. Jeremy M. Miller, "A Critique of the Reynolds Decision," *Western State University Law Review* (1984): pp. 178 and 179.

26. Ibid., p. 180.

27. Ibid., pp. 169 and 170.

28. Ibid., p. 171.

29. Ibid., p. 188.

30. Ibid.

31. Ibid., p. 190.

32. Ibid., p. 191.

33. Keith E. Sealing, "Polygamists out of the Closet: Statutory and State Constitutional Prohibitions against Polygamy are Unconstitutional under the Free Exercise Clause," *Georgia State University Law Review* vol. 17, no. 3, Article 4: http://digitalarchive.gsu.edu/gsulr/vol17/iss3/4, p. 733.

34. Ibid., pp. 733 and 734.

35. Sealing, ibid., p. 734.

36. Martha M. Ertman, "Race Treason: The Untold Story of America's Ban on Polygamy," *Columbia Journal of Gender and Law* (2010), p. 289.

37. Ibid., p. 307.

38. Ibid., p. 313.

39. Ibid.

40. Claire A. Smearman, "Second Wives' Club: Mapping the Impact of Polygamy in U.S. Immigration Law," *Berkley Journal of International Law* (2009): p. 439.

41. Kristin Eliasberg, "Sodomy Flaw: How the Courts have Distorted the History of Anti-Sodomy Laws in America," March 25, 2003, http://www.slate.com/articles/news_and_politics/jurisprudence/2003/03/sodomy_flaw.html.

42. Ibid.

43. Supreme Court's decision, *Lawrence vs. Texas*, 2003, http://supreme.justia.com/us/539/558/case.html.

44. Ibid.

45. Linda Greenhouse, "The Supreme Court: Homosexual Rights; Justices, 6–3, Legalize Gay Sexual Conduct in Sweeping Reversal of Court's '86 Ruling," *The New York Times,* June 27, 2003, .http://www.nytimes.com/2003/06/27/us/supreme-court-homosexual-rights-justices-6-3-legalize-gay-sexual-conduct.html?src=pm.

46. Cassiah M. Ward, "I Now Pronounce You Husband and Wives: *Lawrence v. Texas* and the Practice of Polygamy in Modern America," *William & Mary Journal of Women and the Law* (2004), p. 150.

47. Supreme Court's decision, *Lawrence vs. Texas.*

48. Ibid.

49. Justice Scalia's dissenting opinion on *Lawrence v. Texas,* 2003, http://www.law.cornell.edu/supct/html/02-102.ZD.html.

50. Elizabeth F. Emens, "Monogamy's Law: Compulsory Monogamy and Polyamorous Existence," Chicago: Public Law and Legal Theory Working Paper No. 58, The Law School, The University of Chicago, February 2003, http://www.law.uchicago.edu/files/files/58-monogamy.pdf.

51. Shayna M. Sigman, "Everything Lawyers Know about Polygamy Is Wrong," *Cornell Journal of Law and Public Policy* vol. 16 (2006–2007): p. 166.

52. Ibid., p. 172.

53. Ibid., p. 173.

54. Email interview by Page of Janet Bennion, November 15, 2010.

Bennion is citing crime statistics from the Violence Policy Center. They report state-by-state information on homicides, which is based on information received, and apparently unpublished, by the Federal Bureau of Investigation. Nevada has the most murders of women by men; Vermont is second; Alabama is third; North Carolina is fourth; and Tennessee is fifth. The center's press release can be found at http://www.vpc.org/press/1009dv.htm.

55. Page interview with a Salt Lake City civil rights attorney on November 29, 2011.

56. "FLDS: Former President Allowed to Back out of Plea Deal, Granted Jury Trial," *Standard Times*, (San Angelo, Texas), http://www.gosanangelo.com/news/2011/nov/28/nielsen-allowed-to-back-out-of-plea-deal-granted/.

57. Page interview with a Salt Lake City civil rights attorney.

58. Telephone interview of Paul Murphy by Douglas Page on December 8, 2011.

59. Ibid.

60. Telephone interview of Rodney Parker by Douglas Page on November 30, 2011.

61. Ibid.

11

The Benefits of Legalizing
Plural Marriage

Although we believe polygyny and same-gender marriage can be advocated from a common legal basis, it need not be the case that the preference for one means someone is required to support the other. Jamie M. Gher, in a 2008 article in the *William and Mary Journal on Women and the Law*, writes, "that while polygamy and same-sex marriage share some common linkages, advocates should continue to distance same-sex marriage from plural marriage to avoid relinquishing the movement's hard-earned cultural capital and societal support."[1] She warns same-gender marriage advocates to avoid "maligning polygamy" and, instead, "direct their time and energy toward respecting diversity while fighting for equality."[2]

Other scholars have focused on the specific amendments to the U.S. Constitution for the implications on polygyny. Sarah Barringer Gordon, for example, in a history about the "Mormon question" notes that the debate about plural marriage has shifted from the First Amendment, which is the free exercise of religion amendment, to the Fourteenth Amendment, which provides for equal protection under the law and, thus, provides a firmer basis for constitutional rights as applied to marriage law.[3]

Cultural differences are significant in equal protection advocacy. Alison D. Renteln, for example, writes, "One of the most important principles of justice is equal protection of the law. Failure to allow the consideration of cultural information in a court of law sometimes violates the fundamental idea."[4] Case studies of connections between cultural communities and the law are a growing interest not only in the law but also in academic disciplines. In a thoughtful book by Jill Norgren and Serena Nanda titled *American Cultural Pluralism and Law*, U.S. court cases bearing on culture, gender, race, and class are considered.[5]

Sarah Song, in her book *Justice, Gender and the Politics of Multiculturalism*, devotes a chapter to polygyny in the United States. She considers the issue of freedom of FLDS women to exit their communities if they are oppressed as a key social issue. Song concludes that "a legal regime of qualified recognition of polygamy can, I think, more effectively ensure Mormon women's rights to exit their communities than outright proscription."[6]

Song later writes about an earlier U.S. Supreme Court decision, from 1946, which continued to outlaw plural marriage. She notes Justice Frank Murphy's dissent on the court's ruling. Song writes: "citing anthropological findings that monogamy, polygamy, polyandry and group marriage were four different forms of marriage practiced by different cultures, Justice Murphy argued that Mormon polygamy was 'a form of marriage built upon a set of social and moral principles' and ought to be recognized as such."[7]

Retired University of Michigan History Professor Marvin B. Becker, in an expansive article entitled "An Essay on the Vicissitudes of Civil Society with Special Reference to Scotland in the Eighteenth Century," writes that society (and, therefore, government) cannot cure every citizen or resident from their prejudices, prevent, at all times, criminal behavior or stop behavior that some might consider morally disturbing. The solution, he writes, to working around these issues comes from the law:

> civil society cannot deal with the proposition that racism must be eradicated, but it can work to prevent illegal discrimination. It cannot end rape or "take back the night," but it can insure that legal procedures will be fairer to women. It cannot end homophobia, but it can punish employers for job discrimination. In other words, it cannot satisfy grand and overarching claims calling for fundamental changes in culture or social psychology. . . . The great social questions involve issues incapable of reconciliation; they must be reduced or broken down into interest components.[8]

To put this essay in context of our topic, it is impossible for any government or society to prevent children from being born in a variety of approved or disapproved relationships. Adults, by and large, want and desire love (or at least sex) and sometimes their sexual encounters will lead to extramarital pregnancy. Since society cannot stop unmarried adults from having sex, and the possible resulting unmarried births, is there something else it can do to ameliorate the situation? Yes, we say, it can allow plural marriage because that just might improve the chances of turning an infant into a well-educated, self-sufficient adult.

Another issue for society to consider, when thinking about the legalization about plural marriage, is whether the current laws are helping women in polygamous communities. The failure to legalize plural marriage, one legal scholar suggests, is that it allows government officials to "ignore polygynist communities and the abuses that occur therein." By doing so, writes Emily Duncan, "state governments indirectly condone and thus perpetuate abuse and neglect" in polygynous communities. If polygyny was legal, she says, there would be "greater regulation of the practice, compelling polygynist communities to emerge from the shadows, and openly assist the women and children who live in them."[9]

She goes on to say that polygyny isn't prosecuted because these marriages aren't recorded and some law enforcement officers, as well as politicians, see plural marriage as a constitutional right. That said, Duncan describes a lot of suffering in polygynist communities because their lifestyle is so far underground. Teenage girls are married to much older men—often against their will—and, therefore, have high-risk pregnancies. Duncan also says many of these women often suffer abuse.

LEGALIZING POLYGYNY: KEEPING FAMILIES AND WOMEN SAFE

If polygyny was legal, Duncan writes, it "would alleviate some of the abuses prevalent in polygynous communities because it will lead to greater regulation" and bring them into the open for all citizens to examine.[10] Legalization of polygyny would help law enforcement officials because, as the codirector of Principle Voice, a pro-polygamy group said, "it would be all about going after the crimes, not the culture."[11] Legalizing polygyny would also force "patriarchs to register their multiple marriages" so the government can accurately calculate with much greater accuracy whether each family is eligible for aid, and if so, how much." It would also expose "polygynous communities" and provide plural wives with greater opportunities in the "outside world."[12]

Still, there's an issue that appears in polygynous marriage, at least in the United States, that doesn't seem to materialize with monogamous marriage, and that's an FLDS woman potentially being coerced into marrying—or creating a "celestial bond"—with a plural husband. While "the relationships referenced by polygamy supporters are between 'consenting adults,' it does not follow that the women participating in such relationships are acting out of free will," as Cassiah Ward writes:

> The effect that polygamy may have on the women who are essentially forced participants creates a duty on the part of the State to proscribe such situations. There is even a state interest in protecting the many women who marry into polygamous relationships. Although there may not be any actual physical coercion, the potential for psychological and religious coercion that comes to fruition through the indoctrination of the original teachings of Joseph Smith and the seclusion of these women from the rest of society still exists.[13]

So the worst-case scenario for anyone who's opposed to the Supreme Court's *Lawrence* ruling is that any adult, it would appear, can enter into any kind of intimate relationship with another adult.

There remains a question, however, about the legality of polygyny. Justice Scalia would appear to think that the court's ruling on *Lawrence* means it's an "anything goes" society in the United States with intimate relationships as long as all parties are consenting adults. Other Supreme Court justices may think the *Lawrence* ruling is not without restrictions on adult behavior, so far as intimate relationships are concerned, even if all parties are consenting adults.

Even if this unfettered freedom exists, Ward's warnings about women only entering into plural marriages on their own free will are valid. If polygyny becomes legal, is there a way to protect a woman from being forced into a plural marriage? One legal scholar suggests there's a means of protecting all spouses in plural marriages by making them partners and, thus, providing them with a voice in a household's day-to-day management as well as its most intimate issues.

MAKING POLYGYNY WORK UNDER THE LAW

Adrienne Davis, a law professor at the Washington University School of Law in St. Louis, writes that one of the reasons for and benefits of polygyny—at least for women—has to do with improving their relationship not only with their husband but also providing them with in-house assistance for their multiple obligations. She writes:

> Polygamy presents another option. For some women, increasing the ratio of women to men in a household might be more effective than pressuring husbands to "change" and conform to women's expectations. Done properly—that is, among women committed to feminist principles—polygamy can provide a "sisterhood" within marriage, generate more adults committed to balancing work/family obligations, and allow more leisure time for each wife. As Luci Martin, Vice Chairman of Utah's National Organization of Women, once remarked, "[Polygamy] seems like a pretty good idea for professional women, who can proceed with their careers and have someone at home they can trust to watch their children."[14]

The question she then attempts to answer is if polygyny is legal, how can the country make sure everyone, including multiple spouses, is protected. Would family law apply to a polygynous marriage or is there some other kind of law that could be used?

The problem for any wife in a polygynous marriage is that "multiplicity means that one wife doesn't know whether one will end up as a mono-wife or as one of ten co-wives . . . polygamy's serial entrances and exits means that these unions are constantly forming and constantly dissolving, which engenders substantial uncertainty and vulnerability for plural spouses."[15]

In addition, as it is currently practiced in the United States, polygyny puts too much power with the husband. And while perhaps this doesn't apply to Kody Brown or Joe Darger, a plural husband with few morals can always threaten his existing wives with "economic or emotional diminution" by adding another wife.[16] And so the question becomes "is there a way to protect all parties, including the wives, from these potential pitfalls?"

She suggests that the best way to protect all the wives (and, potentially, all husbands) in a plural marriage setting is through partnership law. While it might seem odd to apply partnership law to an intimate setting like marriage, it's not entirely out of the question either.

"Like partnerships, marriages typically generate wealth and assets through their members' combined efforts, which can confuse ownership and frustrate titling at dissolution (that is, divorce or death)," Davis writes.[17] She also explains that partnership law has already been used on monogamous marriages: "In the eleven community property states, the law has already recognized these similarities, explicitly incorporating commercial partnership norms into its default principles. More recently, reform of dissolution principles in family and inheritance law in non-community-property states has been driven by the recognition that intimate associations are also characterized by partnership principles."[18]

In essence, Davis writes, partnership law, applied to plural marriage, could allow multiple wives and potentially multiple husbands] to leave the marriage without dissolving the household. Rules would be set out that could be applied to all spouses, covering the economics of the household and prevent a polygamous husband [or wife] from marrying without seeking approval from all the spouses in the household.

The worst criticism any devout, fundamentalist Mormon could say about applying partnership law to a plural marriage is that it makes marriage far more egalitarian—at least in the eyes of the law—than they might prefer. On the other hand, partnership rules like the ones put forth by Professor Davis could also make it far easier for law enforcement and the courts to regulate polygamy—which is already done with monogamous marriages—thus making plural marriage far more acceptable within a predominantly monogamous marriage culture.

It is difficult to believe that if plural marriage becomes legal in the United States, it would only be permissible between one man and multiple wives. While it might not enter into the thinking of a Supreme Court Justice, what would various interest groups, including the National Organization of Women, think if plural marriage were only constitutionally acceptable between one husband and multiple wives? They'd probably claim that women have as much of a right to multiple husbands as men have a right to multiple wives, citing the Fourteenth Amendment as part of their argument. Then there's the issue of same-gender marriage being expanded in a plural setting and, finally, there are two other groups of people whose civil rights are beginning to be recognized, at least in California, the transgendered and bisexuals. Wouldn't they have plural marriage rights if polygyny were legal or decriminalized?

While we don't have any particular insight as to how the justices might rule on a plural marriage case brought before the Supreme Court—and certainly we're not lawyers—it seems that everyone, both men and women, could enter into plural marriage. Thus, polyandry, polygamy as well as group marriage, would likely be legal—all because of the Due Process and Equal Protection Clauses of the Constitution's Fourteenth Amendment.

AN ATTORNEY'S LIMITED KNOWLEDGE

Judge Richard A. Posner, who sits on the U.S. Court of Appeals for the Seventh District in Chicago, has said there are limits to an attorney's knowledge, especially on sexual matters. Lawyers, he wrote in his book *Sex and Reason*, come with little knowledge of sex. He writes:

> The narrowness of legal training is an old story but a true one. . . . A [lawyer specializing] in the Fourteenth Amendment is expected to know a lot of judicial opinions and legal doctrinal niceties, but is neither expected nor likely to know much about the history, nature, and practice of sexual regulation. It is not helpful, in this regard, that sex remains a taboo subject in our society. . . . The less that lawyers know about a subject, the less that judges will know; and the less that judges know, the more likely they are to vote their prejudices.[19]

Perhaps this should be considered a call for attorneys to interview and hire more culturally trained social scientists, so they gain an understanding of sexual behavior in nonmonogamous cultures, even those in the United States.

CANADA AND PLURAL MARRIAGE

It's difficult to write about the latest polygyny ruling from British Columbia's Supreme Court because the case is so fluid. Similar to the polygyny decision in the United States, there's no shortage of criticism and endorsement of the court decision. Polygyny was determined to be in violation of

Canada's Constitution and its Charter of Rights and Freedoms, which is similar to the U.S. Bill of Rights, in November 2011, by British Columbia's Supreme Court and, according to the attorney for the FLDS group, the case, one way or another, will be appealed, perhaps even to Canada's Supreme Court.[20]

At issue in British Columbia was a polygynist community in Bountiful, which, as *MacLean's* magazine reported, "has operated with impunity for more than 60 years, despite allegations of forced marriages of underage girls, child abuse and the trafficking of wives across the Canada-U.S. border."[21] This fundamentalist Mormon community is led by Winston Blackmore, who reportedly has 30 wives and 100 children and, according to the *Economist,* includes about 1,000 residents, "progeny of half-a-dozen men."[22] The commune was set up in 1947 "after a few men excommunicated by the mainstream Mormon Church in Utah moved north."[23]

There are no statistics, or even estimates, as to how many people are living within a plural marriage setting in Canada "in part because the relationship is illegal and there is a reluctance to identify as being a polygamist."[24]

Plural marriage has been illegal in Canada since 1892. As Law Professor Nicholas Bala writes, Canada made polygyny illegal to discourage "immigration by polygamous American Mormons families, who at the time were being actively prosecuted by the United States government under laws which prohibited polygamy in that country."[25]

British Columbia Supreme Court Justice Robert Bauman wrote that polygamy's ban in Canada is constitutional "under Section 1—allowing 'reasonable limits' on absolute rights that can be 'demonstrably justified'—because the harm that flows from polygamous relationships outweighs any violation of constitutionally protected rights."[26] Justice Bauman wrote that he "concluded that this case is essentially about harm; more specifically, Parliament's reasoned apprehension of harm arising out of the practice of polygamy. This includes harm to women, to children, to society and to the institution of monogamous marriage."[27]

Justice Bauman, whose decision against polygyny in British Columbia was hundreds of pages long, went through much of the history and some of the legalities of plural marriage. It included the history of marital practices, various philosophies on marriage, including monogamy and polygyny, and laid out, very clearly, how the justice came to rule that Canada's ban on polygyny remained against the law.

Justice Bauman writes that, "The law seeks to advance the institution of monogamous marriage, a fundamental value in Western society from the earliest of times. It seeks to protect against the many harms which are reasonably apprehended to arise out of the practice of polygamy."[28] What is surprising about the Justice's ruling, however, is that it gives every appearance of contradicting itself. The *National Post* reports that "Chief Justice Robert Bauman wrote that Section 293 of the Criminal Code, the law banning polygamy, does, in fact, run counter to sections of the Charter of Rights and Freedoms [Canada's Bill of Rights]." The *National Post* also reported that:

> In particular, he [Bauman] made reference to Section 2, which protects such fundamental freedoms as freedom of religion, and Section 7, which guarantees the autonomy of the individual. He ruled, however, that the ban remains constitutional under Section 1—allowing "reasonable limits" on absolute rights that can be "demonstrably justified"—because the harm that flows from polygamous relationships outweighs any violation of constitutionally protected rights.[29]

Robert Wickett, an attorney in Vancouver for the Fundamentalist Church of Jesus Christ of Latter-day Saints, says there's a way to live within the law given Justice Bauman's ruling.

Justice Bauman, he said, "lays out for prosecutors and defendants what is lawful and not lawful. He has not said that three people living together is unlawful, but only three people living together in a form of 'marriage' that had a sanctioning event or a religious ceremony. And so people looking at that definition, then, you could imagine how they structure their affairs to stay within this definition,"[30] Wickett added.

In particular, Wickett cites Justice Bauman's ruling, where he quotes from Canadian criminal law, which says the following:

"Section 293 provides:
   293(1) Everyone who

(a) practices or enters into or in any manner agrees or consents to practice or enter into

   (i) any form of polygamy, or
   (ii) any kind of conjugal union with more than one person at the same time, whether or not it is by law recognized as a binding form of marriage; or

(b) celebrates, assists or is a party to a rite, ceremony, contract or consent that purports to sanction a relationship mentioned in subparagraph (a)(i) or (ii), is guilty of an indictable offence and liable to imprisonment for a term not exceeding five years.

   (2) Where an accused is charged with an offence under this section, no averment or proof of the method by which the alleged relationship was entered into, agreed to or consented to is necessary in the indictment or upon the trial of the accused, nor is it necessary on the trial to prove that the persons who are

alleged to have entered into the relationship had or intended to have sexual intercourse."[31]

The problem with this definition, as Wickett told this book's co-author, is that it's too broad. As it stands now, Wickett says, three people living together—even if they haven't entered into any kind of "spiritual" or "marital" relationship—can be arrested for practicing polygyny. So if there's any part of this case that Wickett says he can win on appeal it has to do with the definition of polygyny under Canadian law.

Besides the legal issues, perhaps the biggest issue working against the community in Bountiful is, as McGill University Law Professor Angela Campbell writes, its cloistered and insular living conditions:

> Bountiful . . . has developed through what Peters has described as a culture of secrecy typical of fundamentalist Mormon communities. Residents of Bountiful conduct all aspects of their lives within their community. . . . The community has also acquired an increasing ability to meet residents' health and social needs, which risks intensifying its insularity as residents will be less likely to move beyond community borders to access necessary resources and services . . .
>
> . . . the fact that the community lives a very rural and quiet lifestyle, wears traditional dress and practices polygamy as one of its core social and religious tenets would likely lead to its characterization as peculiar, different, perhaps even suspect by other Canadians . . . they remain a fringe group also because their lifestyle might not be accepted or necessarily understood by most Canadians.[32]

Wickett confirmed Professor Campbell's point, saying Canada's population doesn't understand the FLDS because they're so isolated from the rest of society.[33]

"In Salt Lake City, you have polygynists that are part of the community. They're Mormons but they don't believe a prophet determines who you marry. They have plural marriages, many children and they dress like everyone else," Wickett said.[34] "In Bountiful, they're FLDS and they believe the prophet determines who you marry," he added. Wickett says he expects "his guys" to be charged with violating Canada's criminal code on polygyny.

The biggest issue in Justice Bauman's ruling was the harm, he says, that polygamy causes both women and children. Plural marriage causes underage marriage, puts women at an "elevated risk of physical and psychological harm," and that infants born into a polygynous family face a higher mortality rate than those born to monogamous couples, the Justice wrote.[35]

Queen's University Law Professor Beverley Bains questions why there is so much attention on saving women from polygamy when so little is done in saving them from abuse in monogamy. She notes, "criminalizing a marital state makes no sense particularly when many new Canadians come from countries where polygamy is accepted. . . . If Canada wants to claim to be a multi-cultural country, we have to reassess laws that have no other justification except Christian morality."[36]

Law Professor Bala says "polygamy . . . is illegal not only because it violates the concept of monogamy, but also because it undermines monogamy."[37] Bala cites much law and Christian ideology in his article that appears in the *Canadian Journal of Family Law*. He dismisses arguments about same-gender marriage leading to polygyny, writing that the argument is "weak, as it raises very different social and constitutional issues from the recognition of same-sex marriage."[38]

Bauman's ruling was about the value of monogamy—and specifically heterosexual monogamy because of its long history in Canada—as upholding Western civilization. But now that same-gender marriage is allowed in Canada, one observer writes, society's values changed. "Put bluntly, if heterosexuality is no longer legally, morally, or socially relevant to marriage, why should monogamy continue to be so important?" wrote Neil Addison in London's *Guardian* newspaper.[39]

NOTES

1. Jamie M. Gher, "Polygamy and Same-Sex Marriage—Allies or Adversaries within the Same-Sex Marriage Movement," *William & Mary Journal of Women and the Law* (2008): p. 559, http://scholarship.law.wm.edu/wmjowl/vol14/iss3/4.

2. Ibid, p. 559.

3. Sarah Barringer Gordon, *The Mormon Question: Polygamy and Constitutional Conflict in Nineteenth Century America* (Chapel Hill: The University of North Carolina Press, 2002).

4. Alison D. Rentelen, "In Defense of Culture," in *The Courtroom in Engaging Cultural Differences: The Multicultural Challenge in Liberal Democracies*, ed. Richard Schweder, Martha Minow, and Hazel Rose Markus (New York: Russell Sage Foundation, 2002), p. 200.

5. Jill Norgen and Serena Nanda, *American Cultural Pluralism and Law* (Westport, CT: Praeger Press, 1996).

6. Sarah Song, *Justice, Gender and the Politics of Multiculturalism* (Cambridge: Cambridge University Press, 2007), p. 162.

7. Ibid., p. 157.

8. Marvin B. Becker, "An Essay on the Vicissitudes of Civil Society with Special Reference to Scotland in the Eighteenth Century," *Indiana Law Journal* (April 1, 1997): p. 469.

9. Emily J. Duncan, "The Positive Effects of Legalizing Polygamy: 'Love Is a Many Splendid Thing,'" *Duke Journal of Gender Law & Policy* (2008): p. 316.

10. Ibid, p. 333.

11. Ibid., p. 334.

12. Ibid., pp. 334–335.

13. Cassiah Ward, "I now Pronounce You Husband and Wives: Lawrence vs. Texas and the Practice of Polygamy in Modern America," *William & Mary Journal of Women and the Law* (2004): pp. 144 and 145, http://scholarship.law.wm.edu/wmjowl/vol11/iss1/4.

14. Adrienne Davis, "Regulating Polygamy: Intimacy, Default Rules, and Bargaining for Equality," *Columbia Law Review* (December 2010): p. 1972.

15. Ibid., p. 1991.

16. Ibid., p. 1992.

17. Ibid, pp. 2004 and 2005.

18. Ibid., p. 2005.

19. Richard A. Posner, *Sex and Reason* (Cambridge, MA: Harvard University Press, 1992), pp. 346 and 347.

20. Page interview with Robert Wickett, attorney for FLDS in British Columbia, December 12, 2011.

21. Ken MacQueen, "Polygamy: Legal in Canada," *Maclean's,* June 25, 2007.

22. "Hunting Bountiful: Ending Half a Century of Exploitation," *The Economist,* July 8, 2004.

23. "Hunting Bountiful."

24. Nicholas Bala, "Why Canada's Prohibition of Polygamy is Constitutionally Valid and Sound Social Policy," *Canadian Journal of Family Law* (2009): p. 9.

25. Ibid., p. 7.

26. Charles Lewis, "B.C. Polygamy Ruling Offers 'Road Map' to Avoid Prosecution: Lawyer," *National Post,* November 23, 2011.

27. The Honorable Chief Justice Robert Bauman, "In the Supreme Court of British Columbia, a Reference by the Lieutenant Governor in Council set out in Order in Council No. 533 dated October 22, 2009 concerning the Constitutionality of s. 293 of the *Criminal Code of Canada,* R.S.C. 1985, c. C-46," November 23, 2011.

28. Ibid.

29. "B.C. Supreme Court Rules Polygamy Ban is Constitutional, but Flawed," *The National Post,* November 23, 2011.

30. Ibid.

31. Justice Bauman's ruling, November 23, 2011.

32. Angela Campbell, "How Have Policy Approaches to Polygamy Responded to Women's Experiences and Rights? An International Comparative Analysis," May 31, 2005, p. 6. Available at SSRN: http://ssrn.com/abstract=1360230 or http://dx.doi.org/10.2139/ssrn.1360230.

33. Page-Wickett interview, December 12, 2011.

34. Ibid.

35. Justice Bauman's ruling, November 23, 2011.

36. Tracey Tyler, "A Many-Ringed Circus," *Toronto Star,* February 21, 2009, http://www.childbrides.org/canada_TS_a_many-ringed_circus.html.

37. Bala, "Why Canada's Prohibition of Polygamy is Constitutionally Valid and Sound Social Policy," p. 8.

38. Ibid., p. 5.

39. Neil Addison, "Polygamy in Canada: A Case of Double Standards," *The Guardian*, November 30, 2011., http://www.guardian.co.uk/commentisfree/belief/2011/nov/30/heterosexuality-canada-law-monogamy-polygamy.

12

Religious Foundations:
A Cultural Critique

How should churches, mosques, and synagogues respond in light of our national family crisis and increased calls for cultural pluralism? A myriad of legal considerations involving property ownership, inheritance, taxes, child disciplinary obligations, and health insurance, to name but a few, will require special study and legal reflection. We consider here the moral-ethical context since changes in the law are pointless unless religious institutions, where our national moral consciousness is shaped, become committed to a theology of cultural pluralism, especially concerning family matters.

Divorce is a major problem in the United States and the blended family is on the rise. Plural marriage might serve as a potential alternative for divorce in a significant number of cases, thus alleviating its detrimental impact on many children. Nevertheless, divorce would continue to be necessary, particularly since the psychodynamics of certain marriages may be even more stressful and harmful to children than divorce. Religious communities that seek to minimize divorce might well explore plural marriage as an option from a theological point of view.

RELIGIOUS TOLERANCE

Putting the debate about marriage into perspective requires us to review some of the major, controversial issues in the last 500 years. One of them is the idea of religious tolerance, which, eventually, involved the thought that two people who agree on little, including how each practices their faith, can live side by side in peace. This becomes very pertinent, especially when discussing which martial practices can be allowed.

Religious tolerance may have its roots in Europe's Protestant Reformation in the 16th century. Little did Luther know that he was setting Europe on a collision course with itself that would last for just over 130 years on what it meant to be a faithful Christian. While Europeans may have become more tolerant of religious practices that weren't their own, as a result of the Peace of Westphalia in 1648, the debate over what it means to be tolerant of others not sharing the same lifestyle, as well as what it means to be a true Christian, or faithful to God's directions, especially when it comes to the issue of same-gender marriage, continues today.

England, in both the 16th and 17th centuries, struggled with tolerance over differing faiths, religious practices, the role of an established church, as well as the outlook of that established church—Catholic or Protestant— and a government's boundaries in peoples' personal lives. Many suffered painful deaths because of their faith. The sectarian issues with the Church of England in the 17th century forced many Puritans to leave England and establish colonies in Massachusetts, where they thought they would be free to practice their faith without any interference from London.

As John Barry writes in his book *Roger Williams and the Creation of the American Soul* (2012), Williams, a devout Christian, learned that the government tolerance he was searching for wasn't to be found in the Puritan colonies. They were just as forceful in making sure everyone abided by their rules in the New World as William Laud, the archbishop of Canterbury, was in making sure his rules were followed in England. The church and the government, whether it was in England or in Massachusetts, Williams learned, was, practically speaking, one body. As a result of his disagreements with those who ruled in Massachusetts, he was forced to flee the colony, establishing Providence, later Rhode Island, as a place that kept government regulations and religious faith separate.

Thomas Curry points out that Williams "loathed religious persecution, which he believed was anti-Christian, anti-Protestant, inhumane and useless." Both Catholics and Protestants, as Williams saw it, died "heroically for their beliefs."[1] Williams, like his mentor, Edward Coke, separated the Ten Commandments. The government, Williams thought, could not rule on the "First Table of the Commandments," matters of faith and worship; the government could only regulate the Second Table, because they were about the moral behavior that God demanded.[2]

It wasn't until 1689, nearly 70 years after the Puritans started arriving in Massachusetts, that England's Parliament established the Act of Toleration, which recognized religious diversity. As Curry points out, in England it allowed non-Anglican Protestants "a bare toleration to practice their religion." In America, this act of Parliament made non-Anglican Protestants considerably freer, not experiencing "the same deprivation of civil rights as their coreligionists in the mother country."[3]

The idea of religious tolerance was advanced through many writings in the 17th and 18th centuries, including by John Locke and French writer Voltaire. There were, of course, others who weighed in on the topic. Locke, in one of his last writings, maintained "religious societies . . . did not impede the ends of civil government."[4] As Perez Zagorin writes: [Locke] outlined a very wide area of religious freedom and pluralism exempt from interference or imposition by the state. At the same time, he made it clear that certain practices, like infanticide or sexual promiscuity, that were illegal according to human law could not become lawful by their use in religion."[5]

Voltaire would appear to have gone further than Locke on the issue of religious tolerance asking his fellow French citizens, who were primarily Catholic, about the extent to which they would go to defend their beliefs because they saw their faith as "the first work of God."[6] Zagorin writes:

> To such people he [Voltaire] put the question of whether they wished in good faith that the Catholic religion, because it was divine, should rule by means of hatred, ferocity, prisons, tortures and murders. . . . Did Catholics therefore "want to maintain by executioners the religion of a God who died at the hands of executioners and preached only gentleness and patience."[7]

Religious tolerance, advanced by Locke, Voltaire and other European writers, as well as the experiences in England and in Europe, played a role in 1789, after the American Revolution was over and after the U.S. Constitution had been written, in one of the most pressing political issues facing the First Congress, the Bill of Rights. James Madison, who had been a delegate to the constitutional convention in Philadelphia and would later become president of the United States, pushed for passage of the Bill of Rights because he wanted to prevent one faith from becoming a national religion. Curry writes that in 1789, "Americans at the time universally understood an establishment of religion to mean a government preference for one church, sect or religion."[8]

The passage of the Bill of Rights, as some political scholars maintain, and as Curry points out, doesn't prevent "government sponsorship on an equitable basis of all religions or religion in general."[9] Still, it remains questionable as to whether the government can show no preference for a particular religion by assisting one or any faith. This idea of government neutrality in religious matters, thought to be mandated by the First Amendment's prohibition against the government establishing a church, might prohibit the Supreme Court from ever ruling in favor of Fundamentalist Latter-day Saints

(Mormons) retaining a constitutional right to plural marriage. Or, perhaps to maintain the government's religious neutrality, the Supreme Court will determine that all Americans retain the constitutional right to any kind of plural marriage they seek. Such a ruling might equally allow Fundamentalist Latter-day Saints to practice plural marriage for religious reasons as much it might allow other heterosexuals as well as gays, lesbians, bisexuals, and the transgendered a plural marriage option for spiritual reasons as well as secular ones.

AMERICAN PERSPECTIVES

Some American traditions of theology will be considered. We have already discussed Islam and its African American variant of plural marriage in previous chapters. We also take up a Christian, African American theology in this chapter.

The political right has generally opposed departures from the heterosexual, monogamous family as an erosion of American and/or Christian values. What some call American fundamentalism (Turner 2004) is primarily a Protestant religious movement but "there has also been a remarkable convergence of opinion between fundamentalism, the political right, [and] Catholic conservatives."[10]

On the American liberal theological front, differences in the Anglican Communion, for example, have arisen over some American Episcopal churches which recognize same-gender marriages and openly gay bishops while others oppose these actions. In fact, Rowan Williams, the Archbishop of Canterbury, recently stated, "Profound differences among the world's 77 million Anglicans over gay clergy and same sex unions could divide . . . yielding two styles of being Anglican."[11] Debates about plural marriage in the Protestant tradition have occurred in Africa and will be considered later.

In Kilbride's tradition, Roman Catholicism, Father Charles E. Curran's moral theology (1993, 2002, 2008) has staked out a position in favor of cultural pluralism. Father Curran embraces a concept of *Catholicity* that he applies to Roman Catholic and mainline Protestant churches but not to Fundamentalists. By "Catholic," he means a church open to all humanity, which strives to penetrate all dimensions of existence with a union of different aspects such that Catholicity does not exclude differences but demands them.

His historical-critical (constructionist) method opposes a literal interpretation of scripture as inadequate for our times (see also Spong 1991 for a similar Episcopalian perspective). Along with church tradition and human reason, Father Curran believes that theology can profit from "experience" or by a dialogue with the human arts and sciences. As a prime example, he cites the changing attitude of most Christian churches to their present but not past intolerance for slavery.

Curran favors a form of non-natural law theology that searches for "coherence" among beliefs and practices, not from human "reason" reflecting on "human nature" alone, but by emphasizing social discourse in a truly Catholic (universal) social community. In this view, his church is primarily a Catholic worldwide community of moral discourse involving a genuine openness to dialogue with persons and communities sometimes now excluded from the church.

Curran's support for an experience-based theology resists current dogma with its insistence on an essential unchanging human nature grounded in universal moral truths, which downplay or ignore cultural diversity and historical circumstances in philosophical or theological moral discourse.[12] Current Roman Catholic positions on marriage and family debate in America have aligned the Catholic Church with Christian Fundamentalists as noted above. Father Curran, on the other hand, notes, "Today we are much more conscious of the great diversities of culture . . . different understandings of human realities such as marriage and the family as culture, social, political and economic institutions and structures"[13]

While Curran recognizes historical contingency and experiential significance in morality, he holds that some beliefs, from a Roman Catholic perspective, are nevertheless universal, not by virtue of being "natural" but by being socially invented as such and based on faith in a universal creed. He writes, for instance, "One significant contribution that the whole Judeo-Christian approach makes to a universal morality concerns speaking out for the rights and concerns of poor people at all times and in all places."[14]

Although Curran does not specifically consider marriage and family from his perspective, he applies it to moral issues such as war and peace, reproductive practices, racism, and ecology (2008). Certainly, however, this theological perspective could be extended by theologians and others into the family debate proposed here for plural marriage.

On a pragmatic note, in New York, Christian opposition to same-gender marriage was softened by exemptions written into the law allowing for same-gender marriage (Fraga, June 28, 2011). These exemptions, for example, indicated that clergy need not preside over same-gender wedding ceremonies and that refusal to do so will not allow a civil claim or state action of any kind. This is a good model for plural marriages as well so as to allow freedom of religion in the United States. Accordingly, we hope Christian readers will evaluate our materials as supportive of, if not changes in church theologies per se (thoughtful material here we hope for seminarians and future church leaders) but a willingness to tolerate presently civil and religious marriages undertaken outside their churches. We are, therefore, recommending at this time a pro–civil same-sex marriage option for secular marrying entities, like justices of the peace.

We also remind all readers that every religious community, which claims to be global, universal, and not just American in outlook (Catholicism, Episcopalian, Lutheran, and others) are especially invited to consider the American cultural context in more global perspective as we have done in this book. We take up an international theological perspective later in this chapter.

We emphasize that Christianity is best understood as a Judeo-Christian tradition. Rabbi Mordecai M. Kaplan is an intellectual giant of the 20th century whose thought has given rise to reconstructionism, an American Jewish religious movement (see Goldsmith, Schult, and Seltzer 1990). Reconstructionism, influenced by philosopher John Dewey, is especially concerned with ethical beliefs that work or function in a pluralistic society rather than with supernaturalism, beliefs about spiritual beings. In Kaplan's opinion, supernaturalism tied religious belief to the authoritarianism of past generations. "Transnatural" religion, on the other hand, considers religion to be a product of history and in a process of continuous development. For Kaplan, God, in the tradition of the process philosophers, such as Alfred North Whitehead and Charles Hastshorne, is present in the ever-developing "organicity" of the universe. There is a creative process at work transforming humanity for the better. On this view, Kaplan redefined Judaism as an "evolving religious civilization."[15]

In Kaplan's theology, there is much potential for a rethought family agenda as an evolving reconstructive theology where religious experience is not so much a matter of "true" or "false" belief as it is of pragmatic and functional self-actualization where the healthful and moral are integrally related. Surely, constructionist scholars and theologians in search of bridgeheads across disciplines could profit greatly by Kaplan's "stoerics," "a normative science of human life in all its aspects."[16]

Reconstructionists, for example, have supported same-gender marriage. In a Summary of Boundaries report published by the Jewish Reconstructionist Federation, it is stated that, "We retain an unwavering commitment to forming inclusive communities, welcoming to gay, lesbian, bi-sexual and transgendered Jews, as well as multicultural families, Jews of color, and other groups traditionally excluded from full participation in Jewish communal life. Issues relating to the gay and lesbian family are included in religious school curricula. Our rabbis are free to perform same-sex commitment or marriage ceremonies if it is their practice to do so."[17]

There is no evidence that the two theologians, and their many followers considered above, do more than provide a relevant theoretical, theological framework for the rethinking of marriage and family morality along the lines proposed in this book. These theologies are well-suited for the American experience of cultural pluralism as it is applied to our marriage culture. We hope a thoughtful debate will ensue. It is our hope that our national marriage culture can be rethought and debated such that millions of American adults and children can be welcomed into religious communities with all the rights, privileges and spiritual benefits this entails.

INCULTURATION: AFRICAN POLYGYNY AND AMERICAN THEOLOGICAL APPLICATIONS

We now turn for insight to theological discourse in Africa, for example, where a constructionist perspective has emerged, specifically to address polygyny in a context where it is widely practiced. In Africa, as elsewhere, the term *inculturation* is used in reference to current attempts being made there to reformulate Christian doctrine into the culture patterns of local societies (see Ferm 1986; Waliggo et al. 1986). Arij Roest Crollius defines inculturation as follows:

> Recapitulating, we can describe the process of inculturation in the following way: the inculturation of the Church is the integration of the Christian experience of a local Church into the culture of its people in such a way that this experience not only expresses itself in elements of this culture, but becomes a force that animates, orients, and innovates this culture so as to create a new unity and communion, not only within the culture in question but also as an enrichment of the Church universal.[18]

Inculturation is a necessary response by international Christian churches in light of the existence of more than 9,000 independent African churches that have broken away from the mission churches in the last century. Although inculturation embraces such customs as traditional religious rituals, ancestor beliefs, healing practices, and burial customs, the question of polygyny is perhaps the most pressing pastoral and theological topic today.

In a provocative book on the church and marriage in Kenya, *Church and Marriage in East Africa,* Bishop Henry Okullu (of the Anglican-derived Church of the Province of Kenya) observes that he has become painfully aware that polygyny is the single largest pastoral problem in western Kenya. Although details vary, both Catholic and Protestant denominations currently stigmatize polygamous marriage.

For example, a polygamist man must routinely send away all but one wife, if he is to be allowed to take the sacraments. Children of additional wives are considered illegitimate and not acceptable for baptism. Some churches accept polygamists, provided all sexual relations are terminated except for one couple, who is then eligible to be married.

Bishop Okullu decries this state of affairs, for it keeps many people out of church. Although he favors monogamy as the Christian ideal, he believes that monogamists are often defensive and unforgiving in their attitudes. He believes polygyny has much to recommend it, such as limiting divorce and negative consequences for children.

In Catholic theology, Father Michael C. Kirwen (1974) questions dogmatic Roman Catholic teachings on African marriage. His own work considered the levirate as practiced among some societies in Kenya and Tanzania. Father Kirwen notes that this custom where women marry their deceased husband's brother, as in the Hebrew Bible, would make little sense in a European society where "individuals" marry and where strong family lineages are not the basis for social organization. For this reason, European-derived Catholic policy is maladaptive in its opposition to the levirate in all instances. Such a policy has not "incarnated" itself to local custom. Father Kirwen believes that this failure is a grave pastoral problem, an unending source of anxiety and frustration to clergy and laity alike.

Father Kirwen provides an excellent critique of the neo-scholastic theology of the 19th century whose canons were the basis for a pre-Vatican II "manualist" theology taught to missionaries of his generation in the 1960s and thereafter. Such marriage canons were foundationalist in assumption and thought to be suitable for all cultures everywhere, although, in fact, they were European in cultural assumption. Marriage, in this view, is between two people, legally *independent* of their families. In manualism, no other model for marriage is mentioned or even hinted at. Ironically, the post-Vatican II revolution set in motion by Pope John XXIII has not yet officially taken hold in Africa concerning marriage. In fact, His Holiness wrote: "the church . . . does not identify herself with any particular culture not even with the occidental culture to which her history is so closely bound."[19]

Father Eugene Hillman (1975) has called for a reconsideration of polygamy in Christian Africa. He observes that polygamy is practiced widely in the Hebrew Bible and that it is not explicitly condemned in the New Testament—arguments frequently made by African parishioners themselves. Moreover, the Council of Trent, which made polygamy anathema in the 16th century, did not consider the situation of non-Western cultures. Therefore, in the "constructionist" view of theology, the Trent dogma should not be taken as "absolutist" and true for all cultures without reflection. Given the many reasons why polygamy is functional in Africa, Hillman thinks that it should be rethought theologically. Hillman himself suggests that the Lutheran Church in Liberia provides a good model where persons arguably who already practice polygamy in good faith should not be prevented from participating in the sacramental life of the church. Once they become Christians through baptism, however, no more polygamous marriages should be allowed.

Right Reverend David Gitari (Church of the Province of Kenya), in a comprehensive study of polygamy (1985), has reviewed Anglican attempts to cover the polygamy question. He finds international conferences wholly inadequate when the question is even considered. Even African-derived canons are concerned primarily with how to "discipline" the polygamist rather than with how to care for him pastorally. He thinks this shows that African theological thought has been overly westernized.

In a view similar to that presented in this book, Reverend Gitari writes that polygyny, as ideally practiced, is in the abstract "more Christian" than divorce and remarriage, as seen from the vantage point of the abandoned wives and especially their children. In conclusion, Reverend Gitari recommended to a CPK synod in 1982 that, while the church teaches monogamy, it must be sensitive to the widespread practice of polygamy. Although generally requiring that a Christian who becomes a polygamist be excluded from Holy Communion, it is imperative to consider special factors on a case-by-case basis.

Don S. Browning (2003), among his many influential works, has considered marriage and modernization of the worlds' economies from a moral perspective. In a provocative chapter on feminism, family and global trends, he questions from a practical, theological, Christian perspective, how both the churches and public policy should address a declining family situation in East Africa. Famines, HIV/AIDS, civil war, poverty, wealth inequality, among other socioeconomic factors have seen a dramatic rise in, for example, street children, child soldiers, AIDS orphans, child-headed households, and female poverty.

He contrasts the Kilbrides' model (P. and J. Kilbride 1990) with the Shorter and Onyancha family model (1998) where, "the analogy between Catholic and East African visions lead them to believe that the Catholic view of sexuality can tap into the high African value of children and procreation to ground appeals for monogamy, parental responsibility . . . protection of wives and mothers."[20] He states the Kilbrides also want to build on African cultural tradition, but one which would allow plural marriage for Catholics as an option. Browning is agonistic on which model is better; he notes that Kilbrides' model builds on African Christianity too but does not merely extend it as a European perspective, which would oppose polygamy per se.

CONCLUSION

The weight of African "mainstream" theological opinion with European-based power structures is against polygamy in spite of a growing unease with mandatory monogamy and celibacy on the continent. For instance, Hillman's rethinking of polygamy was (respectfully) critiqued in a follow-up study titled *Monogamy Reconsidered* (Blum 1989). Nevertheless, whatever the outcome in Africa, the inculturation debate there is relevant for current theological, constructionist-oriented discourse in the United States. Perhaps the most immediate benefactors from an African theological reflection would be many African American churches where parishioners and clerics alike will probably be increasingly confronted with the "man-sharing" debate and crisis polygamy discussed earlier. Given the great diversity in these churches (see Blackwell 1991), such as black, interracial, Catholic, and Protestant, it is not yet possible to ascertain which churches are most affected by this issue. Wider issues of family dysfunction, divorce, and out-of-wedlock births affect all American faith communities for whom lessons learned in Africa are also relevant.

Specifically, for African Americans, what is needed, first and foremost, are social and economic policies to ameliorate the racism and poverty that is at the heart of the present crisis in black marital relations described earlier. In what is hopefully the short run, however, in light of minimal evidence for racial and economic reform, African American theology might reasonably confront marriage and family morality along the lines of the inculturation debates in Africa. This possibility is reasonable inasmuch as we have noted earlier an African-derived cultural retention in African American family culture (see Herskovits 1958).

An African American Christian theological reflection on African theology, apart from polygamy, is not novel. Josiah Young (1986), for example, considers the notion of whether or not black and African theologies are "siblings or distant cousins." Sharp differences exist to be sure. Black theology is concerned primarily with the consequences of life in a racist society, a response that has produced, among other things, a rich Old Testament-based salvation and other-worldly theology, as compared to much of Africa where "cultural questions" (inculturation) rather than political problems dominate (apart from South Africa). In spite of some theologians who feel that black and African theologies have little in common, Young identifies common ground in the mutual experiences of poverty and a strong sense of community. Significantly, he believes that, "African theologies of indigenization" have much to offer African Americans, although he does not mention polygamy. Surely his reflections would be valuable along with the thought of others discussed in this chapter.

NOTES

1. Thomas J. Curry, *Farwell to Christendom: The Future of Church and State in America* (New York: Oxford University Press, 2001), p. 25.

2. Ibid., p. 25.

3. Ibid.

4. Perez Zorgin, *How the Idea of Religious Toleration Came to the West* (Princeton, NJ: Princeton University Press, 2003), p. 263.

5. Ibid.

6. Ibid., p. 297.

7. Ibid.

8. Curry, *Farwell to Christendom*, p. 36.

9. Ibid.

10. Bryan Turner, "Religion, Romantic Love and the Family," in *The Blackwell Companion to the Sociology of Families*, ed. Jacqueline Scott, Judith Treas, and Martin Richards (Malden, MA: Blackwell Publishing, 2004), p. 298.

11. Alan Cowell, "Archbishop Sees 'Two-Track' Anglican Church," *The New York Times*, July 29, 2009, http://www.nytimes.com/2009/07/29/world/europe/29church.html?_r=1.

12. Rev. Charles E. Curran, *Catholic Social Teaching 1891–Present: A Historical, Theological and Ethical Analysis* (Washington, DC: Georgetown University Press, 2002), p. 91.

13. Ibid.

14. Ibid., p. 93.

15. Emanuel Goldsmith, Mel Scult, and Robert Seltzer, *The American Judaism of Mordecai M. Kaplan* (New York: New York University Press, 1990), p. 260.

16. Ibid.

17. This report is found at http://jrf.org/jrfres_PF/showres_pf.php?rid=487.

18. Arij Roest Crollius, *Creative Inculturation and the Unity of Faith* (Rome: Centre "Cultures and Religions" Pontifical Gregorian University, 1986), p. 43.

19. Michael Kirwen, "The Christian Prohibition of the African Leviratic Custom: An Empirical Study of the Problem of Adapting Western Christian Teachings on Marriage to the Leviratic Care of Widows in Four African Societies," (Unpublished doctoral dissertation, University of Toronto, Canada, 1974), p. 20.

20. Don S. Browning, *Marriage and Modernization: How Globalization Threatens Marriage and What to Do about It* (Grand Rapids, MI: William B. Eerdmans Publishing Company), p. 183.

13

A Love and Commitment
Not to Be Feared

It must be the times in which we live. Because it strikes us as odd that it is easier for people to accept divorce than it is for them to support plural marriage.

We base this thought on the many conversations the coauthor has had with people when he's told them about this book. Their reactions have included the following: "Why would anyone want plural marriage? They abuse women and children." "If people hate their wives or their husbands, just get divorced. Don't add a spouse." "There's a reason we have divorce. So people can end bad marriages." "No woman wants more than one husband." "Men don't know how to live with one wife. They don't need two—or more!" "Plural marriage? That's a little out there."

Maybe it's because so many people have been touched by divorce in the last 30 years that the idea of marital break-up is easier to accept than the idea of plural marriage.

Or perhaps Americans just casually accept the idea of marital failure. It's just a matter of time, some people might say to themselves, before a couple they know, including themselves, whose wedding they may have attended, wind up in a courtroom, asking a judge to end their marriage.

Perhaps this acceptance is part of the fall out from the divorce culture, which Barbara Dafoe Whitehead warned about many years ago.[1] In fact, in a recent survey by the Gallup Organization, in 2008, it was learned that 70 percent of all adults found divorce "morally acceptable."[2] As for children, more than 23 million are growing up in households headed by either a single or divorced parent, the Census Bureau reports.[3] In light of much evidence that divorce is harmful for children perhaps that is why Americans want children raised in intact, two-parent families.

According to the last Census, there are more than 27 million divorced adults in the United States and nearly 80 million adults who are never married, which means the country now has more than 100 million adults who are single or divorced. That's about 43 percent of all adults.[4]

So what's better, going all out to keep marriage as it is—an institution solely for two people, with, perhaps, a minor change, allowing two people who share the same gender to marry—or expanding marital opportunities so children living in single-parent houses have an opportunity to grow up under improved economic circumstances?

To us, the latter, while certainly controversial for a society that outwardly claims to be monogamous, is the better idea. It improves children's chances, giving them better childhoods, and more likely turning them into healthy, educated, well-adjusted adults. The former—standing on ceremony on behalf of monogamy—diminishes many children's prospects for the future.

The difficulty most Americans have in accepting plural marriage is that they keep returning to the model they have seen too often on television or read about in newspapers or magazines: it is an abusive system—with adults marrying children—and puts far too much power in the hands of a patriarch.

We are suggesting people look on plural marriage with a new set of eyes—as a much more equitable system of marriage that allows not only men to have plural spouses but also women, too, legally of course. We are proposing this so to recognize what already exists often in the shadows of criminalization and secrecy. We favor a system whereby children grow up with at least two parents, providing them with the guidance they so need and require with the benefits of public legality.

And, indeed, based on the economics we know, as shown in an earlier chapter, married women are in a stronger economic position when compared to all other women of all other marital statuses. That means married women beat out—financially at least—their single and divorced counterparts. Since many single and never married women, especially those in their 20s, are giving birth and bringing up children, isn't there a way we can offer many of them an improved financial position, not only for them but also for their children? We believe there is by expanding marital options through plural marriage.

Based on the latest information from the U.S. Census Bureau, the United States is teetering on the threshold of having more single than married adults, more than 120 million married adults to just over 106 million who are either never married or divorced.[5] As was seen in an earlier chapter, fewer than half of all adults who are married are living with their spouses. The traditional outlook on marriage—something that is only for two people of the opposite gender—does not appear to be the solution that is going to increase the ranks of the married anytime in the near future. So it is best that we consider and debate—and hopefully make legal—the option of plural marriage as described in this book.

In a legal, plural marriage, as law professor Adrienne Davis has outlined, there is a means by which marital assets can be equitably broken up. She suggests that plural marriages be guided by partnership law, which is similar to how some states, California especially, divide assets in a marital breakup.

Plural marriage works for some and doesn't work for others in the same way that monogamous marriage works for some but not for others. "It depends" is our principle based on a strong empirical research often in more than one culture or nation. By saying "it depends," we're saying that some people have the partners, personality, means and lifestyle to make plural marriage—and even monogamous marriage—successful while others do not.

Many studies show younger Americans and Europeans are less committed to marriage than previous generations. Kilbride finds college students, overall, to be keenly aware of the disruptions caused by divorce. As a result of these experiences, few seem willing to defend the status quo—heterosexual, monogamous marriage—in American family culture. What does this mean for the future of marriage?

STRANGENESS

Polygamy today remains a stigmatized practice despite much more public knowledge about it. But the strangeness of polygamy is, in fact, not so strange when compared to many another cultural practices.

Consider this for example: "For some Japanese men, body pillow girlfriends based on comic book characters now take the place of the real thing."[6] Lisa Katayama writes that in Japan, where 25 percent of men between ages 30–34 are virgins, their difficulties in coping with modern romantic life may explain why they turn to life-size dolls. One informant told Katayama that he "knows it's weird for a grown man to be so obsessed with a video game character . . . 'when I die I want to be buried with her in my arms.'"[7] Anthropology students tell Kilbride that using dolls as romantic partners is spreading across the United States. Nevertheless "romantic doll use in Japan is a part of thriving subculture of men and women who indulge in real relationships with imaginary characters."[8]

In fact, there's a company, based in California, called Real Doll. Google it. You'll get the idea, fast!

In our view, marriage in its many forms is preferable to doll substitutes, especially from a child-centered perspective. For example, since much of the work of raising children in the world's cultures is done in the context of marriage, this practice cannot substitute for parenting functions within marriage. We were struck by a news account from South Korea about a married couple so preoccupied with catering to the imaginary needs of its virtual child that its human baby starved to death.[9]

The term "strange," commonly applied to polygamy, is in fact, upon cross-cultural examination, including the observations just considered, not so strange at all. As we have seen in the book, it is a form of marriage and family culture that's widespread today just as it was in the past. The attitude "it depends" also applies to our opposition to extreme cultural relativism (the idea that each cultural practice can *only* be evaluated in its cultural context). On this philosophical view, a relationship with a life-size doll in Japan, and polygamy, are equally valid, enjoying approved status in at least one culture or subculture. We think marriage, even in its many forms, is far more preferable to doll substitutes. Marriage brings people together, which is better than "making love" to a doll.

The media and entertainment industries play a significant role in the attitudes the general public holds toward a number of issues. Television shows like *Big Love* and *Sister Wives* as well as other family-based shows on the air today, show that family life is far different that it was in the 1950s and 1960s.

In *Big Love* a man in Utah has three wives who live in separate houses side by side. Family life is made routine to the viewers as issues of sexuality, work, religion, and morality play out against the backdrop of life in contemporary America. *Sister Wives* is similar to *Big Love* but is based on the real lives of a polygynous family, which recently moved to Nevada.

On *Big Love*, John Tierney, in *The New York Times*, wrote, "the story of a husband with three wives in Utah will not terrify Americans. Polygamy does not come off as a barbaric threat to the country's moral fabric . . . not one that could ever be a dangerous trend in America."[10] He concluded his piece writing with "these three wives . . . sound much like the women in polygamous marriages I've talked to in rural Africa. . . . Overall, they figured it was better to share one prosperous husband than to marry someone else without land, cows, or a job."[11] Tierney notes that polygamy isn't necessarily worse than the current American alternative, divorce and remarriage, sometimes referred to as serial monogamy or, as is said in Africa, "nonsimultaneous polygamy."

The father in Big Love, unlike so many fathers in America, is committed to maintaining his marriages and relationships with his wives and children. How much more in favor of "family values" can you get than that?

Despite Tierney's optimism that *Big Love* will not terrify Americans, the evidence, as of late, is not encouraging. A recent, fair and balanced *National*

Geographic article entitled "The Polygamists"[12] aroused primarily negative letters to the editor.

Factual knowledge about polygamy matters as societies everywhere have a vested interest in a healthy marriage and family culture. For those opposed to marriage in any but one form, they need to ask themselves that if there is only a minimal marriage opportunity—heterosexual monogamy—how will children be reared?

Although marriage is often difficult, there is strong evidence that marriage has some significant health benefits.[13] In this extensive survey we learn, "scientists have continued to document the 'marriage advantage'; the fact that married people on average appear to be healthier and live longer than unmarried people."[14] Studies show a marriage advantage, for example, in pneumonia, surgery, cancer, and heart attacks.

People in stressful marriages enjoy no advantage. An extensive study of men and women in their 50s and 60s found that, "when the married people became single again . . . by divorce . . . death of a spouse, they suffered a decline in physical health from which they never fully recovered."[15] Remarriage after divorce helped only some. Divorce, it appears, often a routine solution for marital woe, is detrimental and not only for children.

State government action concerning marriage is very much in the forefront of public policy today involving a few states that have legalized same-gender marriage. Efforts for a constitutional amendment at the federal level to prohibit all but heterosexual monogamy appear to be on the back burner, at least for now.

University of Chicago Law School Professor Martha Nussbaum, considered earlier, identifies a number of issues to be addressed should polygamy be legalized. She believes that, "children would have to be protected so the law would have to make sure that issues such as maternity/paternity and child support were well articulated . . . polygamous unions would . . . be difficult to administer—but not impossible with good will and effort."[16] For Nussbaum, issues related to marital dissolution include: property rights after divorce or death, legal and financial responsibility for minors and custody rights with divorce, and of course income tax assessments.

Nussbaum (2000) proposes a capabilities approach in evaluating public policy objectives by assessing quality of life outcomes. She proposes specific capabilities as fundamental to human existence, which would serve as a framework for evaluation and policy. Her universalist perspective includes, for example, an expectation for a normal life span, freedom of bodily movement, and opportunities for social interaction and having an emotional life without fear and anxiety. She notes that a capabilities perspective means, "having the social bases of self-respect and non-humiliation; being able to be treated as a dignified being whose worth is equal to that of others. This entails provisions of non-discrimination on the basis of race, sex, sexual orientation, ethnicity, caste, religion, national origin."[17] Applying Nussbaum's policy framework to polygamy in the United States, it is clear that public policy needs to be directed to improve the quality of life of those whose pursuit of the good life, though unconventional, is unnecessarily stigmatized.

The most serious policy issue mentioned by Nussbaum is likely taxes, already a matter of growing concern in the United States and around the world. One of the letters critical of the polygamy article on FLDS in the *National Geographic* mentioned taxes. The letter, in part, states,

> If an FLDS man has four wives, only one of them is legally married in the eyes of the state and federal government. The other three are single women with no income, no assets, and multiple children who apply for and consume every state and federal entitlement benefit for which they are eligible. These communities thrive through the generosity of the American taxpayer and the willingness of state authorities to turn a blind eye to the misuse of entitlement funds.[18]

In Canada, a recent piece reports the term "bleeding the beast" is used by some FLDS to describe strategies to take money from the government. This article does not fail to cite obvious problem cases like "self-styled 'Bishop of Bountiful' Winston Blackmore, whose 22 wives and 119 children all draw taxpayers' funds while pursuing their . . . illegal life style."[19] The story concludes that unemployed wives with children often obtain child tax benefits based on one low income mother's rate, a situation it could be noted would not be possible if all wives were legal and therefore taxed.

Taxes are an issue in other countries beyond Canada and the United States. In the United Kingdom, a man who marries polygamously in a country where it is legal can draw benefits from the government as all of his wives are recognized as dependents.[20] For those who wish to limit tax abuses of polygamy, this example indicates that making it legal first and then taxing fairly, probably will not be popular among those who presently profit by informal and unregulated polygamy.

David Popenoe (1999 and 2000), a national authority on marriage and the family, proposes recommendations to strengthen heterosexual monogamy, which, for him, is superior to other forms of the family including, for example, same-gender marriage and single parent homes. He believes that a father and mother, united through marriage, have biologically based, complimentary differences needed for positive child development. Popenoe lauds such sex typed parenting differences whereby some studies show mothers are overall "responsive" and fathers are "firm." He states further, "many studies have shown that men interact with children in a different way than women, suggesting that the father's mode of parenting is not interchangeable with that of the mother's . . . men emphasize play more than caretaking."[21]

Popenoe is correct to develop policy recommendations even if only to strengthen two-parent, heterosexual households which are central in our national cultural family ideology. Strengthening families through marriage is also in the interest of all families. We disagree with his argument that marriage should be exclusively heterosexual and monogamous. We want to strengthen marriage, too, so by seeing its rights, privileges and responsibilities extended to same-gender couples as well as polygamous men and women. In fact, we are pro-family values, not simply pro-nuclear family values. Popenoe's argument to bolster the "essential father" by marital links to his child's mother is precisely what we're proposing as an argument in favor of plural marriage—absent the shackle of essentialism so often applied to it.

People, for centuries, through songs, novels, poems, first-person accounts, politics, religious faith, and rigorous academic study have attempted to explain and define love. Yet it remains mysterious. How do you know when you're in love? Is the emotion of love that one person experiences for someone exactly the same that another person experiences for someone they love? Can you love two people, maybe more, simultaneously? Is that wrong?

What's worse—a society that loves (even if it does make room for many different combinations of lovers) or a society that doesn't love at all? This question, explored in variety of literature, including George Orwell's *1984* to Aldous Huxley's *Brave New World* and Margaret Atwood's *The Handmaid's Tale*, would likely lead most readers to conclude that a society that loves—even if some of the love expands the boundaries beyond what the majority considers acceptable and normal—is far better than one that doesn't.

Why is love so important? Because in the 21st century, as with the previous one, it's a reason two people marry in America; if it fades away from the marriage, it's a reason people seek a divorce.

How can a government sanction only one version of legally allowable, committed relationships, especially when there are plenty of examples showing heterosexual, monogamous marriage doesn't work for everyone? Does a government that only permits monogamous marriage alienate lonely, divorced and never-married men and women?

How can two Abrahamic faiths, Judaism and Christianity, place limits on marriage, when another one, Islam, allows polygyny? Do you need to be in love to marry? Do you need to hate to file for a divorce?

Can plural marriage, which creates extended families, become the next social safety net? Are young men, in their late teens or early 20s, at a heightened risk of not marrying women their age if plural marriage is legal? Could plural marriage save one couple from divorce by adding a spouse and spare their children the emotional and economic upheaval such breaks up can cause, not to mention frequent harmful impact on children?

Are these questions we shouldn't ask because they make people uncomfortable?

If we have done our job effectively, we've left you with more questions than answers. That's why the title of this book ends with a question mark, not an exclamation point.

NOTES

1. One of the most thorough articles ever written about divorce's affects on family life was authored by Barbara Dafoe Whitehead and appeared in the April 1993 edition of *The Atlantic Monthly*, titled, "Dan Quayle Was Right." The article's title was referencing former vice president Dan Quayle's response to a popular television show, *Murphy Brown*, where the lead character gave birth without being married. Dafoe Whitehead's article can be found at http://www.theatlantic.com/magazine/archive/1993/04/dan-quayle-was-right/7015/.

2. "Cultural Tolerance for Divorce Grows to 70 %," May 19, 2008, http://www.gallup.com/poll/107380/cultural-tolerance-divorce-grows-70.aspx.

3. "Table D1: Characteristics of Children Under 18 and their Designated Parents: 2009," United States Census Bureau, August 2010, http://www.census.gov.

4. "Selected Social Characteristics in the United States, 2010 American Community Survey, 1-year estimates," United States Census Bureau, http://factfinder2.census.gov/faces/tableservices/jsf/pages/productview.xhtml?pid=ACS_10_1YR_DP02&prodType=table.

5. Ibid.

6. Lisa Katayama, "Love in 2-E," *The New York Times Magazine*, July 26, 2009, pp. 20.

7. Ibid.

8. Ibid., 21.

9. Tanya Valdez, "Couple Starved Real Baby while Raising Virtual Baby," *The Examiner*, March 6, 2010, http://www.examiner.com/article/couple-starved-real-baby-while-raising-a-virtual-baby.

10. John Tierney, "Who's Afraid of Polygamy," *The New York Times*, March 11, 2006, http://query.nytimes.com/gst/fullpage.html?res=9C04EEDA1331F932A25750C0A9609C8B63.

11. Ibid.

12. Scott Anderson, "The Polygamists," *National Geographic*, February 2010, http://ngm.nationalgeographic.com/2010/02/polygamists/anderson-text.

13. Tara Parker-Pope, "Is Marriage Good for Your Health?" *The New York Times*, April 18, 2010, http://www.nytimes.com/2010/04/18/magazine/18marriage-t.html?pagewanted=all.

14. Ibid.

15. Ibid.

16. Martha Nussbaum, "Debating Polygamy," *The Faculty Blog,* The University of Chicago Law School, http://uchicagolaw.typepad.com/faculty/2008/05/debating-polyga.html.

17. Martha Nussbaum, "Women and Cultural Universals," in *Pluralism: The Philosophy and Politics of Diversity,* ed. Maria Baghramian and Attracta Ingram (New York: Routledge, 2000), p. 212.

18. *National Geographic,* June 2010, "Letters," page 8.

19. Suzanne Fournier, "B.C. Polygamist Leader 'See no Sin' in Taking Tax Money," *National Post,* June 16, 2009, http://www.nationalpost.com/related/topics/polygamist+leader+sees+taking+money/1702751/story.html.

20. "Polygamous Husbands can Claim Cash for their Harems," *The Daily Mail,* April 18, 2007, http://www.dailymail.co.uk/news/article-449221/Polygamous-husbands-claim-cash-harems.html.

21. David Popenoe, "Modern Marriage: Revisiting the Cultural Script," in *The Gendered Society Reader,* ed. Michael S. Kimmel, with Amy Aronson (New York: Oxford University Press, 2000), p. 162.

14

Fear and the Slippery Slope
toward Tolerance

If one grants one civil right to one group of people living outside of the country's mainstream, then they are on their way to granting a similar right to another group of people who also live outside society's majority population and its legally approved boundaries. This is the crux of the slippery slope argument against same-gender marriage.

Thus, if the United States allows same-gender marriage, those opposed to it say, the country will be forced to slide down the "slippery slope" to legally allowing another vile and odious practice, plural marriage.

It is said that same-gender marriage is such a risky marital practice to make legal that to allow gays and lesbians the right to marry is to place society in a world that's unknown, perhaps even into the abyss. This form of marriage alters adult male and female relationships as they have come to be known, understood and accepted for generations in the Western world, risks the lives of children, both morally and physically, and—worse!—endangers society itself and the country, say opponents of same-gender marriage. Heterosexual monogamy, it is frequently said, is the cause of stable democracies just as poverty, it is said, is caused by single parenthood.

The argument continues: to allow one, new marital practice, in this case same-gender marriage, automatically leads to the legal acceptance of another alternative marital practice—plural marriage—which seems to be contrary to the country's culture, religious practices, and its laws. What's worrisome, the women who enter into these unions, including the resulting children, won't have any legal recourse or protections, opponents infer.

This is why the United States can only allow heterosexual, monogamous marriage, opponents say. There is far more at stake than simply one person's civil right to marry: There future of the United States of America is argued to be at stake.

To accept these arguments is to believe the following:

1. Once alternative forms of marriage are approved, everyone will seek out a plural marriage or a same-gender one, making traditional, monogamous, heterosexual marriage a distant memory;
2. This will permanently damage society and, as a result, bring about the downfall of the country;
3. That various governments haven't any legal ability to protect children;
4. That potential spouses maybe always coerced into a plural marriage and, once married, never have any legal recourse to extract themselves from a harmful or less than satisfying marital union and;
5. That a local police force is without the ability to investigate abuse against anyone.

Stanley Kurtz has taken up much of this in a series of articles in a conservative magazine, the *Weekly Standard*. He writes:

> Among the likeliest effects of gay marriage is to take us down a slippery slope to legalized polygamy and "polyamory" (group marriage) [sic]. Marriage will be transformed into a variety of relationship contracts, linking two, three or more individuals (however weakly or temporarily) in every conceivable combination of male and female. A scare scenario? Hardly. The bottom of the slope is visible from where we stand.[1]

For Kurtz, then, the potential problem with legally accepting same-gender marriage is that it puts the United States on the path to accepting plural marriage and, eventually, destruction. As he sees it, there's too much at risk by accepting same-gender marriage.

Examining the legal arguments against plural marriage, Ronald C. Den Otter, a political science professor at California Polytechnic State University, offers up a series of arguments to counter Kurtz's position. He writes about the government's legal position against plural marriage, which it currently maintains through the Supreme Court's 1879 *Reynolds* decision. He says that "no one has yet formulated an argument that successfully establishes that civil marriage ought to have a numerical limitation and that the burden is on the state to demonstrate that the failure to recognize plural marriage is consistent with the principles of freedom and equality that underlie fundamental rights and equal protection clauses of jurisprudence."[2]

Kurtz sees a larger problem with allowing plural marriage, saying that because this practice involves more than one wife, it's akin to allowing adultery:

Why is state-sanctioned polygamy a problem? The deep reason is that it erodes the ethos of monogamous marriage. Despite the divorce revolution, Americans still take it for granted that marriage means monogamy. The ideal of fidelity may be breached in practice, yet adultery is clearly understood as a transgression against marriage. Legal polygamy would jeopardize that understanding, and that is why polygamy has historically been treated in the West as an offense against society itself.[3]

In other words, instead of considering the idea that plural marriage is about marriage and family, his understanding of plural marriage is sexual. Kurtz sees it only as a sexual practice, not something that involves love and responsibility and, as many devoted practitioners see it, one that often involves fidelity.

To be sure, part of Kurtz's problem is that the article we're referencing here was written in 2003, before much new research had become available on plural marriage. That said, his article is an important one to point out because many people view plural marriage in a similar light—one that is only about sex. But as University of Nevada anthropologist William Jankowiak told the coauthor of this book, people involved in plural marriage in the United States, based on his many years of research in the field, aren't selling a sexual system. They're promoting family. We have emphasized this theme in our book.

Kurtz acknowledges that in those societies that are polygamous, "only 10–15 percent of men may actually have multiple wives."[4] But the greater problem—and this is a stretch because he's asking us to believe that adultery is unique to polygamous countries—is "polygamists are often promiscuous—just not with their own wives."[5] Kurtz cites coauthor Kilbride in his article, writing:

> Anthropologist Philip Kilbride reports a Nigerian survey in which, among urban male polygamists, 44 percent said their most recent sexual partners were women other than their wives. For monogamous married Nigerian men in urban areas, that figure rose to 67 percent. Even though polygamous marriage is less about sex than security, societies that permit polygamy tend to reject the idea of marital fidelity—for everyone, polygamists included.[6]

While the quotation is correct, it is similar to sound bites from political campaigns. It is out of context. The reader needs to keep in mind that this "promiscuousness," referenced by Kurtz, is part of a courting pattern in the polygamous culture in Nigeria. Sexual relations between men and women in Nigeria often result in marriage even for married men. In addition, Kilbride reports, from the same article, that a majority of women would be pleased if their husbands took a second wife, obviously a situation very differently from the United States.

Kurtz's other point is that a culture rich in heterosexual, monogamous marriage provides a set of morals that keeps people's undesirable feelings—like their desire to engage in an extramarital affair—under control.

The most reliable information on infidelity in the United States, as reported by the *New York Times*, shows that, any given year, about 12 percent of all married men and about 7 percent of all married women have an affair.[7] Based on the numbers of married people in the United States, as provided by the Census Bureau, this means nearly 12 million married people in the United States are having an affair any given year, which is nearly 10 percent of all married people in the country, based on the latest statistics.[8]

There's another report, from the *Denver Post*, which is based on a 2006 survey from the University of Chicago's National Opinion Research Center, that said, "20.2 percent of married men said they had been unfaithful, along with 16.7 percent of women."[9] This means that nearly 23 million people, at some point during their married lives, have strayed from their fidelity vows.[10]

So while the percentages of those engaging in an extra-marital affair in the United States are not as high as they are in Nigeria—if we accept Kurtz's arguments that all sexual activity outside of marriage in Nigeria is part of an affair—it's difficult to take the position that the monogamous culture of the United States is greatly superior to that of this African nation.

Kurtz also states that plural marriage "undermines the ethos of monogamy" within marriage and, as a result, "gay marriage itself threatens the ethos of monogamy" and, thus, traditional marriage.[11] But it would seem, based on what we know about the numbers of those who aren't faithful to their wedding vows, or the number of divorces any given year (nearly 1 million) that heterosexual monogamists are doing a better job of bringing down traditional marriage than anyone else. Might it be that there is a slippery slope from exclusive heterosexual monogamous marriage to divorce?

Kurtz's argument also doesn't take into consideration the American view about infidelity, as we have just noted. Based on another report in the *New York Times*, the attitude among most Americans is that infidelity is wrong and that, if anything, "the overwhelming of majority of Americans either practiced monogamy or aspired to it."[12] Kurtz's assumption, then, that legalizing same-gender or plural marriage would irreparably harm the American attitude toward monogamy stands on shaky ground because it assumes that people will give up their morals. Moreover, as we have seen, marriage is much broader than this, involving economics, cultural values, and biological factors, to name but three.

In fact, based on what Professor Den Otter writes, Americans, even if polygamy were made legal, wouldn't be flocking to it. He writes:

According to a recent Gallup Poll, 90 percent of Americans believe that the practice of polygamy is immoral. That figure indicates that the polyamory movement faces a daunting task: to not only encourage Americans to see plural marriage as a morally acceptable practice but also to persuade legislators and judges to change laws that ban plural marriage or treat polyamorists unequally.[13]

Den Otter also says if plural marriage were contested in court, the lawyers fighting to have it remain illegal would need to argue why it's imperative the government make sure all marital relationships are egalitarian. He writes:

Assuming [the government] has a duty to minimize gender inequality in personal relationships, must it therefore prohibit plural marriage? Or is it possible that one can have a feminist sensibility and still permit such marriage? Those who will not accept that possibility may ultimately be justified in their refusal, but they owe a clear explanation to the rest of us about why plural marriage is so odious. . . . In other words, opponents of plural marriage must appeal to justifications of gender equality or non-coercion. They may not base their exclusion of plural marriage on reasons that are unrelated to these two principles.[14]

Notably absent from these discussions—from both Kurtz and Den Otter—is that they're assuming, going forward, plural marriage would continue to be one husband with more than one wife. Never are they considering the argument made by University of Chicago Law School professor Martha Nussbaum that plural marriage, were it to gain legal acceptance in the United States, could potentially allow both women and men to have multiple spouses.[15]

Den Otter expands on the idea that plural marriages lack equality among the genders. But a number of today's traditional, monogamous marriages aren't equal for either participant and the law doesn't regulate this. He writes:

it is not obvious that for a feminist, polygamy is worse than monogamy. In a patriarchal society, gender inequality is just as likely to exist in monogamous relationships . . . the law is largely silent on 'what should go on inside the marriage.' It is not clear why a plural marriage is likely to be so much more inegalitarian than a monogamous one.[16]

In an earlier chapter, anthropologist Janet Bennion takes up this issue and shows how plural marriage can work in patriarchy for women in some FLDS communities.

Den Otter thinks that if plural marriages were decriminalized, the government would be a stronger position to investigate and prevent "incest, child abuse and statutory rape."[17] In addition, he says, legal recognition of plural marriages puts women—because they are usually the weaker partners in these relationships—on a much a stronger footing, writing, "A woman who wants to leave a plural marriage but is not a wife in the eyes of the law is not entitled to any spousal support even when she has performed unpaid domestic labor for years."[18]

Legal recognition, then, of plural wives (and husbands) might just reduce someone's desire to add another spouse. Because once someone is married to someone else, that relationship isn't dismissed, or even diminished, legally at least, without first passing a judge's review.

THE SLIPPERY SLOPE

Does same-gender marriage lead to plural marriage? This certainly is not the case in Africa and other regions of the world where plural marriage is common and same-gender marriage is rare or most often absent. There's an argument, as Kurtz provides, that same-gender marriage leads to other forms of marriages being legally recognized:

> gay marriage is increasingly being treated as a civil rights issue. Once we say that gay couples have a right to have their commitments recognized by the state, it becomes next to impossible to deny that same right to polygamists, polyamorists, or even cohabiting relatives and friends. And once everyone's relationship is recognized, marriage is gone, and only a system of flexible relationship contracts is left.[19]

Kurtz writes that the reason to prohibit same-gender marriage, and the resulting other marital forms that could come about because of this form of marriage's legal acceptance, is because, "children need the stable family environment provided by marriage. In our individualist Western society, marriage must be companionate—and therefore monogamous. Monogamy will be undermined by gay marriage itself, and by gay marriage's ushering in polygamy and polyamory."[20] At risk, as Kurtz sees it, is nothing less than society itself. "Marriage is a critical social institution. Stable families depend on it. Society depends on stable families."[21]

Den Otter notes that same-gender marriage advocates have refrained from taking up the legality of plural marriage, writing, "those who are in favor of same-sex marriage have gone out of their way to demonstrate that the legal recognition of same-sex marriage will not inevitably lead to the legal recognition of plural marriage."[22]

Richard A. Posner, a judge on the United States Court of Appeals for the Seventh District in Chicago, and a University of Chicago Law School lecturer, has written extensively about some of the issues surrounding polygamy and compared some of them to heterosexual monogamy. The problem with plural marriage, he writes, is that it is contrary to an ideal that has been part of Western culture for centuries, companionate marriage. He defines this form of marriage as follows:

> The term signifies marriage between at least approximate equals, based on mutual respect and affection, and involving close and continuous association in child rearing, household management, and other activities, rather than merely the occasional copulation that was the principle contact between spouses in the typical Greek marriage. The equality and companionship envisaged in such a marriage are in tension with the traditional double standard, if only because the husband is expected to refocus his affective energies within rather than outside the home.[23]

There are plenty of reasons to oppose plural marriage, too, Posner writes. They include the following: "The literature (on plural marriage) harps on the insensitivity, brutality, and tyranny of the polygamous husband; he is the lord and master; he treats his wives like chattels, like slaves. These complaints may be exaggerated, but there are several reasons for believing that they contain a kernel of truth."[24]

Other reasons to oppose plural marriage, Posner writes, include the fact that "the more wives a man has, the likelier he is to manage his household (or households) on a hierarchical rather than an egalitarian basis."[25] Polyandry, Posner says, because it "tends to create a relationship that is commercial, impersonal . . . tending more to . . . businesslike"[26] than to be emotional and personal, the ideal of Western companionate marriage.

Posner, like Kurtz, says the problem for many people "acculturated to monogamy," as the majority of Americans likely see themselves, is that a "polygamous culture is bound to seem promiscuous." In addition, the idea of "temporary marriages,"[27] part of the Islamic culture, only adds to this impression, Posner writes:

> Temporary marriage reinforces this impression. And note how it can make the Islamic limit of four wives illusory: since a temporary wife does not count against the limit, a man can, for example by specifying the duration of the temporary marriage at ninety-nine years, obtain a de facto permanent fifth wife.[28]

For all the reasons to be against plural marriage, Posner writes, there's also the issue of society as it stands today, which allows a variety of relationships. In addition, one of the biggest changes over the last 40 to 50 years is the economic independence of women. Because women are often holding professional jobs, Posner writes, "the cost to a child of being without a father will not be fully reflected in a the woman's decision whether to become or remain married."[29] As result of the change of women's economic status, Posner predicts that we will see worrisome trends in many forms of relationships:

> polygamy, de jure or de facto, in a society of non-companionate marriage; monogamy in a society of companionate marriage; and monogamy with an admixture of de facto polygamy in modern Western nations, where marriage is companionate but many women have children outside of marriage because they are no longer dependent on men, and where in addition to the decline of the traditional morality, and in particular of the limitations on divorce, reduces the felt immorality of polygamy—its conflict with the society's sexual laws and norms.[30]

In other words, like or it not, Western society, which is culturally monogamous, at least when it comes to marriage, shows great tolerance for plural relationships. Much of this is due to the fact that women are significantly in the work force and their financial means allows them to determine the types of relationships they will maintain. Some will certainly gravitate to traditional, heterosexual monogamous marriage whereas others may have a series of relationships with different men (perhaps even with different women), which may or may not result in children. Any children may or may not grow up with their father. The previous cultural norm that may have reduced sexual relations outside of marriage has changed, allowing women, as well as men, to engage in sex before or without marriage, never feeling that they're practicing infidelity, being promiscuous or even adulterous.

TOLERANCE

Let's accept Kurtz's argument. Let's consider, indeed, if America signs off on same-gender marriage, it will lead to the legal recognition of plural marriage. Why is this a problem? We have shown in this book that the problem for this position is that it is not based on fact. The two marital forms are unrelated, historically, culturally, socially, and religiously.

As Den Otter has shown, plural marriages sometimes, as do some monogamous ones, treat women unequally. Can we live with this? Is the United States the tolerant society some think it is? Furthermore, what does tolerance entail?

Den Otter writes that the ability of Americans to live with those who don't live like they do can be challenging. People have a right, Den Otter says, as troubling as it might be for other people to accept, to enter into relationships that are not ones they prefer. He writes, "In a liberal society, there is a presumption in favor of letting people decide for themselves what kind of romantic or familial relationships they want to have, even if those relationships are unconventional or hard to fathom."[31] We have taken the philosophical position of limited relativism that presses us to live with practices that we do not approve but willingly tolerate if others do.

In the case of plural marriage, women and children are not always at a disadvantage compared to monogamy. As we have shown in this book, it depends on the circumstances. The reason a number of people cannot tolerate plural marriage is because, as they know the practice, it inevitably hurts women and children.

As for marriages that some people want but that don't seem right to others, Den Otter quotes from Professor Nussbaum: "to rule that marriage as such should be illegal on the grounds that it reinforced male dominance would be an excessive intrusion upon liberty, even if one should believe marriage irredeemably unequal."[32]

Our view is also consistent with David C. Williams. In an article in the *Indiana Law Journal*, he talked about tolerance as it applies to civil society. He writes:

> one chief cultural value supporting civil society in a diverse republic is tolerance. If our culture is tolerant, then we are likely to have tolerant revolutions, tolerant democracies, and tolerant metaphysics. If it is not, then we will not . . . a politics of interest can destroy civil society when those in charge become intolerant of the interests of others.[33]

In addition, it should be understood that the concept of tolerance involves living in peace with others—not necessarily approving of lifestyles that are contrary to one's own beliefs.

PREVIOUS, UNFOUNDED SLIPPERY SLOPES

There's always this thought—no matter the issue—that if society provides a civil right for a group of people that, up until that moment, didn't have it, the risk of this new right outweighs the potential benefits and, therefore, the lid on the idea needs to be tightly fastened. This new civil right is too risky, and since we cannot accurately predict its impact on society, we can only imagine the worst case scenario this new right will have should it be legally allowed, the argument against new civil rights goes.

If Americans were prone to accepting this line of thinking, there's a better then even chance the country would be like Canada, part of the British Commonwealth. In other words, if Americans weren't the risk takers that they tend to show they are, there would never have been a revolution that separated it from Great Britain.

Abolitionists, President Lincoln, members of his cabinet, his party, and his generals and admirals didn't know the full impact of freeing black men, women, and children from slavery. The only thing they knew—with any certainty—was that blacks were enslaved and one geographic section of the country, the South, was working hard to maintain its political strength and, thus, slavery as part of the American landscape.

Americans had little idea what suffrage would look like once women gained the right to vote. What sort of impact would women have on American elections? It was anyone's guess in the 19th and early part of the 20th centuries when the issue was hotly contested. Resistance to the idea of women voting also included their role within society. They were the nurturer and the caretaker, running the home and making sure children were brought up to become proper adults. What business did they have in voting?

The only thing those who were pressing for suffrage knew was that women had made economic contributions over the centuries, if not to society at large, then certainly for their families, by running farms and holding down jobs when urbanization took hold in American life. Pushing the issue along was the fact that, after the Civil War, black men were free and had become full citizens, even if their voting rights weren't fully respected in every precinct. It made sense, as they saw it, to provide women with an equal voice in American elections.

The Lovings, as mentioned in a previous chapter, their attorney and Supreme Court justices, had no idea what the result of their case would be. The critics asked: would white men be flocking to black women? Would black women decide to marry white men? Would black men only marry white women? What would all this mixing of the races, if they had children, do to the American populace? Fear did, at first, rule the day and could have continued to rule the day on this "slippery slope."

The only thing the Lovings' lawyers and Supreme Court justices knew was that two people who had committed themselves to marrying one another, who didn't share the same ethnicity, had a right to be married wherever they lived in the United States. They were citizens, so how could their marriage rights be abridged? Trust in the U.S. Constitution paid off.

All of these issues successfully played out and the country continued, demonstrating the flexibility and the strength of the American populace.

Plural marriage, we believe, is as equally challenging to American law and society as these earlier "slippery slopes." The impact plural marriage would have on American society, were it to become legal, is anyone's guess. The worst-case scenario, as mentioned by University of Chicago Economics professor Gary Becker and Judge Richard A. Posner,[34] is that rich men (and women) would snap up single people left and right, essentially, because of their wealth, buying themselves spouses, perhaps even a harem.

Given what we know about the behavior of American women, while some may very well find the thought of being a rich person's spouse financially attractive, as in Saudi Arabia, as we have seen, it is also likely a number of women would remain single—even after they have given birth—perhaps even never marrying. Or maybe some women would marry in hopes of achieving a financially lucrative divorce.

A single, working mother with a college degree, holding down a top-paying job, might find that she has more to give up by marrying a rich man than by remaining unmarried. The same could be said for single, working fathers, who are also college-educated and are holding down top-paying jobs if they were to give consideration to marrying a rich woman.

The risk of not making plural marriage available in the United States is that the country continues to limit the availability of marriage and family life. In addition, more children will be born to unwed parents. If our cultural ideal is that children need at least two parents—so they will become productive, law-abiding, educated, self-sufficient adults—can we allow consenting adults the opportunity to engage in an alternative form of marriage? The facts speak for themselves.

NOTES

1. Stanley Kurtz, "Beyond Gay Marriage," *The Weekly Standard*, August 11, 2003, http://www.weeklystandard.com/author/stanley-kurtz.

2. Ronald C. Den Otter, "Is there really any Good Argument against Plural Marriage?" 2009, page 4. This is an unpublished paper and is available at http://works.bepress.com/ronald_den_otter/1/.

3. Kurtz, "Beyond Gay Marriage."

4. Ibid.

5. Ibid.

6. Ibid.

7. Tara Parker-Pope, "Love, Sex and the Changing Landscape of Infidelity," *The New York Times*, October 27, 2008, http://www.nytimes.com/2008/10/28/health/28well.html.

8. The latest information from the Census Bureau reports there are a total of 123,809,000 married adults in the United States. Since they're only measuring heterosexual married couples, in the most recent Census, the numbers of married men and married women are determined by dividing the total number into two, giving us 61,904,500 married men and the same number of women. This means, based on the infidelity statistics provided, that 7,428,540 married men have an affair each year and that another 4,333,315 married women have an affair annually for a total of

11,761,855. There appears to be a lack of information as to whether these affairs are heterosexual or involve gay or lesbian partners.

9. William Porter, "Surviving Infidelity," *The Denver Post*, October 13, 2009, http://www.denverpost.com/headlines/ci_13546193.

10. The numbers used here are based on the latest U.S. Census Bureau data on the number of married adults in the United States. See endnote 8. Based on what's being reported by the National Opinion Research Center, 12,504,709 married men and another 10,338,052 married women have, at some point, engaged in an extramarital affair for a total of 22,842,761.

11. Kurtz, "Beyond Gay Marriage."

12. Michael Norman, "Getting Serious about Adultery; Who Does it and why They Risk It," *The New York Times*, July 4, 1998, http://www.nytimes.com/1998/07/04/arts/getting-serious-about-adultery-who-does-it-and-why-they-risk-it.html?pagewanted=all&src=pm.

13. Den Otter, "Is there really any Good Argument against Plural Marriage," page 5.

14. Ibid, pp. 8 and 9.

15. Martha Nussbaum, "Debating Polygamy," *The Faculty Blog*. The University of Chicago Law School, http://uchicagolaw.typepad.com/faculty/2008/05/debating-polyga.html.

16. Den Otter, "Is there really any Good Argument against Plural Marriage," pp. 29 and 30.

17. Ibid, p. 34.

18. Ibid., p. 35.

19. Kurtz, "Beyond Gay Marriage."

20. Ibid.

21. Ibid.

22. Den Otter, "Is there really any Good Argument against Plural Marriage," p. 25.

23. Richard A. Posner, *Sex and Reason* (Cambridge, MA: Harvard University Press, 1992), p. 45.

24. Ibid., p. 255.

25. Ibid., p. 256.

26. Ibid.

27. Ibid., p. 258.

28. Ibid., pp. 258 and 259.

29. Ibid., p. 259.

30. Ibid., p. 259 and 260.

31. Den Otter, "Is there really any Good Argument against Plural Marriage," p. 42.

32. Ibid., pp. 47 and 48.

33. David C. Williams, "Civil Society, Metaphysics, and Tolerance," *Indiana Law Journal* (April 1, 1997): p. 492.

34. This thought is discussed in a book written by Gary S. Becker and Richard A. Posner, titled *Uncommon Sense: Economic Insights, From Marriage to Terrorism*

(Chicago: University of Chicago Press, 2009), in their chapter titled "Polygamy," pages 25–30. Professor Becker writes that biggest argument against polygamy is "the claim that it exploits women" (p. 26). He also mentions that in a society where polygamy would compete with monogamy, women, before marrying, "could write a contract" (p. 26) stipulating the terms of the marriage. Posner warns, in the same chapter, that "legalizing polygamy would reduce the supply of women to men of lower incomes and thus aggravate inequality" (p. 28).

References and Further Reading

Abanes, Richard. 2002. *One Nation Under Gods: A History of the Mormon Church.* New York: Four Walls Eight Widows.

Abbott, Elizabeth. 2011. *A History of Marriage: From Same Sex Unions to Private Vows and Common Law, the Surprising Diversity of Tradition.* New York: Seven Stories Press.

Adams, Walter Randolph and Frank Salamone. 2000. *Anthropology and Theology.* Lanham, MD: University Press of America.

Addison, Neil. November 30, 2011. "Polygamy in Canada: A Case of Double Standards." *The Guardian,* http://www.guardian.co.uk/commentisfree/belief/2011/nov/30/heterosexuality-canada-law-monogamy-polygamy.

Altman, Irwin and Joseph Ginat. 1996. *Polygamous Families in Contemporary Society.* New York: Cambridge University Press.

American Psychological Association (APA). July 18, 2004. *Sexual Orientation, Parents & Children.*

Anapol, Deborah. 2010. *Polyamory in the 21st Century: Love and Intimacy with Multiple Partners.* Lanham, MD: Rowman & Littlefield.

Anderson, Scott. February 2010. "The Polygamists: An Exclusive Look inside the FLDS." *National Geographic,* pp. 34–61, http://ngm.nationalgeographic.com/2010/02/polygamists/anderson-text.

Arrison, Sonia. August 27–28, 2011. "Living to 100 and Beyond." *The Wall Street Journal.* http://online.wsj.com/article/SB100014240531119048754045765288 41080315246.html.

Aschenbrenner, Joyce. 1983. *Lifelines: Black Families in Chicago.* Prospect Heights, IL: Waveland Press.

"Asia's Lonely Hearts." August 20, 2011. *The Economist,* http://www.economist.com.

Baines, Beverly. February 21, 2009. "Polygamy Trial: A Many-Ringed Circus." *Toronto Star,* http://www.childbrides.org/canada_TS_a_many-ringed_circus.html.

Bala, Nicholas. 2009. "Why Canada's Prohibition of Polygamy is Constitutionally Valid and Sound Social Policy." *Canadian Journal of Family Law* vol. 25, no. 2: pp. 165.

Banks, Ralph Richard. 2011. *Is Marriage for White People? How the African American Marriage Decline Affects Everyone*. New York: Dutton.

Barash, David and Judith Lipton. 2001. *The Myth of Monogamy: Fidelity and Infidelity in Animals and People*. New York: Henry Holt and Company.

Barlow, Philip L. 1991. *Mormons and The Bible: The Place of the Latter-day Saints in American Religion*. New York: Oxford University Press.

Barry, John M. 2012. *Roger Williams and The Creation of the American Soul: Church, State and the Birth of Liberty*. New York: Viking.

Bauers, Sandy. December 9, 1992. "Seasonal Adjustments." *The Philadelphia Inquirer*, pp. F1, F4.

Bearak, Barry. May 30, 2010. "Malawi's President Pardons Gay Couple Sentenced to 14 Years in Prison." *The New York Times*, p. 8.

Becker, Gary S. and Richard A. Posner. 2009. *Uncommon Sense: Economic Insights, From Marriage to Terrorism*. Chicago: University of Chicago Press, 2009.

Becker, Marvin B. April 1, 1997. "An Essay on the Vicissitudes of Civil Society with Special Reference to Scotland in the Eighteenth Century." *Indiana Law Journal* vol. 72, no. 2: pp. 463–487.

Bennett, Jessica. July 28, 2009. "Only You. And You. And You." *Newsweek*, http://www.thedailybeast.com/newsweek/2009/07/28/only-you-and-you-and-you.html.

Bennion, Janet. 1993. "Female Networking in Contemporary Mormon Polygyny." Paper presented at the Scientific Study of Religion Meetings, Washington, DC.

Bennion, Janet. 1998. *Women of Principle: Female Networking in Contemporary Mormon Polygyny*. New York: Oxford University Press.

Bennion, Janet. 2004. *Desert Patriarchy: Mormon and Mennonite Communities in the Chihuahua Valley*. Tucson: University of Arizona Press.

Bennion, Janet. 2011. "The Many Faces of Polygamy: An Analysis of the Variability in Modern Mormon Fundamentalism in the Intermountain West." In *Modern Polygamy in the United States*, ed. Cardell K. Jacobson with Lara Burton, pp. 163–184. New York: Oxford University Press.

Bergstrand, Curtis R. and Jennifer Blevins Sinski. 2010. *Swinging in America: Love, Sex, and Marriage in the 21st Century*. Santa Barbara, CA: Praeger.

Bernstein, Nina. March 23, 2007. "In Secret, Polygamy Follows Africans to N.Y." *The New York Times*, http://www.nytimes.com/2007/03/23/nyregion/23polygamy.html.

Betzig, Laura. 1986. *Despotism and Differential Reproduction: A Darwinian View of History*. New York: Aldine.

Billingsley, Andrew. 1993. *Climbing Jacob's Ladder: The Enduring Legacy of African American Families*. New York: Simon & Schuster.

"Blacks Upbeat about Black Progress, Prospects: A Year After Obama's Election." January 12, 2010. Pew Research Center Publications, http://pewresearch.org/pubs/1459/year-after-obama-election-black-public-opinion.

Blackwell, James. 1991. *The Black Community: Diversity and Unity.* New York: HarperCollins Publications.

Bledsoe, Caroline and Gilles Pison, eds. 1994. *Nuptiality in Sub-Saharan Africa: Contemporary Anthropological and Demographic Perspectives.* Oxford: Clarendon Press.

Blum, William. 1989. *Forms of Marriage: Monogamy Reconsidered.* Nairobi, Kenya: Amecea Gaba Publications.

Boaz, David. April 25, 1997. "Privatize marriage: A Simple Solution to the Gay Marriage Debate." Slate.com, http://www.slate.com/articles/briefing/articles/1997/04/privatize_marriage.html.

Book of Deuteronomy, Chapter 25, verses 5–6, Holy Bible, (with the Apocryphal/Deuterocanonical Books), The New Revised Standard Version. 1989. New York: American Bible Society.

Bramlett, Matthew D. and William D. Mosher. May 31, 2001. "First Marriage Dissolution, Divorce and Remarriage: United States," Centers for Disease Control and Prevention, http://www.cdc.gov/nchs/data/ad/ad323.pdf.

Brinig, Margaret and Douglas Allen. 2000. These Boots are Made for Walking: Why Most Divorce Filers are Women. *American Law and Economics Association* vol. 4, no. 2: pp. 376–379.

Brook, James. August 23, 1998. "Utah Struggles with Revival of Polygamy." *The New York Times,* http://www.nytimes.com/1998/08/23/world/utah-struggles-with-a-revival-of-polygamy.html?pagewanted=all&src=pm.

Browning, Don S. 2003. *Marriage and Modernization: How Globalization Threatens Marriage and What to Do about It.* Grand Rapids, MI: William B. Eerdmans Publishing Company.

Cairncross, John. 1974. *After Polygamy Was Made a Sin: The Social History of Christian Polygamy.* London: Routledge & Kegan Paul.

Campbell, Angela. May 31, 2005. "How Have Policy Approaches to Polygamy Responded to Women's Experiences and Rights? An International Comparative Analysis." In *Status of Women Canada, Polygamy in Canada: Legal and Social Implications for Women and Children: A Collection of Policy Research Reports.* Ottawa: Status of Women Canada, 2005), http://papers.ssrn.com/sol3/papers.cfm?abstract_id=1360230.

Carroll, Al. 2007. "Peopling North America." In *Native America from Prehistory to First Contact,* ed. Rodney P. Carlisle and J. Geoffrey Golson. Santa Barbara, CA: ABC-CLIO.

Centers for Disease Control and Prevention. August 27, 2010. Births, Marriages, Divorces, and Deaths: Provisional Data for 2009. National Vital Statistics Reports, U.S. Department of Health and Human Services, http://www.cdc.gov/nchs/products/nvsr.htm.

Chapman, Audrey. 1986. *Man Sharing.* New York: William Morrow & Co.

Cherlin, Andrew. 2009. *The Marriage-Go-Round: The State of Marriage and the Family in America Today.* New York: Alfred A. Knopf.

"The Church of the West." February 7, 2002. *The Economist,* http://www.economist.com/node/976398.

Cook, Alexandra and Nobel Cook. 1991. *Good Faith and Truthful Ignorance: A Case of Transatlantic Bigamy*. Durham, NC: Duke University Press, pp. 45.

Coontz, Stephanie. 2005. *Marriage, a History: From Obedience to Intimacy or How Love Conquered Marriage*. New York: Viking.

Coontz, Stephanie. January 14, 2008. "The Future of Marriage." *Cato Unbound*, http://www.cato-unbound.org.

Cooper, Michael. June 2, 2011. "Improved Tax Collections Can't Keep Pace with States' Fiscal Needs, Survey Finds." *The New York Times*, http://www.nytimes.com/2011/06/02/us/02states.html.

Courlander, Harold. 1976. *A Treasury of Afro-American Folklore*. New York: Crown Publishers.

Cowell, Alan. July 29, 2009. "Facing Gay Rift, Anglican Sees 'Two-Track' Church." *The New York Times*, http://www.nytimes.com/2009/07/29/world/europe/29church.html.

Crollius, Arij A. Roest. 1986. *Creative Inculturation and the Unity of Faith*. Rome: Centre "Cultures and Religions" Pontifical Gregorian University.

Cryster, Ann. 1990. *The Wife-in-Law Trap*. New York: Simon and Schuster.

Curran, Charles E. 1993. *The Church and Morality*. Minneapolis: Fortress Press.

Curran, Charles E. 2002. *Catholic Social Teaching 1891–Present: A Historical, Theological, and Ethical Analysis*. Washington, DC: Georgetown University Press.

Curran, Charles E. 2008. *Catholic Moral Theology in the United States: A History*. Washington, DC: Georgetown University Press.

Curry, Thomas J., 2001. *Farewell to Christendom: The Future of Church and State in America*. New York: Oxford University Press.

Darger, Joe, Alina Darger, Vickie Darger, and Valerie Darger. 2011. *Love Times Three: Our True Story of a Polygamous Marriage*. New York: HarperOne.

Davis, Adrienne. December 2010. "Regulating Polygamy: Intimacy, Default Rules, and Bargaining for Equality." *Columbia Law Review*, vol. 10, no. 8, pp. 1955–2046.

Davis, Jeanie Lerche. November 17, 2008. "Cheating Wives: Women and Infidelity." *USA Today*. http://www.webmd.com and Jayson, Sharon, Getting reliable data on infidelity isn't easy. http://www.usatoday.com.

Davis Brion, David. 2006. *Inhuman Bondage: The Rise and Fall of Slavery in the New World*. New York: Oxford University Press.

de Laguna, Frederica. 1990. "Tlingit." In *Handbook of North American Indians*, ed. William C. Sturtevant, pp. 203–229. Washington, DC: Smithsonian Institute.

Den Otter, Ronald C. 2009. "Is There Really any Good Argument against Plural Marriage." Unpublished paper available at http://works.bepress.com/ronald_den_otter/1/.

DeParle, Jason and Sabrina Tavernise. February 18, 2012. "Unwed Mothers Now a Majority in Births in 20's." *The New York Times*, http://www.nytimes.com/2012/02/18/us/for-women-under-30-most-births-occur-outside-marriage.html?pagewanted=all.

de Tocqville, Alexis. 1945. *Democracy in America*, vol. 1, ed. Phillips Bradley. New York: Vintage Books.

de Waal, Frans. March 1995. "Bonobo Sex and Society." *Scientific American*, pp. 82–88.

Dixon-Spear, Patricia. 2009. *We Want for Our Sisters What We Want for Ourselves: African American Women Who Practice Polygyny by Consent*. Baltimore: Black Classic Press.

"Domestic Violence Facts." July 2007. National Coalition Against Domestic Violence, http://www.ncadv.org.

Donovan, James. 2002. "Rock-Salting the Slippery Slope: Why Same-Sex Marriage Is not a Commitment to Polygamous Marriage." *Northern Kentucky Law Review* vol. 29, no. 3: 521.

Dornbusch, Sanford and Myra Strober. 1988. *Feminism, Children, and the New Families*. New York: Guilford Press.

Driggs, Ken. Winter 1991. "Twentieth Century Polygamy and Fundamentalist Mormons in Southern Utah." *Dialogue, Journal of Mormon Thought*: pp. 44–58.

Dunaway, Wilma A. 2003. *The African-American Family in Slavery and Emancipation*. Cambridge: Cambridge University Press.

Duncan, Emily. 2008. "The Positive Effects of Legalizing Polygamy: 'Love Is a Many Splendid Thing.'" *Duke Journal of Gender Law & Policy* vol. 15, no. 1: 315–338.

Eckholm, Erik. July 5, 2009. "With Higher Numbers of Prisoners Comes a Tide of Troubled Children." *The New York Times*, p. 13.

Edgar, Don. 2004. "Globalization and Western Bias in Family Sociology." In *The Blackwell Companion to the Sociology of Families*, ed. Jacqueline Scott, Judith Treas, and Martin Richards, pp. 3–17. Malden, MA: Blackwell Publishing.

Eliasberg, Kristin. March 25, 2003. "Sodomy Flaw: How the courts have distorted the history of anti-sodomy laws in America." Slate.com, http://www.slate.com/articles/news_and_politics/jurisprudence/2003/03/sodomy_flaw.html.

Ellis, Joseph. 2010. *First Family: Abigail and John Adams*. New York: Alfred A. Knopf.

Embry, Jesse L. 1987. *Mormon Polygamous Families: Life in the Principle*. Salt Lake City: University of Utah Press.

Emens, Elizabeth F. February 2003. "Monogamy's Law: Compulsory Monogamy and Polyamorous Existence." Chicago: Public Law and Legal Theory, Working Paper No. 58, University of Chicago, http://www.law.uchicago.edu/files/files/58-monogamy.pdf.

Ertman, Martha M. 2010. "Race Treason: The Untold Story of America's Ban on Polygamy." *Columbia Journal of Gender and Law* vol. 19, no. 2: 287–366.

Ferm, Deane. 1986. *Third World Liberation Theologies*. New York: Orbis Books.

Fisher, Helen. 1992. *Anatomy of Love: The National History of Monogamy, Adultery, and Divorce*. New York: W. W. Norton.

Fisher, Helen. 2006. "The Drive to Love: The Neural Mechanism for Mate Selection." In *The New Psychology of Love*, ed. Robert J. Sternberg and Karin Weis. New Haven, CT: Yale University Press.

Fisher, Helen. 2009. *Why Him? Why Her? Finding Real Love by Understanding Your Personality Type*. New York: Henry Holt.

"FLDS: Former president allowed to back out of plea deal, granted jury trial." *Standard Times* (San Angelo, Texas), http://www.gosanangelo.com/news/2011/nov/28/nielsen-allowed-to-back-out-of-plea-deal-granted/.

"The Flight from Marriage." August 20, 2011. *The Economist,* http://www.economist.com/node/21526329.

Forbes, Jack D. January 29, 2004. "What is Marriage? A Native American View." http://nas.ucdavis.edu/Forbes/what_is%20Marriage.pdf.

Forbes, Stephanie. April 3, 2003. "Why Have Just One?: An Evaluation of the Anti-Polygamy Laws under the Establishment Clause." *Houston Law Review* vol. 39: pp. 1521.

Foster, Lawrence. 1981. *Religion and Sexuality: Three American Communal Experiments of the Nineteenth Century.* New York: Oxford University Press.

Fournier, Suzanne. June 16, 2009. "B.C. Polygamist Leader 'See no Sin' in Taking Tax Money." *National Post,* http://www.nationalpost.com/related/topics/polygamist+leader+sees+taking+money/1702751/story.html

Fox, Robin. 1967. *Kinship and Marriage: An Anthropological Perspective.* Los Angeles: Pelican.

Fraga, Brian. June 28, 2011. "Same-Sex 'Marriage'Postmortem." *National Catholic Register.*

Fry, Richard. October 7, 2010. "The Reversal of the College Marriage Gap." Pew Research Center. http://pewresearch.org/pubs/1756/share-married-educational-attainment.

Gartrell, Nanette and Henry Bos. June 7, 2010. "U.S. National Longitudinal Lesbian Family Study: Psychological Adjustment of 17-year-old Adolescents." *Pediatrics:* pp. 2009–3153.

Gher, Jaime M. 2008. "Polygamy and Same-Sex Marriage: Allies or Adversaries within the Same-Sex Marriage Movement." *William and Mary Journal on Women and the Law* vol. 14, no. 3: pp. 559–603.

Gitari, David. 1985. "The Church and Polygamy." *Wajibu,* vol. 1, no. 1, pp. 15–27.

Goldschmidt, Walter. 2006. *The Bridge of Humanity: How Affect Hunger Trumps the Selfish Gene.* New York: Oxford University Press.

Goldsmith, Emanuel, Mel Scult, and Robert Seltzer. 1990. *The American Judaism of Mordecai M. Kaplan.* New York: New York University Press.

Goody, Jack. 1983. *The Development of Family and Marriage and Europe.* New York: Cambridge University Press.

Gordon, Barbara. 1988. *Jennifer Fever: Older Men/Younger Women.* New York: Harper & Row.

Gordon, Sarah Barringer. 2002. *The Mormon Question: Polygamy and Constitutional Conflict in Nineteenth Century America.* Chapel Hill: The University of North Carolina Press.

Gottlieb, Alma. 2004. *The Afterlife Is Where We Come From: The Culture of Infancy in West Africa.* Chicago: The University of Chicago Press.

Graff, E. J. 2004. *What Is Marriage For? The Strange Social History of Our Most Intimate Institution.* Boston: Beacon Press.

Gragg, Rod. 2010. *Forged in Faith: How Faith Shaped the Birth of the Nation, 1607–1776.* New York: Howard Books.

Greenhouse, Linda. June 27, 2003. "The Supreme Court: Homosexual Rights; Justices, 6–3, Legalize Gay Sexual Conduct In Sweeping Reversal of Court's

'86 Ruling." *The New York Times,* http://www.nytimes.com/2003/06/27/us/su preme-court-homosexual-rights-justices-6–3-legalize-gay-sexual-conduct. html?src=pm.

Gura, Philip F. 1984. *A Glimpse of a Sion's Glory: Puritan Radicalism in New England, 1620–1660.* Middletown, CT: Wesleyan University Press.

Gwako, Edwins Laban Moogi. 1998. "Polygyny among the Logoli of Western Kenya," *Anthropost* vol. 93: pp. 331–348.

Hagerty, Barbara Bradley. May 28, 2008. "Philly's Black Muslims Increasingly Turn Toward Polygamy." National Public Radio, http://www.npr.org/templates/story/ story.php?storyId=90886407.

Hall, David D. 2011. *A Reforming People: Puritanism and the Transformation of Public Life in New England.* New York: Alfred A. Knopf.

Handlin, Oscar. 1957. *Race and Nationality in American Life.* Boston: Little, Brown, and, Company.

Hankins, Barry. 2004. *The Second Great Awakening and the Transcendentalists.* Westport, CT: Greenwood Press.

Hansen, Karen and Anita Garey. 1998. "Introduction." In *Families in the U.S.: Kinship and Domestic Politics.* Philadelphia, PA: Temple University Press.

Hare, Nathan and Julia Hare. 1989. *Crisis in Black Sexual Politics.* San Francisco: Black Think Tank.

Hendrix, Steve. January 11, 2012. "South Carolina Braces for Ugly Whispers." *The Washington Post,* http://www.washingtonpost.com/local/south-carolina-braces-for-ugly-whispers/2012/01/09/gIQAEZ5pqP_story.html.

Herlihy, David. 1985. *Medieval Households.* Cambridge, MA: Harvard University Press.

Hernandez, David. 1998. "Children's Changing Access to Resources: A Historical Perspective." In *Families in the U.S.: Kinship and Domestic Politics,* eds. Karen Hansen and Anita Garey, pp. 201–215. Philadelphia, PA: Temple University Press.

Herskovits, Melville. 1958. *The Myth of the Negro Past.* Boston: Beacon Press.

Hillman, Eugene. 1975. *Polygamy Reconsidered.* New York: Orbis Books.

Hochschild, Arlie. Fall 2010. "Global Traffic in Female Service: Nannies, Surrogates, and Emotional Labor." Havens Center for the Study of Social Structure and Social Change, http://www.havenscenter.org/audio/arlie-hochschild-global-traffic.

Holloway, Joseph E. 1990. *Africanisms in American Culture.* Bloomington: Indiana University Press.

Holy Bible (with the Apocryphal/Deuterocanonical Books). The New Revised Standard Version. 1989. New York: American Bible Society.

Hudson-Weems, Clenora. 2006. "Africana Womanism: Black Feminism, African Feminism, Womanism." In *Black Studies: From the Pyramids and Pan Africanism and Beyond,* ed. William "Nick" Nelson Jr., pp. 760–791. New York: McGraw-Hill.

"Hunting Bountiful: Ending Half a Century of Exploitation." July 8, 2004. *The Economist,* http://www.economist.com/node/2907136.

Hymowitz, Kay, S. 2011. *Manning Up: How the Rise of Women Has Turned Men into Boys*. New York: Basic Books.

Hymowitz, Kay. February 19, 2011. "Where Have the Good Men Gone?" *The Wall Street Journal*, http://online.wsj.com/article/SB10001424052748704409004576146321725889448.html.

Ingoldsby, Bron B. 2006. *Families in Global and Multicultural Perspective*. 2nd ed. Thousand Oaks, CA: Sage Publications.

Jacobson, Joyce P. 2002. "How Family Structure Affects Labor Market Outcomes." In *The Economics of Work and Family*, ed. Jean Kimmel and Emily P. Hoffman, pp. 133–158. Kalamazoo, MI: W. E. Upjohn Institute for Employment Research.

Jankowiak, William and Emilie Allen. 2000. "Adoring the Father: Religion and Charisma in an American Polygamous Community." In *Anthropology and Theology: God, Icons, and God-talk*, ed. Walter Randolph Adams and Frank Salamone, pp. 293–313. Lanham, MD: University Press of America.

Jasper, Margaret C. 2009. *The Law of Obscenity and Pornography*. New York: Oxford University Press.

Johnson, Dirk. April 9, 1991. "Polygamists Emerge from Secrecy, Seeking not just Peace but Respect." *The New York Times*, http://www.nytimes.com.

Joyce, Joyce A. 2007. *Women, Marriage and Wealth: The Impact of Marital Status on the Economic Well-Being of Women through the Life Course*. New York: Gordian Knot Books.

Katayama, Lisa. July 26, 2009. "Love in 2-E." *The New York Times Magazine*, pp. 20.

Katchadourian, Herant and Donald Lunde. 1975. *Fundamentals of Human Sexuality*, 3rd ed. New York: Holt, Rinehart & Winston.

Kenworthy, Tom. February 7, 1998. "DNC Chief Denies Sexual Affair With Ex-Aide; Romer Says Relationship Is 'Very Affectionate.'" *The Washington Post*, p. A03.

Kershaw, Sarah. October 14, 2009. "Rethinking the Older Woman-Younger Man Relationship." *The New York Times Magazine*, p. E1.

Kilbride, Philip. 1994. *Plural Marriage for Our Times: A Reinvented Option?* Westport, CT: Bergin and Garvey.

Kilbride, Philip. 2003. "African Polygyny: Family Values and Contemporary Changes." In *Applied Cultural Anthropology: An Introductory Reader*. 6th ed, ed. Aaron Podolefsky and Peter Brown, pp. 201–209. Mountain View, CA: Mayfield Publishing Company.

Kilbride, Philip. 2011. "African Polygyny: Family Values and Contemporary Changes." In *Humankind: An Introductory Reader for Cultural Anthropology*, ed. Loretta A. Cormier and Sharyn R. Jones, pp. 173–187. San Diego: Cognella Academic Publishing.

Kilbride, Philip and Noel Farley. 2007. *Faith, Morality and Being Irish: A Caring Tradition in Africa*. Lanham, MD: University Press of America.

Kilbride, Philip and Janet E. Kilbride. 1990. *Changing Family Life in East Africa: Women and Children at Risk*. University Park: Pennsylvania State University Press.

Kilbride, Philip, Collette Suda, and Enos Njeru. 2001. *Street Children in Kenya: Voices of Children in Search of a Childhood*. Westport, CT: Bergin and Garvey.

King, Wilma. 2005. *African American Childhoods: Historical Perspectives from Slavery*. New York: Palgrave MacMillian.

Kirwen, Michael. 1974. "The Christian Prohibition of the African Leviratic Custom: An Empirical Study of the Problem of Adapting Western Christian Teachings on Marriage to the Leviratic Care of Widows in Four African Societies." Unpublished doctoral dissertation, University of Toronto, Canada.

Kron, Josh. May 9, 2010. "Uganda Panel Gives Setback to Antigay Bill." *The New York Times*, pp. 11, http://www.nytimes.com/2010/05/09/world/africa/09 uganda.html.

Kurtz, Stanley. August 11, 2003. "Beyond Gay Marriage." *The Weekly Standard*, http://www.weeklystandard.com/Content/Public/Articles/000/000/002/938xpsxy.asp.

Lawrence vs. Texas, Supreme Court's decision. 2003. Justia.com, http://supreme.justia.com/us/539/558/case.html.

Lawson, Annette. 1988. *Adultery: An Analysis of Love and Betrayal*. New York: Basic Books.

Lee, Felicia R. March 28. 2006. "*Big Love*: Real Polygamists Look at HBO Polygamists and Find Sex." *The New York Times*, http://www.nytimes.com/2006/03/28/arts/television/28poly.html?_r=1&pagewanted=all.

Leibowitz, Lila. 1978. *Females, Males, Families: A Biosocial Approach*. Belmont, CA: Wadsworth Publishing.

Levine, Nancy and Walter Sangree. Summer 1980. "Women with Many Husbands: Polyandrous Alliance and Marital Flexibility in Africa and Asia." *Journal of Comparative Family Studies* (special issue), vol. 11 no. 3: i–iv. Lewis, Charles. November 23, 2011. "B.C. Polygamy Ruling Offers 'Road Map' to Avoid Prosecution: Lawyer." *National Post*.

Luscombe, Belinda. November 18, 2010. "Who Needs Marriage? A Changing Institution." *Time*, http://www.time.com/time/magazine/article/0,9171,2032116,00.html.

MacQueen, Ken. June 25, 2007. "Polygamy: Legal in Canada." *Maclean's*.

"Marriage in America: the Frayed Knot." May 24, 2007. *The Economist*, http://www.economist.com/node/9218127.

Mather, Mark. May 2010. "U.S. Children in Single-Mother Families." Population Reference Bureau. http://www.prb.org/Publications/PolicyBriefs/singlemother-families.aspx.

Mead, Margaret. 1949. *Male and Female*. New York: HarperCollins Publishers.

Miller, Jeremy M. 1984. "A Critique of the Reynolds Decision." *Western State University Law Review*, pp. 178.

Miller, Leon. 1974. *John Milton among the Polygamophiles*. New York: Loewenthal Press.

Miller, Marion Mills. 1913. *Great Debates in American History*, vol. 8. New York: Current Literature Publishing Co.

Moller, Valerie and Gary John Welch. 1990. "Polygamy, Economic Security and Well-Being of Retired Zulu Migrant Workers." *Journal of Cross-Cultural Gerontology* 5: pp. 205–216.

Moore, John H. 1991. "The Developmental Cycle of Cheyenne Polygyny." *American Indian Quarterly* vol. 15, no. 3: pp. 311.

National Geographic. June 2010. Letters, pp. 8.

Newell, Linda King and Valeen Tippets Avery. 1994. *Mormon Enigma.* Chicago: University of Illinois Press.

Norgren, Jill and Serena Nanda. 1996. *American Cultural Pluralism and Law.* Westport, CT: Praeger.

Norman, Michael. July 4, 1998. "Getting Serious About Adultery: Who Does it and why They Risk it." *The New York Times,* http://www.nytimes.com.

Nussbaum, Martha. 2000. "Women and Cultural Universals." In *Pluralism: The Philosophy and Politics of Diversity,* ed. Maria Baghramian and Attracta Ingram, pp. 197–228. New York: Routledge.

Nussbaum, Martha. May 19, 2008. "Debating Polygamy." *The Faculty Blog.* The University of Chicago Law School, http://uchicagolaw.typepad.com/faculty/2008/05/debating-polyga.html.

Okullu, Henry. 1990. *Church and Marriage in East Africa.* Nairobi: Uzima Press.

O'Reilly, David. June 6, 2010. "Diocese Welcomes Priest—and His Wife." *The Philadelphia Inquirer,* pp. B8.

Padawer, Ruth. April 10, 2009. "Keeping Up with Being Kept." *The New York Times Magazine.*

Paddock, Richard C. October 14, 1991. "Doctor Led Three Lives with Three Wives: Polygamy: Stanford University Professor never Divorced and Kept Households with each Woman. Truth Emerged after his Death in August." *Los Angeles Times,* http://articles.latimes.com/1991-10-14/news/mn-436_1_stanford-professor.

Page, Doug. February 2011. "Changing Families: From Traditional to Whatever Works?" *Bay State Parent,* pp. 10–11. http://www.baystateparent.com.

Palmer, Kimberly. July 2, 2008. "Marriage's Financial Pros and Cons." *U.S. News & World Report,* http://money.usnews.com/money/personal-finance/articles/2008/07/02/marriages-financial-pros-and-cons.

Parker-Pope, Tara. April 18, 2010. "Is Marriage Good for Your Health?" *The New York Times,* http://www.nytimes.com/2010/04/18/magazine/18marriage-t.html?pagewanted=all.

Pashigian, Melissa J. 2009. "The Womb: Infertility and the Vicissitudes of Kin-Relatedness in Vietnam." *The Journal of Vietnamese Studies,* vol. 4, no. 2, pp. 34–68.

"People Who Got Married, and Divorced in the Past 12 Months by State: 2009." U.S. Census Bureau, American Community Survey in 2009. http://www.census.gov/compendia/statab/2012/tables/12s0132.pdf.

Persico, Joseph. 2008. *Franklin & Lucy: President Roosevelt, Mrs. Rutherfurd, and the Other Remarkable Women in His Life.* New York: Random House.

Pew Forum on Religion & Public Life. 2007. "The Religious Composition of the United States." http://religions.pewforum.org.

Pew Research Center. January 10, 2010. "Women, Men and the New Economics of Marriage." http://www.pewsocialtrends.org/2010/01/19/women-men-and-the-new-economics-of-marriage/.

Pew Research Center. June 15, 2010. "Marrying Out: One in Seven New U.S. Marriages is Interracial and Interethnic." http://pewresearch.org/pubs/1616/ameri can-marriage-interracial-interethnic.

Pew Research Center. October 7, 2010. "The Reversal of the College Marriage Gap." http://pewresearch.org/pubs/1756/share-married-educational-attainment.

Pew Research Center. March 9, 2011. "For Millennials, Parenthood Trumps Marriage." http://www.pewsocialtrends.org/2011/03/09/for-millennials-parenthood-trumps-marriage/.

Pew Research Center. December 14, 2011. "Barely Half of U.S. Adults are Married—A Record Low." http://www.pewsocialtrends.org/2011/12/14/barely-half-of-u-s-adults-are-married-a-record-low/.

Pingree, Gregory C. 2006. "Rhetorical Holy War: Polygamy, Homosexuality, and the Paradox of Community and Autonomy." *Journal of Gender, Social Policy and the Law* vol. 14, no. 2: pp. 314–383.

"Polygamous Husbands can Claim Cash for their Harems." April 18, 2007. *The Daily Mail*, http://www.dailymail.co.uk.

Popenoe, David. 1999. "American Family Decline: Public Policy Considerations." In *America's Demographic Tapestry: Baseline for the New Millennium*, ed. James W. Hughes and Joseph J. Seneca, pp. 173–183. New Brunswick, NJ: Rutgers University Press.

Popenoe, David. 2000. "Modern Marriage: Revisiting the Cultural Script." In *The Gendered Society Reader*, ed. Michael S. Kimmel, with Amy Aronson, pp. 151–167. New York: Oxford University Press.

Population Reference Bureau. May 2010. U.S. Children in Single-Mother Families. http://www.prb.org/Publications/PolicyBriefs/singlemotherfamilies.aspx.

Porter, William. October 13, 2009. "Surviving Infidelity." *The Denver Post*. http://www.denverpost.com/headlines/ci_13546193.

Posner, Richard A. 1992. *Sex and Reason*. Cambridge, MA: Harvard University Press.

Pryor, Jan and Liz Trinder. 2004. "Children, Families, and Divorce." In *The Blackwell Companion to the Sociology of Families*, ed. Jacqueline Scott, Judith Treas, and Martin Richards, pp. 322–39. Malden, MA: Blackwell Publishing.

Ranke-Heinemann, Uta. 1991. *Eunuchs for the Kingdom of Heaven: Women, Sexuality and the Catholic Church*. New York: Penguin Books.

Renteln, Alison D. 2002. "In Defense of Culture." In *The Courtroom in Engaging Cultural Differences: The Multicultural Challenge in Liberal Democracies*, ed. Richard Schweder, Martha Minow, and Hazel Rose Markus, pp. 194–216. New York: Russell Sage Foundation.

Reynolds v. U.S., 98 U.S. 145. 1878. http://law2.umkc.edu/faculty/projects/ftrials/conlaw/reynoldsvus.html.

Rice, Andrew. June 11, 2007. "An African Solution." *The Nation*, http://www.thenation.com/article/african-solution.

Ruddick, Sarah. 1989. *Maternal Thinking: Toward a Politics of Peace*. Boston: Beacon Press.

Sangree, Walter. December 1969. "Going Home to Mother: Traditional Marriage among the Irigwe of Benue-Plateau State, Nigeria." *Journal of the American Anthropological Association* vol. 71, no. 6: pp. 1046–1056.

Schneider, Harold. 1972. "Human Sexuality from an Intercultural Perspective." In *Human Sexual Behavior: Variations in the Ethnographic Spectrum*, ed. Donald Marshall and Robert Suggs, pp. 59–70. Englewood Cliffs, NJ: Prentice-Hall.

Scott, Joseph. 1989. "The Sociology of the Other Woman: Man-Sharing." In *Crisis in Black Sexual Politics*, ed. N. Hare and J. Hare, pp. 105–109. San Francisco: Black Think Tank.

Sealing, Keith E. "Polygamists Out of the Closet: Statutory and State Constitutional Prohibitions Against Polygamy are Unconstitutional Under the Free Exercise Clause." *Georgia State University Law Review* vol. 17, no. 3, Article 4:733: http://digitalarchive.gsu.edu/gsulr/vol17/iss3/4.

Segal, Ronald. 1995. *The Black Diaspora: Five Centuries of the Black Experience Outside Africa*. New York: Farrer, Straus and Giroux.

"Sex Scandal First Minister's Wife Iris Robinson Cleared in Toyboy Business Deal Probe." May 27, 2011. *Belfast Telegraph*, http://www.belfasttelegraph.co.uk.

"Sexual Orientation, Parents & Children." July 18, 2004. *American Psychological Association*, http://www.apa.org/about/policy/parenting.aspx.

Shipps, Jan. 1985. *Mormonism: The Story of a New Religious Tradition*. Chicago: University of Illinois Press.

Shipps, Jan. 2001. "Is Mormonism Christian? Reflections on a Complicated Question." In *Mormon & Mormonism: An Introduction to an American World Religion*, ed. Eric A. Eliason, pp. 76–99. Chicago: University of Illinois Press.

Shorter, Aylward and Edwin Onyancha. 1998. *The Church and AIDS in Africa*. Nairobi: Pauline Publications Africa.

Shostak, Marjorie. 1981. *Nisa: The Life and Words of a !Kung Woman*. New York: Random House.

Siegel, Jane. 2011. *Disrupted Childhoods: Children of Women in Prison*. Piscataway, NJ: Rutgers University Press.

Sigman, Shayna M. 2006–2007. "Everything Lawyers Know about Polygamy Is Wrong." *Cornell Journal of Law and Public Policy* vol. 16: p. 166.

Sipe, A. W. Richard. 1990. *A Secret World: Sexuality and the Search for Celibacy*. New York: Routledge.

Smearman, Claire A. September 17, 2009. "Second Wives' Club: Mapping the Impact of Polygamy in U.S. Immigration Law." *Berkeley Journal of International Law* 27, no 2: 382–448.

Solomon, Deborah. March 4, 2010. "The Priest." *The New York Times*, http://www.nytimes.com/2010/03/07/magazine/07fob-q4-t.html.

Some, Kipchumba. June 7, 2009. "Grandfather Catholic Priest Bares It All." *The Standard Online*, http://www.eastandard.net.

Song, Sarah. 2007. *Justice, Gender and the Politics of Multiculturalism*. Cambridge: Cambridge University Press.

Spender, Robert F. and Jesse D. Jennings, eds. 1965. *The Native Americans: Prehistory and Ethnology of the North American Indians*. New York: Harper & Row.

Spong, John. 1991. *Rescuing the Bible from Fundamentalism*. San Francisco: Harper-Collins.

Stack, Carol. 1974. *All Our Kin: Strategies for Survival in a Black Community*. New York: Harper & Row.

Stevenson, Brenda E. 1995. "Black Family Structure in Colonial and Antebellum Virginia: Amending the Revisionist Perspective." In *The Decline in Marriage Among African Americans*, ed. M. Belinda Tucker and Claudia Mitchell-Kernan, pp. 27–59. New York: Russell Sage Foundation.

Stopford, Annie. 2006. "Trans Global Families: The Application of African Ethical and Conceptual Systems to African-Western Relationships and Families." *JENDA: A Journal of Culture and African Women Studies*, no. 8. http://www.africaknowledgeproject.org/index.php/jenda/issue/view/12

Suda, Collette. October 4, 2007. "Formal Monogamy and Informal Polygyny in Parallel: African Family Traditions in Transition." Inaugural Lecture, University of Nairobi.

Sudarkasa, Niara. 1982. "African and Afro American Family Structure." In *Anthropology for the Eighties*, ed. J. Cole, pp. 132–161. New York: Free Press.

Sudarkasa, Niara. 1996. *The Strength of Our Mothers: African & African American Women & Families: Essays and Speeches*. Trenton, NJ: Africa World Press.

Sullivan, Winnifred Fallers. 2005. *The Impossibility of Religious Freedom*. Princeton, NJ: Princeton University Press.

Summary of Boundaries and Opportunities Report. n.d. Jewish Reconstructionist Federation, http://jrf.org.

Takenaka, Ayumi and Mary Osirim. 2010. *Global Philadelphia: Immigrant Communities Old and New*. Philadelphia: Temple University Press.

Talese, Gay. 1980. *Thy Neighbor's Wife*. New York: Doubleday and Company.

Taylor, Paul. June 15, 2010. "Marrying Out: One in Seven New U.S. Marriages is Interracial and Interethnic." Pew Research Center, http://pewresearch.org.

Taysom, Stephen C. 2011. *Shakers, Mormons and Religious Worlds: Conflicting Visions, Contested Boundaries*. Bloomington, IN: Indiana University Press.

Thompson, Krissah. January 22, 2012. "Survey Paints Portrait of Black Women in America." *The Washington Post*, http://www.washingtonpost.com.

Thorne, Barrie and Marilyn Yalom, eds. 1982. *Rethinking the Family: Some Feminist Questions*. New York: Lungman.

Tierney, John. March 11, 2006. "Who's Afraid of Polygamy." *The New York Times*, http://query.nytimes.com/gst/fullpage.html?res=9C04EEDA1331F932A25750 C0A9609C8B63

Turner, Bryan S. 2004. "Religion, Romantic Love, and the Family." In *The Blackwell Companion to the Sociology of Families*, ed. Jacqueline Scott, Judith Treas, and Martin Richards, pp. 289–306. Malden, MA: Blackwell Publishing.

Tyler, Tracey. February 21, 2009. "A Many-Ringed Circus." *Toronto Star*, http://www.childbrides.org/canada_TS_a_many-ringed_circus.html.

U.S. Census Bureau. 2006–2010. "American Community Survey, Selected Social Characteristics in the United States." http://factfinder2.census.gov/faces/tableservices/jsf/pages/productview.xhtml?pid=ACS_10_5YR_DP02&prod Type=table.

U.S. Census Bureau. 2009. "Number of Times Married by Sex by Marital Status for the Population 15 years and Over." 2009 American Community Survey, http://www.census.gov/prod/2011pubs/acs-13.pdf.

U.S. Census Bureau. 2010a. "American Community Survey 1-Year Estimates." American Fact Finder, Sex by Age (Black or African American Alone), http://www.census.gov/newsroom/releases/pdf/20110920_acs_webinar.pdf.

U.S. Census Bureau. 2010b. "American Community Survey 1-Year Estimates." Selected Social Characteristics in the United States, http://www.census.gov.

U.S. Census Bureau. 2010c. "Family Type By Presence and Age of Own Children." http://www.census.gov.

U.S. Census Bureau. 2011a. "Living Arrangements of Children Under 18 and Marital Status of Parents by Age, Sex, Race and Hispanic Origin and Selected Characteristics of the Child for All Children," http://www.census.gov/population/www/socdemo/hh-fam/cps2011.html.

U.S. Census Bureau. May 2011b. "Number, Timing, and Duration of Marriages and Divorces: 2009," http://www.census.gov/prod/2011pubs/p70-125.pdf.

U.S. Census Bureau. n.d. "Fertility 2010 American Community Survey 1-Year Estimates http://factfinder2.census.gov/faces/tableservices/jsf/pages/productview.xhtml?pid=ACS_10_1YR_S1301&prodType=table

U.S. Department of Health and Human Services. August 27, 2010. "Births, Marriages, Divorces, and Deaths: Provisional Data for 2009." National Vital Statistics Reports, Centers for Disease Control and Prevention, http://www.cdc.gov/nchs/data/nvsr/nvsr58/nvsr58_25.pdf.

U.S. Department of Health and Human Services. May 21, 1991. "Monthly Vital Statistics Report." National Center for Disease Statistics.

U.S. Department of Justice, Bureau of Justice Statistics. December 2009. "Prisoners in 2008." http://bjs.ojp.usdoj.gov/content/pub/ascii/p08.txt.

Valdez, Tanya. March 6, 2010. "Couple Starved Real Baby while Raising Virtual Baby." *The Examiner,* http://www.examiner.com/article/couple-starved-real-baby-while-raising-a-virtual-baby.

Van Wagoner, Richard. 1986. *Mormon Polygamy: A History.* Salt Lake City, UT: Signature Books.

Vigoda, Ralph. March 15, 1995. "Polygamy Is not a Bad Idea." *Philadelphia Inquirer http://articles.philly.com/1995-03-15/living/25700789_1_polygamy-plural-mar riagefamily-life.*

Violence Policy Center. September 15, 2010. Press release: "Nevada Ranks #1 in Rate of Women Murdered by Men According to VPC Study Released Annually for Domestic Violence Awareness Month in October." http://www.vpc.org.

Volokh, Eugene. May 22, 2008. Same-Sex Marriage and Slippery Slopes. *Hofstra Law Review* vol. 33: pp. 122.

Waliggo, J.M., et al. 1986. *Inculturation: Its Meaning and Urgency.* Kampala, Uganda: St. Paul Publications.

Wallace, Rob, Katie Thomson, and Lauren Sher. February 2, 2010. "Jenny Sanford Exclusive: Husband Refused to Be Faithful in Wedding Vows." ABCNews, http://abcnews.go.com/2020/jenny-sanford-south-carolina-gov-mark-sanford-refused/story?id=9727121#.T70TL1IjlvE.

Ward, Cassiah M. 2004. "I Now Pronounce You Husband and Wives: Lawrence v. Texas and the Practice of Polygamy in Modern America." *William & Mary Journal of Women and the Law*, pp. 150, http://scholarship.law.wm.edu/wmjowl/vol11/iss1/4.

Ware, Helen. February 1979. "Polygyny: Women's Views in a Transitional Society, Nigeria 1975." *Journal of Marriage and the Family* vol. 41, no. 1: 185–195.

Washington, Robert and Steve Nangendo. Sept. and Dec. 1997. "Knowledge about AIDS and Sex Practices among Young Kenyan Adults." *Scandinavian Journal of Development Alternatives*, vol. 6, nos. 3 & 4, 130–141.

Watanabe, Yasushi. 2004. *The American Family across the Class Divide*. Ann Arbor, MI: Pluto Press.

Weir, Alison. 1991. *The Six Wives of Henry VIII*. New York: Grove Press.

Weston, Kath. 1991. *Families We Choose: Lesbians, Gays, Kinship*. New York: Columbia University Press.

White, Gregory and Paul Mullen. 1989. *Jealousy: Theory, Research and Clinical Strategies*. New York: Guilford Press.

Whitehead, Barbara Dafoe. April 1993. "Dan Quayle Was Right." *The Atlantic Monthly*, http://www.theatlantic.com/magazine/archive/1993/04/dan-quayle-was-right/7015/.

Whitehead, Barbara Dafoe. 1997. *The Divorce Culture*. New York: Random House.

Wiencek, Henry. 2003. *An Imperfect God: George Washington, His Slaves and the Creation of America*. New York: Farrar, Straus, and Giroux.

Williams, David C. April 1, 1997. "Civil Society, Metaphysics, and Tolerance." *Indiana Law Journal*, vol. 72, no. 2, 489–495.

Williams, Michael W. 1990. "Polygamy and the Declining Male to Female Ratio in Black Communities: A Social Inquiry." In *Black Families: Interdisciplinary Perspectives*, ed. Harold E. Cheatham and James B. Stewart, pp. 171–197. New Brunswick, NJ: Transaction Publishers.

Wilson, Stephan and Lucy Ngige. 2006. "Families in Sub-Saharan Africa." In *Families in Global and Multicultural Perspective*. 2nd ed., ed. Bron Ingoldsby and Suzanna Smith, pp. 247–272. Thousand Oaks, CA: Sage Publications.

Winslow, Ben. August 20, 2008. "Foster care for Jeffs' Apparent Child Bride." *Deseret News*, http://www.deseretnews.com.

Wolfe, Leanna. 1993. *Women Who May Never Marry*. Atlanta: Longstreet Press.

Wolfe, Leanna. 1998. "Adding a Co-Wife." *Loving More Magazine*, no. 15, pp. 22–25.

Wolfe, Leanna. 2006. "Exploring Nonmonogamy." Unpublished manuscript, http://drleannawolfe.com/.

Woodworth-Ney, Laura E. 2008. *Women in the American West*. Santa Barbara, CA: ABC-CLIO.

Wrixon, Ann. June 10, 2010. "Children Raised by Lesbian Parents Have Excellent Outcomes." *IAC*, http://adoptionhelp.org/blog/2010/children-raised-by-lesbian-parents.

Wykes, S. L. October 8, 1991. "Respected Doctor Had Multiple Wives, Secret Bank Account." *San Jose Mercury News,* hosted at http://nl.newsbank.com.

Wykes, S. L. October 8, 1991. "Stanford Doctor Had Secret Life—Three Wives." *San Jose Mercury News,* http://nl.newsbank.com.

Wykes, S. L. October 11, 1991. "Bigamist's Family Stunned Anger Outweighs Grief after Physicians Death." *San Jose Mercury News,* http://nl.newsbank.com.

Yamani, Maha A. Z. 2008. *Polygamy and Law in Contemporary Saudi Arabia.* Berkshire, UK: Ithaca Press.

Young, Ann Eliza. 1875. *The 19th Wife Featuring, One Lady's Account of Plural Marriage and its Woes Being the Chronicle of Personal Experience of Ann Eliza Young—19th and Rebel Wife of the Leader of the Utah Saints and Prophet of the Mormon Church, Brigham Young Written by Herself.* New York: Easton & Co.

Young, Josiah U. 1986. *Black and African Theologies.* Maryknoll: Orbis Books.

Young, Kimball, 1954. *Isn't One Wife Enough?* New York: Holt.

Zeitzen, Miriam. 2008. *Polygamy: A Cross-Cultural Analysis.* Oxford: Berg.

Zimmerman, Carle C. 1949. *The Family of Tomorrow: The Cultural Crisis and the Way Out.* New York: Harper.

Zimmerman, Carle C. 2008. *Family and Civilization,* ed. James Kurth. Wilmington, DE: ISI Books.

Zorgin, Peter. 2003. *How the Idea of Religious Tolerance Came to the West.* Princeton, NJ: Princeton University Press.

INTERVIEWS CONDUCTED BY DOUGLAS PAGE

Janet Bennion, anthropologist, Lyndon State College, Vermont.

Patricia Dixon-Spear, professor, African American Studies Department, Georgia State University.

William Jankowiak, anthropologist, University of Nevada at Las Vegas.

Linda McClain, law professor, Boston University.

Paul Murphy, spokesman, Office of the Utah State Attorney General.

Rod Parker, attorney in Salt Lake City.

Andrea Press, sociologist, University of Virginia.

Bruce Schulman, professor, Boston University.

"Susan and Dave," a suburban Boston couple involved in the polyamorous community. Their names have been changed.

Robyn Trask, executive director, Loving More.

Robert Wickett, attorney, Vancouver, British Columbia, Canada.

Adrien Wing, law professor, University of Iowa.

Index

About the Authors

PHILIP L. KILBRIDE is professor of anthropology and former chair of the department of anthropology at Bryn Mawr College, where he has taught since 1969. He has published widely in the area of family studies, childhood, and ethnicity, both concerning the United States and East Africa. He has published on the plight of children living on the streets in Kenyan cities suffering from family breakdown there. His specialty is ethnographic research.

DOUGLAS R. PAGE is a freelance writer and reporter. His work has appeared in the *San Francisco Chronicle*, *The Journal-Gazette* (Fort Wayne, Indiana), *News & Tech*, and *Bay State Parent* magazine. He's worked at United Press International, the *Chicago Sun-Times*, and Tribune Media Services. He holds an MBA from Northwestern University's Kellogg School of Management and a BA from DePauw University, Greencastle, Indiana. He resides in Massachusetts with his wife and two children.